CHILDREN IN RESIDENTIAL CARE
Critical Issues in Treatment

Commentary

"This compilation of articles by well-known authors in the field offers a thoughtful discussion of some of the most pressing problems in the residential care of children. Clinical issues such as sexual acting out, behavior management, separation, and peer influence are discussed first, with practical treatment suggestions for practitioners. The second section deals with important management issues such as quality assurance, evaluating effectiveness of treatment, coping with burnout, and institutional abuse."

—*Book Briefs*

"To all of the authors, 'clinical issues' means what occurs in the daily lives of the youngsters in care. The effectors of treatment, those who need the important knowledge, skill, and understanding, are those who interact most often with the youngsters in their daily lives . . . The fact that so many of the critical issues in residential treatment are considered makes this volume a very valuable resource."

—Jacquelyn Sanders in *Social Service Review*

"This excellent compilation . . . provides in-depth discussions of some of the most critical issues and guidelines for addressing those issues. A section on clinical issues deals with such concerns as crisis intervention, discipline and behavior management, helping the child cope with separation and loss, and the impact of various life events while the child is in care. Gwynn, Meyer, and Schaefer's article on the influence of the peer culture in the institution and on treatment is especially helpful, providing insight into its operation and impact on the institution. Equal attention is focused on several significant management issues, ranging from quality assurance and permanency planning to coping with staff burnout. This is a valuable addition to the literature and will be beneficial to anyone interested in residential child care, particularly students, clinicians, and supervisors in child welfare settings."

—Joseph C. O'Rourke in *Readings*

CHILDREN IN RESIDENTIAL CARE
Critical Issues in Treatment

Edited by

Charles E. Schaefer, Ph.D.
and
Arthur J. Swanson, Ph.D.

Jason Aronson Inc.
Northvale, New Jersey
London

First Softcover Edition 1993

Copyright © 1993 by Jason Aronson Inc.
Copyright © 1988 by Van Nostrand Reinhold

Library of Congress Cataloging-in-Publication Data

Children in residential care.

  Includes index.
  1. Child psychopathology—Residential Treatment. I. Schaefer, Charles E.
II. Swanson, Arthur J. (Arthur John), 1953–   . [DNLM: 1. Residential Treatment—
in infancy & childhood.   WS 350.2 C5365]
RJ504.5.C48   1988   362.2'1   87-16140
ISBN 0-442-27966-3 (hardcover)
ISBN 1-56821-000-0 (softcover)

Manufactured in the United States of America. Jason Aronson Inc. offers books and cassettes. For information and catalog write to Jason Aronson Inc., 230 Livingston Street, Northvale, New Jersey 07647.

Contributors

Philip Barker, M.B.
Professor of Psychiatry and Pediatrics
University of Calgary
Calgary, Alberta, Canada

Kevin J. Corcoran, Ph.D.
Assistant Professor
Graduate School of Social Work
University of Houston
Houston, Texas

Peter H. Cormack, Ph.D.
Director, Professional Education
  Division
Convalescent Hospital for Children
Rochester, New York

David A. Crenshaw, Ph.D.
Clinical Director
Astor Home for Children
Rhinebeck, New York

Andrew Diamond, M.S.W.
Director of Residential Programs
Vista Del Mar Child Care Service
Los Angeles, California

Carol Gwynn, Ph.D.
Psychology Intern
The Children's Village
Dobbs Ferry, New York

Richard M. Kagan, Ph.D.
Director of Research and Quality
  Assurance
Parsons Child and Family Center
Albany, New York

Mark Katz, Ph.D.
Supervising Psychologist
San Diego Center for Children
San Diego, California

Anthony N. Maluccio, D.S.W.
Professor, School of Social Work
University of Connecticut
West Hartford, Connecticut

Rebecca Meyer, Ph.D.
The Children's Village
Dobbs Ferry, New York

John B. Mordock, Ph.D.
Assistant Executive Director
Astor Day Treatment Center
Poughkeepsie, New York

Beverly A. Richard, M.A.
The Children's Village
Dobbs Ferry, New York

Nolan Rindfleisch, Ph.D.
Associate Professor
The Ohio State University
College of Social Work
Columbus, Ohio

Charles E. Schaefer, Ph.D.
Director of Training
Division of Psychological Services
Fairleigh Dickinson University
Hackensack, New Jersey

Arthur J. Swanson, Ph.D.
Assistant Professor of Psychiatry
New York Medical College
Valhalla, New York

John Van Hagen, Ph.D.
Clinical Director
St. Vincent's School for Boys
San Rafael, California

A WORD ABOUT PRONOUNS

Please note that some contributors used the traditional male pronoun "he" to refer to children of both sexes, while others employed the "sex-neutral" but more awkward "he or she" style.

Preface

Residential treatment for children can be defined as a total therapeutic program for those youngsters whose emotional and/or behavioral problems preclude treatment in the community on an outpatient basis. In the spectrum of services for children, residential centers tend to be places of "last resort" and serve children and adolescents who are the most disturbed. In meeting this challenge, residential treatment centers must develop programs that are both comprehensive and of high quality. The goal of this book is to discuss some of the most critical issues underlying effective residential treatment and to offer guidelines for dealing with these issues. The book is directed more toward practical "how to" issues related to effective treatment rather than more general theoretical formulations.

Residential treatment centers offer a unique opportunity for children and those who serve them. Unlike outpatient treatment, residential treatment offers the opportunity to create a total therapeutic environment for the children in residence. The creation of such an environment, however, requires the practitioner to take a broad look at what constitutes clinical work. Individual treatment must necessarily be supplemented by broad-based interventions that require highly skilled clinical and management teams.

The present book is divided into two parts, the first dealing with *Clinical Issues* and the second with *Management Issues* in effective residential treatment. In Part I, clinical issues ranging from handling children's separation experiences to the importance of family work are discussed. Part II, devoted to a variety of management issues, includes articles on combating institutional child abuse and evaluating treatment effectiveness. How successfully an agency handles these and the other critical issues described in this book will, to a large extent, determine how therapeutic its milieu will be for children.

This book will be of interest to a wide range of professionals who work in residential or inpatient settings, including administrators, psychologists, social workers, psychiatrists, child care counselors, teachers, recreation specialists, and psychiatric nurses. Because many of the issues pertaining to residential treatment are also relevant to day treatment, the material in this book will be helpful to practitioners in day treatment centers. It has been our experience that most of the issues discussed in this book are sadly neglected in graduate training. Thus, this book can provide a useful framework for those entering the area and stimulation for those already working in this domain. All of the chapters in the book are new, although a few are based on previously published articles.

CHARLES SCHAEFER
ARTHUR SWANSON

Contents

Introduction

The following chapter by Philip Barker on the future of residential treatment encourages all of us to take a hard look at the type of services residential treatment centers have offered in the past and should be offering in the future. Within the past three decades, society has oscillated between viewing residential treatment centers as panaceas for almost all behavior problems of youth and as totally sinister institutions that serve only to exacerbate children's problems. Neither of these extreme views is correct, and both have been harmful. The future of residential treatment depends upon our identifying the type of childhood problems that are best treated in residential settings, and then documenting the type of services that most effectively and efficiently remediate these disorders.

This provocative introductory chapter by Barker reviews the drawbacks, myths, and pitfalls of residential treatment, identifies the important place residential treatment holds in the continuum of services for youth, and suggests ways that residential centers can improve their effectiveness. Many of the recommendations for improvement will be elaborated upon in succeeding chapters of this book. It is the opinion of the editors that a continual process of critical self-analysis and self-improvement is needed by those working in residential treatment centers to ensure the most effective treatment of children in care.

1

The Future of Residential Treatment for Children

Philip Barker

Residential treatment centers for disturbed children have a long history (Barker, 1974a). In many places they were established before outpatient services for such children existed. They seem at first sight a logical approach to the treatment of severely disturbed children. If other measures have failed, what could be better than to place such children in environments where they can receive "intensive" therapy from a team of experts who are with them round the clock? If, moreover, they come from disturbed families, and their family environments are having adverse effects on their adjustment, this might even seem a near-ideal treatment approach. But what seems like an attractive idea has its drawbacks, and we now know that residential treatment is no panacea for children's problems. Some of residential treatment's benefits have also been questioned, in the light of our contemporary understanding of children's psychiatric disorders. This is therefore an opportune time to review the current place and future role of residential treatment in the spectrum of treatment services for children.

THE PROBLEMS

Residential treatment has both practical and theoretical drawbacks.
    The *practical drawbacks* include the following:

1. The treatment may not be successful.
2. Children can become institutionalized and overdependent on treatment centers.
3. Children may learn dysfunctional behaviors from other disturbed children who are in treatment with them.

4. Children may lose contact with, or even be abandoned by, their families.
5. The treatment is very expensive.

We will now briefly examine each of these problems.

Inconclusive results: The results of the residential treatment of disturbed children, while hard to assess (Barker, 1974b), are, at best, inconclusive. The pioneering work of Redl and Wineman (1951, 1952), which illustrates quite well an earlier approach to residential treatment, makes it clear what a very long-term and difficult undertaking the intensive residential treatment of children can be. Moreover, the relative failure of many forms of residential treatment has been documented by Romig (1978) and by Shamsie (1981).

"Institutional neurosis" (Barton 1966): This is a major hazard of residential treatment. Children may become overdependent on institutions in which they are living; after some initial rebellion, they may learn to conform to routine, accept having decisions made for them, and lose their drive and initiative. Disturbed children may be particularly at risk, as their emotional bonds with their families are often weak. Furthermore some conditions—infantile autism, for example—are themselves characterized by difficulty in forming relationships, and a tendency to withdraw from social contacts. Both tendencies may be exacerbated in residential settings.

The learning of dysfunctional and even antisocial behaviors: Such learning from other troubled children has often been observed in residential centers. The peer culture can be a very powerful influence, and it can have a variety of undesirable effects. Yet it can be turned to advantage. Vorrath and Brendthro (1985), for example, have described a program that uses "positive peer culture" as a therapeutic tool.

Abandonment by families: Abandonment is an ever present possibility. Some families discover that they function happily and with less stress without the child who is in the residential center. They find excuses for visiting less often, and for dropping out of the treatment process; meanwhile the child can become alienated and act out feelings of abandonment and resulting rage. On the other hand, in some enmeshed families the short-term separation of parent(s) and child can itself be therapeutic—as, for example, in treating some of the more severe cases of school refusal (Barker, 1968).

The expense of treatment in residential centers: This can be a serious practical problem. Some families can afford only brief periods of residential treatment for their child, and many cannot afford it at all. Funding by governments or third-party insurers often is necessary, but it may be unavailable.

Theoretical objections to residential treatment also exist, and need to be taken into account as we plan the future of this treatment modality. They include the following:

1. Children's behavior is highly context-dependent.
2. Traditional psychoanalytic views, and especially the use of individual psychodynamic theory, are increasingly being questioned as a practical basis for the treatment of disturbed children.
3. As psychoanalytic views become less fashionable, the problems of individuals are coming to be understood more and more in terms of the social systems to which they belong.
4. Institutional solutions to human problems are losing favor in many societies.

We will now consider each of these objections briefly.

The context of children's behavior: That children's behavior is highly context-dependent is well established. The epidemiological studies of Michael Rutter and his colleagues in the Isle of Wight (Rutter et al., 1970), and more recently those of the Ontario Child Health Study (Boyle et al., 1987; Offord et al., 1987), illustrate this well. Both revealed little overlap between the children showing disturbed behavior at home and those showing it at school. Moreover, children's behavior is known to vary widely with different adults and in different peer groups. We know too that competent residential treatment staff can, for example, usually establish control of children with behavior disorders, or ensure school attendance in those with school refusal, but such behavioral changes often do not persist when the children return to the environments in which their problems developed.

The limitations of the psychoanalytic approach: In its early days residential treatment was often based on then-popular psychoanalytic theories; these tended to overemphasize intrapsychic phenomena, and underplay the importance of ecological factors. Henao (1985, p. 34) puts it well:

Freud's theories and the therapeutic approaches derived from them emphasized psychological development and psychological conflict almost in isolation from interpersonal and social forces. Freud believed that families were an obstacle to treatment.

Henao (1985) goes on to quote Freud (1916–17), who said:

In psychoanalytic treatments the intervention of relatives is a routine danger and a danger one does not know how to meet.

Freud was not a child psychiatrist, and over the years since he expressed these views it has become increasingly clear that we cannot, if we want to be successful, treat children in isolation. Treating adults apart from their families of origin may succeed, especially if they have moved away and are leading lives of their own. But children have developmental needs that must be met, either by their families or by some substitute for the families, and treating them in isolation from their ecological contexts is unrealistic. Yet this is what much residential treatment traditionally has done. It was thought that children would learn, and then internalize, new ideas, moral values, and standards of behavior that they would take with them when they were discharged. They would acquire "controls from within," as Redl and Wineman (1952) put it in the title of their second book. This idea seems reasonable in theory, but how often it works out successfully in practice is unclear. What *is* clear, though, is that this process is a long and difficult one, often requiring years of residential treatment—something that is rarely possible in these days of financial stringency and limited budgets. In any case, few residential treatment centers now operate on these theoretical lines.

The systems approach to the problems of children and their families: Systems thinking (Becket, 1973) is tending to replace, or at least supplement, psychoanalytic thinking. The systems thinker does not see the child, or the child's behavior, as the problem. Instead, the way the family system functions is the focus of attention. The system, moreover, is more than the sum of its parts. "Disturbed" behavior in a family member is regarded as a feature of the functioning of the family system—necessary behavior for the person concerned in that particular system at that time. (For a summary of systems theory and how it is applied to families, see Barker, 1986a, especially pp. 37–43.)

Systems theory provides a ready explanation of the phenomenon we have already discussed—that children can display very different behaviors in different situations. When they move from one system to another, their behavior will be modified according to the nature of the system into which they move. If we accept this view of things—and I believe it has considerable validity—we must rethink our residential treatment programs.

The addition of a "systems" perspective to our approach to residential treatment means that we have to make certain changes in our treatment philosophy and programs. Somehow we have to make the family system the focus of our endeavors, even though the child is temporarily removed from it. I believe that the main objection to many current residential programs is that they fail to do this, even though they may pay lip service to working with the families of the children they admit. Despite an oft-stated commitment by the staff to working with entire family groups, many of the children feel the problems are *theirs,* and that they are to blame for the family's situation. They do not feel that they are part of a troubled family unit. They may even come to believe that it is their duty to "be good," rather than their parents' duty to exercise control over them. Moreover, they may not realize that their parents have as much, or more, need to learn to exercise control as they have to learn new behaviors. All this may lead to deep-seated feelings of guilt in the child—or more likely the exacerbation of preexisting guilt feelings. Such feelings then lead to further antisocial behavior, and the acting-out of the poor self-image the child has acquired.

Disenchantment with institutional approaches to human problems: In developing our treatment programs for disturbed children we must be aware that institutional solutions to human problems are becoming unfashionable. This attitude may be due in part to disappointment with the results of traditional thinking and practices, as well as the practical drawbacks considered above. More important, however, may be the new world view being taken by many. Comments I made about this in an earlier paper apply at least as much now as they did in 1982. I said, in part:

Toffler (1980), in his thought-provoking book *The Third Wave,* argues that from being hunter-gatherers, men first became agriculturalists (the "first wave" of civilization) and then developed an industrial society (the "second wave"). Our current social, educational, religious, and industrial institutions were developed to suit the needs of an industrial society. Residential treatment centers, like institutions for the mentally ill, the retarded, the elderly or the delinquent, may be seen as part of this set-up. Toffler believes that the second wave has now more or less run its course in western societies and is being replaced by the third wave. Mass production is being replaced by "customization," service industries employ more people than factories, and the rights of individuals and minority groups are being asserted in a way which never occurred in the industrial age. Information has become paramount and the electronic transmission of data, the computer, the silicone chip, the satellite, automation, and cybernetics are revolutionizing our civilization.

The nuclear family was the basis of society during the second wave. It provided the factory fodder. To enable it to do so, unproductive family members were removed to institutions such as those mentioned above.

The recent questioning of the benefits of residential treatment may be but a part of the many changes which Toffler discerns as signs of the emerging third wave. The concepts of individual psychopathology, based on the work of Freud, suited the second wave; systems theory, with its emphasis on the exchange of information and on relationships, suits the emerging third wave better. (Barker, 1982, p. 635)

To the above might be added the increasing role being played in our society by "self-help" groups. These are not new (Alcoholics Anonymous has existed since the 1930s), but many more of them, designed to help diabetics, sufferers from cystic fibrosis, the parents of autistic children, those who have lost a child through the "sudden infant death syndrome," cocaine addicts, gamblers—indeed those faced with just about any human problem—have come into being. This seems a healthy development; people are finding they have, within themselves and their social circles, resources that can help them deal constructively with their problems. They turn to professionals for help less than they used to.

The new world view, which Toffler writes about and I have commented on, does not mean that the concepts of individual psychopathology should be abandoned. Individuals do have their own problems, as well as their strengths (which we often overlook in our assessments of children and their families). The question is, to what extent is exploring the psychopathology of individual children profitable and cost-effective? Doing so has the disadvantage that it highlights the child's problems, while doing nothing positive about them. I believe it is better to concentrate on problem-solving, or solution-finding, rather than on the search for causes that may be buried deep in the past.

Perhaps Milton Erickson contributed more to this change of viewpoint than anyone else. The first volume of *Conversations with Milton H. Erickson* (Haley, 1985) shows clearly how Erickson's approach differed from that of traditional therapists. Haley seems to have embarked on these conversations with quite traditional views about psychotherapy; but Erickson, when asked to discuss how he would approach various clinical problems, offered very different ideas. He was always concerned with finding solutions to problems, rather than exploring their causes, and he did this in ways that were both creative and, often, unconventional. (For a fuller discussion of Erickson's approach see Haley, 1985 and Barker, 1986b.)

SOME POSSIBLY MISTAKEN IDEAS CONCERNING RESIDENTIAL TREATMENT

Some commonly held ideas about residential treatment may be mistaken. In plotting a future for residential treatment, it is important to examine these ideas and to consider whether they are valid.

1. *Residential treatment is more intense than other forms of treatment.* This statement is open to question, though much depends on how you measure intensity. Is it an intense relationship with a specific therapist

that is important? Or is it the particular nature of the therapeutic milieu that is provided for the children? Or is it the behavior modification program built into the treatment, intensity being measured by the number of times the child faces specific environmental contingencies designed to bring about modification of his or her behavior? Or is it a matter of the number of hours spent in group or individual therapy? Or is some other criterion the one we should use to measure intensity? Or perhaps several factors should be taken into account?

In fact, most of the things that can be done in a residential setting can be done on an outpatient basis, or at least in a daypatient unit. The "therapeutic milieu" is probably the main exception, though a day unit can provide an effective milieu for many types of disturbed children. I believe that residential treatment may or may not be more intense than other forms of therapy, depending on how the unit's program is organized and on the measure of intensity used.

2. *Children are usually admitted to residential treatment because they need this type of therapy.* The fact is that many children are admitted because those caring for them, or their school, or their home community, have had enough of them—or at least of their disturbed behavior. The main reason for admission may be the need to protect the community, or to give the family or community a break. Such reasons may be legitimate, but they are not always acknowledged.

3. *Residential treatment and residential care are the same.* There often seems to be confusion between the concept of providing care for children who cannot, for whatever reason, live at home, and the provision of treatment for their psychiatric problems. Thus a major residential treatment center in Calgary is called the "adolescent care center"—a name that is emblazoned in large letters on the main building; yet it is unashamedly a treatment center. Even Whittaker's (1979) important book on residential treatment was called *Caring for Troubled Children.*

While good care of disturbed children may certainly promote their healthy development, it is important to distinguish between the care given in foster homes, group homes, detention units, and other places where children are looked after away from their families, and the therapy provided in treatment centers.

4. *It is easy to combine therapy with the family and residential treatment of the child.* In my experience this combination is not easy to achieve. While integrating family work with residential treatment is usually a desirable objective, it also presents major challenges. Even trying to combine the two is in some ways paradoxical. If you want to treat the family unit, why divide it into two by removing one or more members from the others? It may be that integration of the two approaches can be achieved only if the admission of the child is, from the outset, defined as a

procedure intended to bring about change in the family system, rather than as a treatment for the child per se.

Another important point is that the parents of many disturbed children have serious personality problems, often dating back to their own unsatisfactory childhood experiences. Consequently, they themselves may require intensive and expert therapy, not just guidance in how to handle their children.

SOME OTHER AREAS OF CONCERN

Whittaker (1979) has identified four areas of concern related to residential and day treatment programs.

1. Continuity of care is important. Whittaker says that "the controversy over deinstitutionalization is based on a false and misleading dichotomy between residential and community-based programs." All services should be community-oriented and closely in touch with what Whittaker terms "the major systems in which the child participates," that is, family, peer group, school, family doctor, and community at large. The residential center as a separate entity, whether or not geographically far removed from the family and community, makes no sense.

2. Residential and day programs should provide support and treatment for families, not treatment of children in isolation from their families and home communities.

3. No single theory or set of practical prescriptions will meet the needs of all troubled children.

4. Treatment programs should be able to demonstrate what they do in simple, clear, and jargon-free terms, understandable by the general public.

CURRENT INDICATIONS FOR RESIDENTIAL TREATMENT

Despite these problems, I believe that residential treatment has an important place in the range of services that should be available for disturbed children. Admission may be required either because the child's disturbance is so severe that it cannot be managed while he or she lives at home, or because a residential program is what is needed for the presenting clinical problems. Sometimes both factors will apply.

Admission for Reasons other than the Need for the Residential Program Itself

There are three main groups of these reasons:

1. *For the protection of the community.* Some disturbed children pre-

sent real dangers to society; this group includes those with homicidal tendencies, rapists and those who sexually abuse others, and fire-setters. Residential treatment may not always be the treatment of choice, but treatment in a residential setting is dictated by the seriousness of the child's behavioral problems.

2. *For the protection of the child.* In this category we have suicidal children; children who abuse drugs, alcohol, or solvents to a dangerous degree; those who persistently run away and get themselves into dangerous situations; and perhaps some who are the victims of physical or sexual abuse—though there are valid objections to the admission of the victims rather than the perpetrators of the abuse.

3. *Because the child's behavior, though not dangerous to others, is so disturbed as to be more than the community can deal with using available resources.* Into this category fall some children with pervasive developmental disorders, some psychotic children, and others with severe behavior disorders or persistent school attendance problems that have been unresponsive to other treatment measures.

It is important to note that, when admission for any of the above reasons is being considered, the community and its capacity to cope with the child's problem must be taken into account. Not every suicidal or psychotic child needs residential treatment; much will depend on the family's and the wider community's emotional and physical resources. The decision to admit children should be based on assessments of their social systems as well as on their psychiatric status.

Admission Due to Need for the Residential Treatment Program Itself

Sometimes the residential program is what the child needs, whether or not it is dangerous or impractical to maintain the child in the community. Defining the circumstances for which this is the case, however, is more difficult. For one thing, residential treatment centers vary greatly in the programs they offer. Also what they offer has to be compared with what can be offered by other available programs—for example, outpatient therapy for the child, family therapy, or day treatment. The child's family situation is also a crucial factor; treatment of any sort for children's disorders only makes sense if it is based on an understanding of the family context, or—if the child has no functioning family group—on whatever his or her social context is.

In the following situations, residential treatment may be the best approach:

1. *A self-perpetuating cycle of dysfunctional behaviors is well established, and other less draconian, and less expensive, measures have failed.* Regard-

less of how the situations may have started, we sometimes see families in which the dysfunctional behaviors of different members, or family subsystems, seem to be reinforcing each other. For example, the presenting problems may be a boy's behavior; he may be playing truant from school, staying out late, defying his parents' instructions, and getting into trouble with the law. At the same time, as their attempts to control their wayward son fail, the parents (or it may be just a single parent) become increasingly angry with him, and more and more rejecting in their attitudes toward him. As he senses this rejection, the son—who is already feeling angry and unhappy because of the constant criticism and disapproval to which he is subjected—feels still more miserable and unwanted. He spends even less time at home, and probably more in the company of a delinquent peer group, as the parents' attitudes become increasingly negative. Such problems often can be resolved by family therapy, but sometimes this fails, and it seems that the warring factions in the family need a break from each other while skilled treatment for the family continues. In this case, admission is part of a family treatment plan and is often welcomed by all concerned because living in such a situation tends to be stressful for everyone.

When admission is recommended because of a self-perpetuating destructive family pattern, this should be plainly stated to all concerned. The residential treatment plan should be formulated in family terms; that is, admission of the child to the residential center should be suggested not as a treatment for the child, but as a means of tackling the family's problems. The child may be offered a break from the tensions at home, whereas the parents may be offered a respite from their efforts to deal with their child, and the opportunity to learn new ways of interacting with him or her, while the child learns new ways of dealing with the parents.

2. *The treatment required by the child demands technical skills that the parents do not possess, and which cannot readily and quickly be taught.* These skills most likely will be those required to carry out intensive behavior therapy, as, for example, the techniques that seem most effective in the treatment of autistic children and those with other forms of pervasive developmental disorder. Some parents, of course, can learn such skills readily and practice them effectively, but others cannot, and it is necessary to admit their child to a center that provides the needed expertise. Following admission these parents should become partners with the treatment staff in the therapeutic process.

3. *The young person is psychotic and out of touch with reality* to such an extent that he or she cannot be managed by untrained laypeople; or the severity of the child's behavior disorder is so great that only skilled management by highly trained professionals can bring it under control.

IMPROVING THE EFFECTIVENESS OF RESIDENTIAL TREATMENT

Residential treatment thus has its risks and drawbacks, and it is our duty to minimize them as far as possible. I suggest that the following measures can help achieve this.

1. Admission should be for as short a time as possible. This means days if possible, or, failing that, weeks, and months only when necessary. There is also much to be said for setting at least a provisional discharge date at the time of admission.

2. The goals of the treatment program should be clearly defined, ideally in writing, before admission. The establishment of well-defined goals is sometimes overlooked, but the advent of strategic therapy methods has drawn attention to its importance. Both Haley (1976) and Madanes (1981), for example, have pointed out that the development of a therapeutic strategy presupposes the existence of an objective that the strategy aims to achieve. As therapy methods become more refined and parsimonious, and focused strategic plans are used increasingly, the setting of clearly defined goals becomes essential. This applies as much to the residential treatment of children as to any other form of therapy. I have discussed the subject more fully elsewhere (Barker, 1985, Chapter 4; 1986a, Chapter 6); but, in summary, one must consider the following questions in discussing objectives with clients:

(a) The desired state, or "outcome frame" as the developers of neuro-linguistic programming (Dilts et al., 1980; Bandler and Grinder, 1979) call it, must be well defined. This means that a clear description is required of how things will be when treatment is successfully completed.

(b) The objectives of therapy should be framed in positive terms. It is not sufficient to say that a child's temper tantrums should cease. A more important question is, what should replace them? In other words, how should the child respond to situations in which tantrums now occur? Or perhaps the parents do not want their children to be constantly fighting with each other. What should the children be doing in place of fighting?

(c) Besides being stated positively, goals should be operationally defined. It is not enough for people to say that they want "to be a happy family" or "to get along well together." The therapist must know more precisely what the family's definition of a "happy family" is, and just how family members would be interacting if they were "getting along well together." If family members would like to be doing more things together, they should be asked what particular things they want to do together. It may turn out that they are far from agreed on the objective, and that different family members have very different ideas about what they would like their collective activities to be.

(d) The next question is, will there be any drawbacks to the desired state? Will something that provides gratification for some family member be lost, without its being replaced by a satisfactory alternative? For example, if a daughter who would not eat the food her mother prepares starts to eat without protest, will there be less closeness between mother and daughter? If so, will this be a problem for the mother? Or will the change result in less closeness between the parents, who will no longer have the daughter's eating problems to discuss, or to argue about?

(e) Will there be any other consequences, not yet considered, of the proposed objectives?

(f) What has so far stopped the clients from making the desired changes? This question is closely related to the two foregoing ones, but approaches the issue from a different perspective.

(g) Under what circumstances are the changes desired? Most behaviors have value in certain situations. Anger, feelings of unhappiness, and stubborn behavior can all be appropriate in some circumstances; so it is important to define the context of the desired changes.

(h) How quickly should the desired changes occur? Change can necessitate big adjustments by all concerned, which may take time. Asking this question has the added advantage of replacing consideration of whether change will occur with discussion of the timetable for change, the implicit message being that the changes *will* occur. Indeed therapists should always talk and act on the assumption that treatment will be successful; if they do not evidently believe in what is proposed, it is unlikely that those they are treating will. (An exception, of course, is the use of paradoxical injunctions, but this is a different matter.)

3. Problems should be identified as the family's from the start. The patient, or client, is the family, not the child.

4. The parents should be involved in all major decisions affecting the young person, and as many minor ones as possible, throughout treatment.

5. A discharge plan should exist from the time of admission, even though it may need to be modified as new information becomes available. The plan should include where, and into whose care, the child is to be discharged, together with a target discharge date.

6. While in residential treatment the young person should spend as much time as possible in the physical care of the parent(s) or guardians. "Earning" time with the family, or making visits home contingent upon certain behaviors, is generally to be avoided, as that inevitably carries the message that only a "good" child is welcome at home. The primary aim of therapy should be to produce change in the family system rather than to focus on the "problem" child.

7. Prolonged periods of residential treatment—more than, say, six

months—should be considered only after a detailed assessment of the situation has been made by all involved (including the young person him- or herself, the parent(s) or guardians, and other concerned members of the family), and all other possibilities have been ruled out for adequate reasons. Further similar reviews should be held at regular intervals, I suggest at least once every three months, so that the need for continuing residential treatment is examined critically, instead of being accepted as inevitable.

8. Those responsible for the treatment of disturbed children should always bear in mind the children's basic developmental needs. As O'Brien and Gerad (1985, p. 336), quoting Arndt and Gruber (1977), point out:

> It is within the family that individuals first develop the feeling of belonging, a sense of self-worth, the ability to trust others, and a capacity for intimate relationships.

Removing children from their families disrupts these processes, and ensuring that the processes occur in residential settings presents great challenges. Too often I have seen adolescents who have spent several, even most, of their formative years in residential settings, some of them avowedly therapeutic, others claiming to provide no more than "care." Although such young people presumably have had serious problems before removed from their families, it is a tragedy that they often fail to develop any of the above personality strengths while in residential treatment. In fact, long-term residential care may leave young people with feelings of worthlessness, distrustful attitudes toward the world, difficulty with intimate relationships, and the feeling of belonging nowhere and to no one.

How exactly to avoid these difficulties I am not sure, but I suspect that awareness of the dangers; continuing intimate contacts with their families; brief, focused, and goal-oriented periods in residential treatment; and avoidance of moves from one residential setting to another, will all help.

A BLUEPRINT FOR THE FUTURE

So, how is residential treatment for disturbed children likely to develop, in the light of the points we have considered so far?

Probable developments include greater emphasis on the family as the unit of treatment, even though it is the child who is admitted; shorter periods of treatment; the formulation of clearer and more specific therapy goals; and better integration of residential programs with other community treatment resources. Rather than being a treatment modality in its own right, residential treatment will come to be regarded as but one part of a spectrum of services. Admission to a residential center seldom is the first treatment measure implemented; it is considered only when less drastic and costly treatments, carrying less risk of institutionalization and interference with personality development, have been given a fair trial.

Admission usually follows a period of treatment that has involved the whole family, with the child still living at home. If this has failed to achieve the desired results, and if one of the indications described above exists, a residential treatment plan, with clearly defined objectives, is worked out. Progress toward the goals is continuously monitored. If it is unsatisfactory, the benefits of having the child in the residential setting must be reconsidered. The residential placement and treatment of the child should always be just part of a treatment plan that involves the whole family. Family unwillingness to participate constitutes a critical situation. Intensive work to involve the family, or the finding of a substitute family, may be needed.

Discharge planning starts before admission, and is a continuous process thereafter. Both child and family know exactly what is going on, and consider themselves active participants in the planning process. The residential unit is open to family members in an informal way. The key figures in the child's life will not change at the time of discharge home because the same clinical team will continue to be involved, and the same therapists will conduct any individual and/or family therapy that is under way.

Desirable developments, which I hope will characterize the future development of residential programs, include:

1. Clearer descriptions of their aims and programs, in terms meaningful to the lay public, by those running residential treatment centers.
2. Flexible programming that places the convenience of families and community contacts before expediency and the convenience of residential staff.
3. Close liaison between residential centers and relevant professionals in the communities they serve, ideally with extensive cross-staffing, so that children do not feel they are being handed over from one set of adults to another when they are admitted or discharged.
4. Rigorous program evaluation, and research projects designed to measure the effectiveness of different aspects of residential programs, as well as any undesirable side effects of such programs.

There may also be a place for the further development of programs for the admission of whole families, if only for brief periods, as suggested by Dydyk and her colleagues (1982). Writing of the "intensive family therapy unit" at Thistletown Regional Center for Children and Adolescents, these authors describe the admission of whole families, one at a time, to a special unit (in their case a four-bedroom house) for intensive assessment and treatment by a team of therapists, over a period of a few days. This provides at least a short-term alternative to removal of children to residential settings. It can also provide consultation for therapists or agencies who are "stuck" in their management of family systems. It may reveal possible alternatives to residential treatment, but if the latter is still required, it can mean that additional diagnostic information is obtained prior to admission. This helps define the family's treatment needs, and so may shorten any period of residential treatment.

Children who have no "home" in the community, and have no sense of "belonging" anywhere, will not be admitted, as was long ago advocated by Wardle (1974) in an important contribution to the literature on residential treatment. Instead, such children first will be provided with a home, and adults whom they can regard as parent figures. Only then will residential treatment be considered.

The developmental needs of both the children and their parents will be assessed and borne in mind throughout treatment, and a focus of the family work will be on providing for these needs. In many cases, the parents themselves will have pressing therapeutic needs, and residential centers will be as concerned with providing for these needs as they are with the needs of the children in residence. "Re-parenting" of the parents, as described by Kirschner and Kirschner (1986) will often be needed, and the staff will be expert in providing this. They also will have available, within their therapeutic repertoire, many innovative techniques such as those described by Ney and Mulvihill (1985). The staff will understand clearly that if the parents' needs are not met, the long-term results of their treatment of the children in their care are likely to be poor.

The following chapters will elaborate on many of these suggestions and describe a number of other ways to improve the effectiveness of residential treatment for children.

REFERENCES

Arndt, C. M. and Gruber, M. (1977). Helping families cope with acute and anticipatory grief. In E. R. Prichard and J. Collard, eds., Social Work with the Dying Patient and the Family. New York: Columbia University Press.

Bandler, R. and Grinder, J. (1979). Frogs into Princes. Moab, Utah: Real People Press.

Barker, P. (1968). The inpatient treatment of school refusal. British Journal of Medical Psychology, 41, 381–387.

Barker, P. (1974a). History. In P. Barker, ed., The Residential Psychiatric Treatment of Children. New York: Halstead Press.

Barker, P. (1974b). The results of inpatient treatment. In P. Barker, ed., *The Residential Psychiatric Treatment of Children*. New York: Halstead Press.

Barker, P. (1982). Residential treatment for disturbed children: its place in the '80s. *Canadian Journal of Psychiatry, 27,* 634–639.

Barker, P. (1985). *Using Metaphors in Psychotherapy*. New York: Brunner/Mazel.

Barker, P. (1986a). *Basic Family Therapy,* 2nd edition. London: Collins; and New York: Oxford University Press.

Barker, P. (1986b). Milton Erickson's contribution to psychiatry. *British Journal of Psychiatry, 148,* 471–475.

Barton, R. (1966). *Institutional Neurosis.* Baltimore: Williams and Wilkins.

Beckett, J. A. (1973). General systems theory, psychiatry and psychotherapy. *International Journal of Group Psychotherapy, 23,* 292–305.

Boyle, M. H. and Offord, D. R. (1986). Smoking, drinking and use of illicit drugs among adolescents in Ontario, *Canadian Medical Association Journal, 135,* 1113–1121.

Dilts, R., Grinder, J., Bandler, L. C., and DeLozier, J. (1980). *Neuro-Linguistic Programming,* Vol. I. Cupertino, Calif.: Meta Publications.

Dydyk, B., French, G., Gertsman, C., and Morrison, N. (1982). Admission of whole families. *Canadian Journal of Psychiatry, 27,* 640–643.

Freud, S. (1916–17). Introductory lectures on psychoanalysis, lecture 28: analytic theory. In J. Strachey, ed., *The Standard Edition of the Complete Psychological Works of Sigmund Freud.* London: Hogarth, p. 459.

Haley, J. (1976). *Problem-Solving Therapy.* San Francisco: Jossey-Bass.

Haley, J. (1985). *Conversations with Milton H. Erickson, M.D.,* Vol. I: *Changing Individuals.* New York: Triangle Press.

Henao, S. (1985). A systems approach to family medicine. In S. Henao and N. P. Grose, eds., *Principles of Family Systems in Family Medicine.* New York: Brunner/Mazel.

Kirschner, D. A. and Kirschner, S. (1986). *Comprehensive Family Therapy: An Integration of Systemic and Psychodynamic Models.* New York: Brunner/Mazel.

Madanes, C. (1981). *Strategic Family Therapy.* San Francisco: Jossey-Bass.

Ney, P. and Mulvihill, D. (1985). *Child Psychiatric Treatment: A Practical Guide.* Beckenham, Kent: Croom Helm.

O'Brien, J. G. and Gerard, R. J. (1985). A death in the family. In S. Henao and N. P. Grose, eds., *Principles of Family Systems in Family Medicine.* New York: Brunner/Mazel.

Offord, D. R., Boyle, M. H., Szatmari, P., Rae-Grant, N. I., Links, P. S., Cadman, D. T., Byles, J. A., Crawford, J. W., Blum, H. M., Byrne, C., Thomas, H., and Woodward, C. A. (1987). 'Ontario child health study: prevalence of disorder and rates of service utilization.' *Archives of General Psychiatry,* in press.

Redl, F. and Wineman, D. (1951). *Children Who Hate.* Glencoe: The Free Press.

Redl, F. and Wineman, D. (1952). *Controls from Within.* Glencoe: The Free Press.

Romig, D. (1978). *Justice for Our Children.* Lexington, Mass.: Lexington Books.

Rutter, M., Tizard, J., and Whitmore, K. (1970). *Education, Health and Behaviour.* London: Longman.

Shamsie, S. J. (1981). Antisocial adolescents: our treatments do not work—where do we go from here? *Canadian Journal of Psychiatry, 26,* 357–364.

Toffler, A. (1980). *The Third Wave.* New York: William Morrow.

Vorrath, H. H. and Brendthro, L. K. (1976). *Positive Peer Culture.* Chicago: Aldine Press.

Wardle, C. J. (1974). Residential care of children with conduct disorders. In P. Barker, ed., *The Residential Psychiatric Treatment of Children.* New York: Halstead Press.

Whittaker, J. (1979). *Caring for Troubled Children.* San Francisco: Jossey-Bass.

Part I

CLINICAL ISSUES

The following chapters have been selected because they address many of the key clinical issues faced by practitioners in residential treatment. Compared to children in outpatient treatment, those in residential treatment require more comprehensive clinical services. These services include treatment of the individual child and of the child in relation to his or her environment and family. These chapters offer a rich mixture of theory and practice in each of these treatment domains.

2

Helping Children Deal with Separation and Loss in Residential Placement

Arthur J. Swanson
and
Charles E. Schaefer

Separation is one of the most common human experiences. All of us, at different periods in our lives, experience the loss of significant others. While the cause for a loss may vary (loss through death, moving away, estrangement, etc.), its psychological effect often assumes a rather predictable pattern. Children who enter residential treatment are confronted with issues of separation and loss prior to, during, and after their period of stay. Furthermore, children's experiences of separation and loss during placement are often exacerbated by their having endured other losses prior to their placement in residential care. The purpose of the present chapter is twofold: first, to examine issues of attachment and separation and their subsequent effects, particularly how separation is experienced by the child; and second, to offer concrete suggestions for dealing with issues of separation and loss with the family and the child in residential treatment. The focus is not only on helping the child accept separation and loss as inevitable aspects of life, but on using these experiences to enhance the child's emotional growth.

BOWLBY'S THEORY OF ATTACHMENT

John Bowlby, a British psychoanalyst, proposed that attachment is an innate tendency of members of a species to maintain proximity for the purposes of survival (Bowlby, 1969). That is, children have a natural predilection to attach, particularly to one person. In his theory, attachment is distinguished from dependence. Whereas dependence occurs as a result of a child's having physiological needs met, attachment is more of a psychological phenomenon that occurs as a result of an ongoing interaction with an adult or adults in the environment. As the child comes to perceive that the responsible adult is a consistent and reliable caretaker, a "secure attachment" is formed. The development of such an attachment allows the child to experience greater ease in future separations from the primary caretaker and from significant others.

When a child is not provided a secure base, by virtue of a parent's failure to interact consistently with the child at an early stage of development, an "anxious attachment" may be formed. Children who are anxiously attached frequently experience greater fears of separation, due, in part, to their uncertainty as to whether or not they can count on their primary attachment figures. These children often present with excessive demands for attention as they attempt to satisfy their unfulfilled needs for nurturance.

Children who have formed an anxious attachment with the primary attachment figure, and who experience other significant losses, may become acutely sensitive to any kind of separation or loss. As such, they may become frightened or anxious in situations that would not appear alarming to others.

Children entering residential care frequently have not established the secure attachment referred to by Bowlby. Many of the children have been victims of chronic neglect and/or have interacted with multiple caretakers prior to forming a relationship with one primary attachment figure. As a result, these children may be considered to be at great risk for experiencing psychological pain when faced with separation from individuals to whom they are not securely attached. Much of this pain is evidenced through a series of fairly predictable stages of grieving.

STAGES OF GRIEVING

In his observations of normal infants and children separated from their families, Bowlby (1973) identified three basic stages of grieving. The initial stage he labeled *protest,* in which the child rejects the new environment in anger over the loss. In the second stage, the child begins to exhibit *despair,* characterized by withdrawal and sadness over loss of the love object. In the *detachment* stage, the child emancipates himself from the prior attachment and begins to adapt to the new environment. In a study of loss among foster children, Thomas (1967) proposed a *preprotest* phase, characterized by a lack of response to the loss. Such a phase corresponds to Kubler-Ross's (1969) initial stage of *denial,* in which individuals dying of terminal illness fail to accept the reality of their situation. For both children and those dying of terminal illness, this denial stage appears to serve the adaptive function of giving the individual time to mobilize resources to face the impending loss.

Bowlby's stages of grieving demonstrate the range of feelings experienced by normal children who are separated from their families. When that separation occurs as a result of a child's being placed out of the home, the child may experience additional thoughts and feelings. For example, the child may feel that the placement is not for the purpose of seeking treatment but rather as a punishment for bad behavior. In some cases, this is, in fact, the message communicated by the parents. In other cases, however, the child perceives that he is being rejected by the family because he is a "bad kid." In a study comparing children who were "abandoned" to those who lost their parent through death, the former group demonstrated significantly more emotional problems (Mishne, 1979). Abandoned children tended to show less empathy for others, less ability to relate, less capacity to learn, and a limited ability to explore feelings. Mishne believes that abandoned children experience more emotional pain, in the knowledge that their parents have made an active choice not to live with them, whereas parents who have died have made no such choice. Although abandoned children may possess strong feelings of anger toward their parents, these feelings may be too threatening to express, and may be manifested in feelings of guilt and self-doubt.

To the extent that children placed in residential treatment are not securely attached, and perceive that they are being abandoned by their caretakers, they are likely to respond even more strongly to separation from their families than would securely attached children seeking treatment. This is not to say, however, that their responses will follow one predictable pattern of behavior. In fact, children may show a wide range of reactions to placement. One child may present as exceedingly cold and aloof, protecting himself from another possible rejection by refusing to get involved with caregivers in the new setting. Another child may be extremely compliant, in an effort to please others lest he be sent away again. Still another might act aggressively toward others in order to be rejected once again, to confirm his belief that he is unworthy of being loved. Finally, another child might act immaturely, regressing to behavior characteristic of a much younger child to succor nurturance from his new caretakers. Although children may choose one of the above patterns as a predominant manner of interacting, typically they exhibit a range of behaviors occurring either concurrently or at different points in treatment.

Although potential hazards exist in separating children from their parents by placing the children in residential care, in some circumstances such placement proves to be the most therapeutic option. For example, such a setting is appropriate for children who have been abused or chronically neglected and whose special needs preclude either outpatient therapy or placement in a foster home. More generally, in those situations in which families express serious concern over their ability to manage the behavior of their children, residential placement may be indicated. While in placement, the child and the family may gain a necessary respite from one another while beginning, separately at first, and then together, to work toward the child's eventual return home. Viewing the child's separation from his family as part of an ongoing therapeutic process rather than as an entity in itself will assist both the worker and the family to deal with the issue of separation effectively.

Given that separation experiences in life are inevitable and, in the case of some children, unavoidable, the following are some suggestions for helping children cope with the separation feelings they may experience prior to, during, and at the conclusion of placement in residential care. Although the recommendations offered were derived from the authors' work with boys in residential treatment, they would appear to be equally applicable to girls in a similar setting.

RECOMMENDATIONS FOR EASING THE TRANSITION INTO RESIDENTIAL TREATMENT

All too often, children are placed in residential care too abruptly, with poor planning and with little opportunity for them to comprehend and master this extremely stressful situation. Careful preparation of a child for placement can help minimize the harmful effects of such a move and maximize the opportunity every crisis presents for change and growth.

Some procedures to help a child cope with the loss of home and acceptance of a new placement are given in the following paragraphs.

Notify the Child in Advance. Parents should be advised to begin discussion of the possibility of placement in small doses; in other words, planning and discussion should be done in separate, tactful steps. Initially, the child should be told of the possibility of placement. He should be kept informed at each step in the process as placement planning becomes more specific. As the child adapts to proposed changes and is able to accept them at each step in the process, he becomes emotionally prepared to move on to the next step.

In addition, parents should listen to their child's thoughts and feelings about placement and convey their understanding and acceptance of his reactions.

Also, the child should be involved in the planning process as much as possible so he can maintain a sense of control over his own life. For example, allow the child to choose clothes and toys to bring with him when he enters placement.

Parents should describe in detail what life will be like at the institution (the program, facilities, staff, and expectations of the child) and ways to cope with the new environment.

Arrange Preplacement Visiting. Encourage the child (and his family) to visit and become as familiar as possible with the agency before he moves in. He should talk with both staff and other children in the cottage he will enter. The child care worker should talk with the boy alone and encourage him to express his feelings and thoughts about placement.

Comfort and Counsel the Parents. The caseworker should actively assist the parents in expressing and dealing with feelings of guilt, inadequacy, failure, and mourning. Otherwise, the child will perceive his parents' distress about the separation and respond with comparable upset. The more accepting the parents are of placement, the more easily the child will adapt to his new surroundings.

Once the child is placed, it is essential that parents continue to assume a central role in his treatment. This can be accomplished best by carefully delineating parental rights and responsibilities at the outset of treatment. Treatment contracts signed by parents and staff are particularly effective in clarifying these expectations.

Let the Child Bring Some "Transitional Objects." Familiar objects such as toys or clothing brought from home can be a source of comfort to a child entering residential care. Photographs can also help the child deal with separation from his family. Allow the child to hang photos of family members on the wall or to place them on his dresser.

Give the Child a Welcome Gift. A "welcome to the cottage" gift could be given to a boy when he arrives; for example, a car or a small stuffed animal. Some agencies present each new child with a soft teddy bear to provide a source of comfort, as well as an outlet for frustration and anger.

Prepare Staff and the Other Children in the Cottage. When possible, staff and the children in an admitting cottage should be notified a week in advance of an upcoming admission. Pertinent information such as the child's name, age, and reason for referral should be given to the child care staff. Admissions should not occur just prior to a major holiday.

Assign a "Buddy" from the Cottage. The new child could be assigned a "buddy" whose job it is to be a special friend and to orient him to the cottage and the agency during the first two weeks.

Allow Time to "Settle In" at the Cottage. On admission day, the social worker should accompany the child and his parents to the cottage to meet the child care workers. It is usually best for the parents to stay while the child unpacks his bag. The child care worker should ask the parent about the child: his favorite foods, special interests, sleeping habits, and other idiosyncrasies. This settling-in period also gives the parents time to get to know the child care staff, and thus alleviates some of their anxiety about leaving their child with a stranger. If possible, have the new child arrive before the others return from school. In this way, he can receive extra attention from staff and can assimilate things gradually. It is often desirable to hold a child back from school for a day or two in order for him to become more familiar with his new environment and his new caretakers.

It is important that staff avoid enacting what has been referred to as the "adoption process" in the institutional care of children (Palmer et al., 1983). In this process, staff may take on inappropriate parenting functions to the exclusion of the child's parents. Staff may view the family as the cause of the child's placement and as "unworkable." The subtle, or not so subtle, communication of the staff's feelings toward the parents may cause them to avoid contact with staff and reduce their level of involvement in the child's treatment. This may, in turn, be experienced by both staff and child as rejection and abandonment of the child.

Schedule Regular Admission Days. If possible, a cottage or unit should admit children only on certain days, to facilitate the admission process for all concerned. For example, the second and fourth Thursdays of a month could be unit admission days. Children handle stress and change better when others are going through it with them.

Establish Regular Casework Contact. The child's social worker/therapist should see the child within 24 hours of his arrival and meet with him regularly to establish a supportive relationship.

The social worker can help the child to:

- Understand why it is necessary to live away from the family, and realize that his family has his best interests at heart. (The social worker should explain the facts of the child's placement to him and help the child overcome the feeling of being abandoned.)
- Resolve confusion and conflict about having to live away from home, insofar as possible.
- Recognize the limitations of the family situation.
- See that something positive can come from the change (instill hope).
- Understand the purpose and goals of placement. (The child should know what problems brought about his placement and what issues must be resolved before he can return home; often the child needs to be dissuaded of notions that he is serving a "sentence" in residential care, and that he has no control over the timing of his discharge.)
- See that, although he will be well taken care of by staff, no one will try to take the place of his biological parents.
- Find solutions to homesickness, such as writing letters home, calling home occasionally, or listening to a tape recording of a parent's voice.

- Work through ambivalent feelings about his parents.
- Understand the roles of the various staff members working with him.
- Make constructive use of the available resources and relationships.

In conjunction with casework contacts, a "new admissions" group can be formed in which newly admitted children meet for a designated amount of time to discuss issues of separation as well as to become oriented to their new surroundings. Including a more mature child already in residence to act as a co-leader in such a group can prove particularly beneficial to incoming children.

Facilitate Grief Work. Give permission for the child to grieve: to acknowledge the loss of family and home, and to express sadness, anger, and other feelings that accompany such losses. Children need to understand that such feelings are normal and expected.

Assist the child to recognize and label his feelings (guilt, sadness, fear) so he does not have to act them out through withdrawal or aggression. Once the child has some words to describe his inner experiences, he and staff can share the experiences.

Allow the child to go through the grieving process at his own pace. Usually there is a need to work through the various stages of grief over and over until acceptance and readjustment occur. The more disturbed the child is, the more repetition he will need. Staff responses should include respect, understanding, and caring.

Help the child discriminate between appropriate times to ventilate grief (e.g., in your office) and inappropriate times, when he should suppress such thoughts and feelings (e.g., in the classroom).

Encourage the child to find partial replacements or substitutes for his losses and to develop attachments to new things that will give pleasure, such as a new friend or hobby. At the same time, the child needs to understand that he does not have to reject his parents or previous caretakers in order to feel comfortable in his new surroundings.

Discuss with the child ways you have handled separations in your life that proved useful to you. The child may not only learn from your experiences; he may also be comforted by the knowledge that others have had similar experiences and could themselves find effective means of dealing with separation and loss.

HANDLING SEPARATION EXPERIENCES DURING PLACEMENT

Express Caring. The child should be called or visited by other children in his cottage, as well as by staff members, if he is separated from his cottage for a significant period of time. Examples include time spent in the infirmary, at home (for more than four days), or in the hospital.

It is important for the child who is away to get emotional support from his friends in the cottage. Caring for and about others is thus taught to children in the cottage, as well as to the child who is away. If a child has been away for an extended period of time, he should be given a special welcome back.

Respect Private Property. The child should be encouraged to learn to share with other children toys and games that belong to the cottage. However, he should have a secure place to keep personal property, and should be allowed to decide when and with whom to share this property. Often, the personal property a child brings with him represents his ties to his home and family. If a child loses something he cherishes, every effort by staff and other children should be made to get it back or replace it.

Deal with Own Separation Experiences. The departure of staff members or other children from a cottage offers an excellent opportunity for adults to model for the child appropriate ways of handling grief and expressing feelings. Many of the strategies we describe here for helping the child deal with separation can be applied equally well to adults experiencing similar losses. To the extent that staff "practice what they preach," the child will learn to deal successfully with issues of separation and loss.

RECOMMENDATIONS FOR HELPING CHILDREN ADJUST TO DISCHARGE

Discharge from a residential treatment center constitutes a developmental crisis similar to that encountered by the child upon admission. The departing child must repeat the emotional process of separation, this time from staff and peers. The child experiences several types of loss in the act of leaving, including:

1. *Physical losses:* Food, clothing, and shelter, once provided by staff, will begin to be provided by parents or other caretakers. The child may not feel secure that his physical needs will continue to be met after discharge, especially if parental neglect in the past led to his placement.
2. *Psychosocial losses:* Relationships with staff and peers and the child's identity as a member of the cottage group will undergo dramatic changes as a result of the discharge. The child may find it difficult to separate himself from these relationships and may be unwilling to give up his identity as a resident of the cottage.

3. *Socio-cultural losses:* Educational, recreational, and religious needs once again must be served by the child's home community. The child may doubt the community's ability to meet these needs.

The form and substance in which these losses are experienced will be different for each child. The child about to leave a residential placement almost always needs encouragement and reassurance to resolve the developmental crisis posed by departure. During the entire termination phase, but especially around the time of imminent departure, the developmental tasks faced by the departing child and his responses to these tasks often test the clinical skills (and the patience) of staff.

Many therapists view leaving as the central issue in treatment: the successful termination of therapy presents the child a chance to end a key relationship with emotional maturity, and may help him leave behind unresolved needs and longings that linger from infancy (Allen, 1942). So, termination affords an important growth opportunity for children. As therapy ends, the child must learn to look to himself and others for the strength previously provided by the therapeutic milieu. He may also need to realize that some yearnings (i.e., immediate and unending needs for nurturance from authority figures) are impossible to satisfy.

The following are some recommendations for easing the stress of separation for children who are about to be discharged from the agency.

Individual Counseling. Separation issues should be discussed in therapy, starting three to six months prior to the planned discharge. Casework objectives at this time should include the following:

- Help the child face and resolve feelings about leaving the residential facility, the staff, and the other children. [the use of therapeutic stories dealing with separation can be particularly helpful in this regard (Wegner, 1982; Crenshaw et al., 1986)].
- Discuss accomplishments in relation to initial goals; help the child understand why these changes did or did not take place.
- Discuss anxieties and concerns about adjusting to the return home or the move to the new placement.
- Anticipate the child's future problems (although problems may have been resolved, they might re-emerge and cause the child new difficulties).
- Assure the child that community services are ready to serve him if he needs help again.
- Let the child know that your interest in him will continue after discharge; discuss ways to keep in touch and maintain the relationship.

- Involve the child in decision making and problem solving concerning discharge; get the child actively involved in discharge planning so he will not feel helpless when he leaves.

If the child contributes to decisions determining his fate after discharge, that helps him to feel independent and in control of his life; also a child is likely to become involved in and accepting of a plan he has helped to develop. So, involve the child in decisions regarding:

- Whom he will live with on a permanent basis.
- Ways to avoid the problems that led to initial placement.
- Selection of after-school activities.
- Participation in outpatient therapy.

Increased Home Contacts. The six months prior to discharge should involve increased contacts for the child with his family and community. This will allow the child to make a gradual transition from his current placement to his home and community.

Group Therapy. Three months prior to discharge, a "discharge group" might be formed in which staff members encourage children who are about to leave to share their thoughts and feelings about leaving and their expectations for the future.

Goodbye Rituals. Prior to the child's leaving, a group session should be held in the cottage to provide an opportunity for the child to discuss his plans, goals, and feelings, as well as to allow the other children to express their feelings about his leaving, to reminisce, and to express words of encouragement and advice.

In addition, a "goodbye" party should be held in the cottage. This ceremony should include a cake, small gifts from the children remaining behind, and a farewell speech by staff. A framed picture of children and staff in the cottage or a scrapbook would make a practical and appropriate gift. It is also possible to provide children with "discharge papers" signed by peers and staff who are close to the child.

Vicarious Experience. The children remaining in the cottage should be helped by child care counselors to use this departure as an opportunity to confront their own feelings and fantasies about past and future separations and losses. In this way the departure of a child may create motivation for change for those children remaining behind.

Maintain Contact. Departing youngsters should be given the phone number of the cottage. After a week, a staff person and some of the child's friends should call him to say "hello." He should be encouraged to join an alumni association and to come back and visit. Assuming adequate resources are available, after-care services should also be provided.

SUMMARY AND CONCLUSIONS

Bowlby's theories of attachment and grieving have been applied to the separation experiences of children in residential placement. What becomes evident is that although these children may manifest feelings of loss differently, they are, by and large, acutely sensitive to such feelings. Numerous concrete suggestions have been offered to help children with these feelings at the beginning, middle, and end of treatment. The actual details of such suggestions are less important than is the need for each clinician to become sensitive to the separation process. In developing such sensitivity, clinicians need to acknowledge and express their own feelings of loss in order to be accepting of similar feelings expressed by the children in their care. Given a sensitive clinical staff and the regular implementation of specific procedures relevant to separation and loss, children in residential care can learn not only to cope with such experiences but to be strengthened by them.

REFERENCES

Allen, F. H. (1942). *Psychotherapy with Children*. New York: Norton.
Bowlby, J. (1969). *Attachment and Loss*, Vol. 1. New York: Basic Books.
Bowlby, J. (1973). *Separation, Anxiety and Anger*. New York: Basic Books.
Crenshaw, D. A., Holden, A., Kittridge, J., and McGuirk, J. (1986). Therapeutic techniques to facilitate termination in child psychotherapy. Manuscript submitted for publication.
Kubler-Ross, E. (1969). *On Death and Dying*. New York: Macmillan.
Mishne, J. (1979). Parental abandonment: a unique form of loss and narcissistic injury. *Clinical Social Work Journal, 7*, 15–33.
Palmer, A. J., Harper, G., and Rivinus, T. M. (1983). The "adoption process" in inpatient treatment of children and adolescents. *Journal of the American Academy of Child Psychiatry, 22*, 286–293.
Thomas, C. (1967). The resolution of object loss following foster home placement. *Smith College Studies in Social Work, 39* (Vol. 3).
Wegner, C. (1982). The suitcase story: a therapeutic technique for children in out-of-home placement. *American Journal of Orthopsychiatry, 52*, 335–353.

3

Crisis Intervention in Residential Care

Mark Katz

Upon speaking with Johnny, one quickly learns that he is feeling extremely vulnerable and somewhat abused. He wants nothing more than to be accepted, appreciated, and recognized. Instead he feels victimized, exploited, and devalued. Although he seems to long for the opportunity to share more of himself emotionally, the thought of this frightens him. He feels that he has tried this in the past, but that his efforts have been at times unheard. Johnny is feeling alone and unsupported. Beneath his stoic demeanor lies an individual crying out for help.

Johnny came to residential care roughly six months ago. He is twenty-eight years old, and works as a child care worker.

Johnny has learned that there are children in residential care who, by the way in which they communicate to us the rage, desperation, or despair that they feel, are masterful in their ability to evoke in us extremely intense and powerful emotions. As a child care worker, Johnny is particularly at risk for having these emotions emerge because it is his responsibility to respond to these children in their times of greatest crisis.

For Johnny to be truly effective in helping these children, he will need some ongoing help himself. Ideally, the help will come from a cohesive group of care givers—a treatment team that collectively attends not only to the emotional needs and emotional well-being of the children in treatment but also to each other's emotional health as well.

This simultaneous attention to the needs of both child and child care giver is essential if we are to address effectively the issues, struggles, and conflicts that bring many children to residential care, and that often underlie the various crises they experience. It represents a necessary first step in the successful implementation of the assessment and intervention procedures that will be covered in this chapter.

INTRODUCTION

Although we know that many children in residential care are vulnerable to moments of crisis, we sometimes are less sure of what critical information we can derive from these crises to help us reduce the occurrence of similar episodes. Perhaps even more important, we are uncertain about what critical skills we might be able to teach children to help them control their own behavior—eventually, we hope, in the absence of the highly structured surroundings inherent in residential care. In this chapter we will take a close look at the critical information and critical skills that can be derived, at least in part, from knowledge gained in crises. We will discuss ways in which a child care worker can increase his or her awareness of the precipitants or triggers that might underlie a child's out-of-control behavior, and how the child care worker can plan to reduce the likelihood of future out-of-control experiences. Following sections will focus on the specific skills that children can develop in order to control their emotions and actions, and ways in which the child care worker might assist children in developing these skills. A few comments are in order first.

Many children in residential treatment will express their vulnerability by moments of out-of-control behavior. Occasionally they will find themselves overwhelmed by their emotions and unable to control their actions. They may fail to appreciate on these occasions the possible harmful effects of such behavior, either personally or with respect to the welfare of others. At such times, these children may be completely dependent upon skilled child care staff stepping in to provide, as benignly as possible, the safety, security, relief, and control that are lacking.

In their efforts to help the out-of-control child regain control, professional child care staff are asked to pay very close attention to the stage of the episode, and to intervene in a manner that will relate to the level of control that may remain. A child who is just beginning to lose control, for instance, may still be responsive to efforts to provide a safe option, a time-out perhaps, in which he or she can better think through the situation at hand, rather than respond impulsively to it. A child in a more advanced stage, on the other hand, may be much less responsive to such interventions, and the child care worker may have to let the episode run its course.

Various contributors to the field of residential care, such as Trieschman (1969), have been very helpful in providing us a conceptual framework for understanding the notion of stages of out-of-control behavior, and how these different stages may require different types of interventions. Redl and Wineman (1957) have also helped us to appreciate the inherent clinical value of providing our interventions in the context of the child's day-to-day experience in residential care—frequently referred to as the child's life space. If we provide our interventions within the existing milieu, perhaps when an experience is still fresh, the child may be able to learn from the experience. Many specific and practical approaches are available to us in our efforts to assist children to regain control, and to do so safely. A great deal can be learned from the workshops offered, and resource materials provided, by such organizations as the National Organization of Child Care Worker Associations. The organization is continually updating its files on available materials relevant to handling the various crises that emerge in residential care.

CRITICAL INFORMATION AND CRITICAL SKILLS THAT CAN BE LEARNED FROM CRISES*

All out-of-control episodes have a starting point. By paying very close attention to these starting points, we can learn a great deal about what types of situations, experiences, events, or conditions are likely to be difficult for a particular child, and which of them might be likely to precipiate or trigger some form of overreaction. We may be able to learn why one child finds a particular situation difficult, and why another child finds another experience painful or personally threatening. Then, after looking closely at a child's vulnerabilities or existing resources, we might also learn that even with his or her best efforts, the child may still be unable to withstand the pressures of a certain situation or experience. We might become aware of the times in which we are asking "too much, too soon" from the child. From our observations of and interventions in crises, and our discussions with other members of the treatment team, we can begin to assimilate this information, so that we can make needed changes that will allow us to prevent many future out-of-control experiences.

After working through a crisis with a child, we may be able to identify specific skills that the child must develop in order to control his or her own behavior, and ultimately to do so under less structured and less supervised surroundings. We can then formulate interventions to assist the child in developing these critical skills. Specifically, we will be better able to assist the child in acquiring:

1. An increased awarenesss of the specific situations, events, or experiences that represent the greatest risk for out-of-control behavior.
2. The abiljty to anticipate, plan, and think ahead about upcoming events or situations that might trigger an overreaction of some sort.

---

*For purposes of this discussion, the crises referred to will for the most part pertain to latency age children in residential care. Many of the precipitating factors, sources of vulnerability, and critical skills to be learned might also apply to some teenagers in residential care.

3. The ability to identify subjective feelings or sensations that may signal to the child that he or she is susceptible to losing control.
4. A greater capacity to express emotions verbally, and ultimately to gain confidence in relying upon language rather than acting-out forms of behavior to communicate difficult or painful emotional experiences.
5. Specific alternative responses that can be called upon when the child is especially at risk for out-of-control behavior.
6. The ability to evaluate his or her own behavior independently, including his or her effectiveness in anticipating certain difficult moments, and in planning and responding accordingly.

In combination, these skills can be very important for effective problem solving. Once acquired, they can afford these children tools to use later on, to regulate and control their actions and emotions when they are no longer in the highly structured surroundings of residential care.

INCREASING THE CHILD CARE STAFF'S AWARENESS OF THE PRECIPITANTS OF A CHILD'S OUT-OF-CONTROL BEHAVIOR

Once we identify a child's principal areas of vulnerability as they manifest themselves in residential care, we can take a closer look at some probable reasons for these high-risk situations. We can, for example, begin to look more closely at possible conflicts or dynamics that may be underscored by certain situations, the specific deficits or disabilities that may be highlighted by certain task requirements and situational demands, or the very sensitive feelings and painful emotions that may be stimulated by certain experiences. *We may then be able to provide ahead of time the extra support, comfort, guidance, or structure that a child might need, at least initially, to effectively withstand a particularly difficult situation or experience. We will also be in a position to alter the particularly difficult situation if we think that the child does not have the resources needed to handle the situation effectively, even with extra support and direction.* It thus becomes very important for us to use information derived from our own observations of crises, and from discussions with other treatment team members who might have observed the child struggling in other parts of the program, to identify a particular child's areas of vulnerability. In effect, we must determine what situations, experiences, conditions, or events seem to present the child with the greatest risk for some form of out-of-control behavior.

Assessing the Precipitating Factors, Triggering Events, or High-Risk Situations

Although each child brings to residential treatment a unique set of vulnerabilities, the literature on children in residential care highlights various general situations, events, and experiences that may place certain children at greater risk than others for out-of-control behavior. For example, transition periods seem to be much more difficult for some children to handle than others. Transition periods (i.e., those times in which a child is moving from one situation to another) can be relatively short, as is the case when a child goes from the cottage to school in the morning, or perhaps simply from the classroom to a recess period; or they can be of greater duration, as is the case when a child goes on an off-grounds outing, or embarks on a lengthier home visit. Child care staff in residential treatment facilities often speak of a child's increased level of vulnerability during these less structured and less supervised transition periods. Classroom teachers in residential care facilities may note that some children are at greater risk even when they must go from one predictable classroom assignment to a newer, less familiar one.

Some children are at increased risk for out-of-control behavior in what they perceive as competitive situations, where they think they cannot be successful even if they put forth the effort. Often, this feeling relates to the distrust that many children in residential care feel toward their abilities in general. Many of these children have experienced tremendous amounts of failure on many different levels, and they often try to avoid putting themselves in situations that can, in any way, re-create the very painful feelings that accompany such failures. Also many children who come to residential care experience a range of specific learning-related, attentional, or neuropsychological deficits and vulnerabilities, which in some cases may render them at a serious competitive disadvantage, not only at school but also sometimes in response to various scheduled activities on the playground and in the cottage. A child who cannot remember instructions well; cannot remember directions; cannot perform even simple reading, writing, or computation tasks; cannot perform certain visual–motor exercises; or cannot sustain his or her attention very well, may be quite defensive or overreactive in response to tasks, activities, games, or other demands that place heavy emphasis on these skills for their successful performance.

Before or after home visits, or during family visits or family sessions on the grounds, many of these children will experience a variety of fears and anxieties concerning their place in the family, and the status of their relationships with members of the family. Child care staff often note an increase in the frequency of acting-out behavior at the time of family contact, or sometimes just in response to anticipation of such contact. Similarly, increased frequencies of acting-out incidents are also reported after the period of contact, which often may be related to feelings and fears associated with loss and abandonment.

Some children in residential care are at particular risk for out-of-control behavior when they perceive a change or alteration in a relationship with a member of the treatment team. These children can be easily disappointed, hurt, frustrated, and angered by even subtle changes that they believe are occurring (either real or imagined) between themselves and the important child care workers whom they strongly depend upon. Sometimes, simple alterations in the amount of contact that traditionally occurs between a child and child care worker can lead to an increased risk of crisis-related episodes.

Many children in residential treatment experience difficulties in their general capacity to deal with stress. Unlike most other children their age, these children tend to seriously overreact to situations that might in general frustrate or stress them, or invoke in them any feeling of discomfort. Whereas other children might be able to sense some sign of emerging emotional distress, and consequently call upon some coping mechanism or strategy to effectively reduce the discomfort, many children in residential treatment seem to lack this capacity. It is almost as though they have never learned to use emotions or underlying sensations as signals to anticipate difficult experiences. A signaling mechanism such as this could afford them the opportunity to cognitively sort out different response possibilities, which could subsequently reduce their stress.

Many children in residential care are at an increased risk of out-of-control behavior if the level of structure or the degree of supervision is lessened. These children may demonstrate a marked decrease in their ability to effectively control and regulate their actions and emotions in situations that lack structure and definition.

Checklists such as the one that follows may assist a treatment team in their efforts to pinpoint situations, circumstances, and conditions under which a child in residential care may be most vulnerable.

Often a crisis is required to show us that our expectations for a child are too high in a certain situation, or that triggering events and experiences that the child has been exposed to may be emotionally overwhelming. The following are just a few such examples, showing how a team's increased awareness of specific precipitating events, and of a child's particular vulnerabilities, allowed it to make the interventions needed to reduce the frequency of future acting-out experiences.

The first example involved an eleven-year-old child in residential care, who had just been transferred to a new school in the community. He was

RTC Crisis Prevention Checklist

Child's Name: _____   Name of Rater: _____

Age: _____   Date: _____

Directions

The following checklist is intended to help the treatment team in identifying specific factors, situations and/or experiences that may be associated with a particular child's most emotionally vulnerable moments. These moments might be typified by any number of possible reactions, including disruptive or oppositional behavior, withdrawal, aggression, or perhaps more seriously regressive displays. Please treat the following checklist of occurrences as a partial one at best, and do not hesitate to write in any personal observations or impressions that you may have regarding what you feel to be particularly troublesome times and experiences for the child in question.

After reading each item, note whether the specific situation or experience is one that the child in question seems to find difficult to cope with. Place a check mark in the "Yes" column, if you feel this to be the case. If the child shows no unusual responses to the situation or experience, then place a check mark in the "No" column. If you are uncertain as to where the child falls with respect to any of these items, place a checkmark in the "Not Sure" column.

Situations or Experiences That Relate to Transition Type Periods

	YES	NO	NOT SURE
1. When a child has to switch from one task or activity to another (either in the classroom, on the playground, or in the unit/cottage).			
2. When the child goes from the unit/cottage to school in the morning.			
3. When the child goes from the classroom to a recess period.			
4. During the time when the child goes from the classroom to lunch.			
5. On the child's return to the classroom from lunch.			
6. Coming back to the unit/cottage after school.			
7. Going from the unit/cottage to the afternoon activity.			
8. Returning to the unit/cottage following the afternoon activity.			
9. Other transition type period: Please explain.			

_____

_____

Situations or Experiences That Call Into Play a Child's Feelings About His/Her Abilities*

	YES	NO	NOT SURE
10. When the child is asked to read something out loud.			
11. When the child is having to read in general.			
12. When the child has to write something.			
13. When the task or situation at hand requires that the child carry out a series of steps.			
14. When the task or situation at hand requires that the child remember a series of instructions.			
15. When the child is asked to perform an activity that requires a high level of coordination (either visual motor or fine motor).			
16. When a child is trying to express himself or herself, but can't seem to find the right words.			
17. When the child has to listen very carefully to something being said.			
18. When a child has to undertake a task that he/she seems to find difficult (specify task(s) if possible). _____ _____			

Situations That May Offer Less Structure Than Is Usually the Case

	YES	NO	NOT SURE
19. During recess periods.			
20. When the child is having to spend time on grounds, with less supervision than usual.			
21. When the child is involved in unstructured off-grounds activities.			
22. When involved in an off-grounds activity in general.			
23. On home visits, when a child has free time to do as he/she pleases.			
24. When the teacher or child care worker leaves the classroom/unit/cottage for a brief period of time.			
25. During weekends.			
26. During school holidays.			
27. Other unstructured or less structured type of situation (please specify if possible). _____ _____			

Social, Interpersonal, or Interactional Type Situations

	YES	NO	NOT SURE
28. During play time situations with age mates.			
29. During situations in which the child is feeling criticized (whether or not the feedback that the child received was intended as criticism).			
30. During group meetings in the unit/cottage.			
31. During group discussion periods in the classroom.			
32. When the child is playing in a game that requires taking turns.			
33. When someone says "no" to the child.			
34. When a child loses in a game.			
35. During activities that are viewed as competitive.			
36. Other social type situations (please specify if possible).			

_____

_____

Situations or Experiences That Involve Contact or Even Thoughts About the Family

	YES	NO	NOT SURE
37. The day the child is to go on a home visit.			
38. The time surrounding a child's return from a home visit.			
39. During or just after a phone conversation with a family member.			
40. At the time when the family is known to be going through a stressful period (divorce, separation, illness, hospitalization, other stressors?).			
41. Just prior to or following the birth of a child at home.			
42. A time when a child anticipated having contact with a family member, but the contact didn't materialize.			
43. Prior to, during, or following family conferences (specify if possible).			

_____

_____

	YES	NO	NOT SURE
44. While the child is on a home visit.			
45. Other situation that involves family contact.			

Situations Involving Daily Routines, Mealtime, and Bedtime

	YES	NO	NOT SURE

46. The time period during which a child is awakened in the morning, and is asked to carry out his morning responsibilities.

47. During breakfast time.

48. During lunch time.

49. During dinner time.
50. If the child is taking medication, just prior to or following medication (please specify if possible).

_____

_____

51. During quiet times in the evening.

52. Around bedtime.

53. While the child is doing his evening chores.
54. Other situation involving some aspect of the daily routine (please specify). _____

_____

Situations That Involve Some Type or Change or Alteration in the Child's Environment

	YES	NO	NOT SURE

55. Being asked to accept a new responsibility.

56. Being exposed to a new academic task in the classroom.

57. Going to a new class.

58. Transferring to a new unit/cottage.

59. When a scheduled activity is changed or canceled.

60. During staff shift changes.
61. The time in which the child learns of an unexpected change occurring at home (please specify if possible).

_____

_____

62. During times in which the tension or stress level of the unit/cottage or in the classroom is unusually high.

63. Other situations that involve changes or alterations in the daily milieu (please specify).

_____

_____

Situations or Experiences That May Evoke Certain Relationship Issues

	YES	NO	NOT SURE

64. The day that a special staff member is off.

65. Just prior to or during a special staff member's vacation.
66. When a staff member is feeling especially angry or disappointed about the child.

67. When only male staff members are on shift.

68. When only female staff members are on shift.

69. Following a reprimand from a staff member.
70. When a staff member is feeling that he or she is unable to control matters involving the child, or other children.
71. When a staff member is not able to follow through with something that had been promised to the child.
72. Other situations involving the child and an individual with whom he or she enjoys a relationship (please specify).

_____

_____

---

*Some of the situations listed here may in fact highlight an area in which the child has a specific disability or deficit of some sort that places him/her at a decided disadvantage. "Yes" responses may warrant appropriate assessment of abilities that are called into play within the specific situation.

appearing quite defensive in his new class, and on two separate occasions had stormed angrily out of the classroom. His sixth grade teacher stated that his tension started to rise during the morning reading exercise, when each child was requested to read out loud to the rest of the class. The child had belligerently refused to do this, and as a result was asked to sit in the corner and write 100 times, "I will behave in class." Any sentences that were sloppy or contained incorrect spellings had to be rewritten. This consequence seemed to incite the child further; on two occasions he stormed out of class, each time refusing to return for the rest of the school day. The teacher unfortunately had never been made aware of the child's serious reading disability. The child was reading three to four years below his grade level. Also he historically had been very vulnerable and extremely volatile in classroom situations where the expectations clearly exceeded his abilities. To make matters worse, also unbeknownst to the teacher, the child had a serious writing impairment, which made his writing assignment an almost impossible task. Once the teacher, with the help of the treatment team, was able to rearrange the classroom tasks in line with the child's abilities, so that the child could in fact be successful, his adjustment improved noticeably.

In another case, a child care worker noticed that most of a particular nine-year-old child's recent out-of-control episodes had occurred between Sunday evening and Monday morning. Actually, for three Monday mornings in a row the child refused to go to school, and angrily reacted to the staff's attempts to find out what the problem was. He refused to talk, and emphatically denied that anything was wrong. For three weeks in a row he suffered the consequences of his behavior, losing privileges that he had worked quite hard to gain. During the weekly staff meeting, the child care worker, in association with other members of the child's treatment team, decided to take a closer look at the circumstances that preceded the child's out-of-control behavior. It was soon learned that each episode occurred not long after the child's return from a home visit. Circumstances in the home were then examined more closely, and it was learned that the child's mother, a former drug user, had again been taking drugs, especially on the weekends while the child was home. For the last several Sunday evenings she had been barely coherent, to the degree that a family friend had to take the child back to the facility. Also it was soon learned that the child was extremely fearful that if he told anyone about his mother's drug problem, he would be removed from her care permanently. He was also very worried about her well-being and about whether "she would take too many drugs and die." The situation at home was understandably too much for the child to withstand emotionally, and he communicated this predicament behaviorally to the staff on the Sunday evenings and Monday mornings following his home visits. When the team learned of the child's unbearable bind, his child care worker was able to spend a great deal of time with him, allaying some of his fears and anxieties. The treatment team also was able to reprioritize their family goals, and refocus their efforts on the mother's drug abuse. Rather than consequences for his behavior, the child appeared to need emotional support, and some visible sign from someone that his mother was going to be helped with her problems and would be all right. The child's adjustment, though still erratic during the weeks that followed, improved gradually in response to the important changes that the team made, in regard to both the child's emotional needs and the changing circumstances at home.

INCREASING A CHILD'S AWARENESS OF HIGH-RISK SITUATIONS OR TRIGGERING EVENTS

If we can choose the right words, and communicate them at the right times, we may be able to provide a child with an understanding of a specific, concrete, and identifiable situation or event during which he or she may be at the greatest risk for some form of out-of-control behavior. Our doing this affords the child the opportunity to think ahead. Some children do have the ability to anticipate things in advance and call upon a different, more effective response instead of an overreactive one when the risky or troubling situation occurs; having identifiable triggering experiences can be very helpful to them in beginning to reduce the frequency of out-of-control episodes.

A child care worker recently assisted a nine-year-old child in successfully reducing the number of his tantrum episodes by helping him understand the usual triggering events, and then rewarding him for the times that he was able to pay attention to, and respond differently to, these events. Specifically, the child care worker showed the child that his temper outbursts would often occur when he heard someone say "no" to him. (Sometimes, when he was confronted about his temper outbursts, his behavior would escalate further and further out of control.) The child was first asked to practice paying very close attention to how many times he heard the word "no" in the course of a day, in whatever context it occurred. He was then asked to practice responding differently to the word "no" when he heard it applied to himself. The child was capable on his own of coming up with a variety of better response possibilities. The child care worker would meet with the child several times during the week and reward him with points from the agency point system when he demonstrated that he had heard the word "no" and had behaved himself well. The child care worker also rewarded him on the spot when she was able to observe, during the course of the child's day, that he was effectively handling hearing the word "no." Other team members were asked to pay close attention to the child's efforts, and to reward him for these efforts in a similar manner.

HELPING A CHILD ACQUIRE THE ABILITY TO ANTICIPATE, PLAN, AND THINK AHEAD

Some of the children in residential care who appear to be the most susceptible to out-of-control experiences also seem to be the most unskilled in thinking ahead, and in anticipating and planning for situations that they find particularly troubling. These children may need practice in thinking ahead, and the child care worker can be very helpful in this regard. For example, the child care worker may be able to provide the child with opportunities to think beforehand about a situation or experience that might represent for the child an increased risk for out-of-control behavior. A new and different response to the situation can be discussed, which may serve to avert a potential crisis. The child care worker also can be helpful in providing the child with a great deal of recognition and reinforcement for the times in which he or she demonstrates the ability to anticipate a potentially difficult situation, and to think ahead about other, more effective ways of handling the situation.

An example of how child care workers might be able to help a child practice thinking ahead was very creatively demonstrated in the case of an eight-year-old child who appeared to be at his greatest risk for serious acting-out behavior on the days when his child care worker was off work. On these days, the child often felt that he did not have to listen to the other staff or cooperate with their requests. His child care worker, who noticed that the child had little appreciation of the time span between days, and little understanding that certain things happened on certain days, devised a process in which the child could begin to practice thinking ahead about things. (The child appeared to live minute to minute, and to talk to him about the difference between his behavior Saturday through Wednesday versus Thursday and Friday seemed to make little sense to him.) A weekly calendar was made, and the child was asked to practice filling in, in advance, the activities or events that would be occurring on different days, and at different times during the day. The child care worker would reward the child for keeping his calendar current, and also for being able to demonstrate that he could remember when certain things occurred, without looking at the calendar. Then the child care worker had the child note on the calendar the days of the week that the child care worker would be off. They would discuss the matter of different behaviors and different attitudes occurring on days on versus days off, why these differences might be occurring, and how the child could practice being more consistent from one day to the next throughout the week. The child care worker and the child devised a plan whereby the child would pay very close attention to his behavior on the days when the child care worker was not there. (The child also was asked to place on his calendar some notation for each day of the week, to serve as a behavioral reminder.) The child care worker and child also agreed upon having a designated staff member pay attention to the plan on the child care worker's days off. Special rewards were given when the child was able to demonstrate consistent improvement throughout the week, including the days when the child care worker was away. The total intervention process eventually was reported to be relatively successful, and the child did seem to reduce the frequency of acting-out behaviors during the absences of his child care worker. Perhaps even more importantly, the child was given a tool that, with the help of the staff, he could use to anticipate other events that were significant to him.

HELPING A CHILD TO IDENTIFY CERTAIN
EMOTIONAL WARNING SIGNS OR SIGNALS

As stated previously, some children in residential care seem to be less effective than many of their age mates in recognizing the emotions or sensations that they might experience just before losing control. These children seem less proficient than most others their age in using emotional warning signs of an approaching situation that might personally overwhelm them if some direct and immediate action is not taken. Lacking this ability, these children tend instead to be flooded by their emotions, thereby setting the stage for some form of out-of-control reaction. Learning to spot one's unique *early* warning signs can allow one to take any number of immediate actions that ultimately can serve to interrupt the escalating emotional experience. As with helping children in residential care develop other critical skills, child care workers can be instrumental in helping children develop this ability. A child care worker might begin by paying close attention to what seem to be the child's early warning signs. Often, there are behavioral correlates to these early warning signs, and these behaviors may be easy to spot. For example, some children may become much more abrupt or negative in their actions. Other children may grow increasingly scattered and disorganized. Still other children may grow increasingly rigid, and may choose defensively to withdraw from direct contact. Once a child care worker can identify some characteristic behavior pattern that seems to precede out-of-control episodes, the child can be assisted in appreciating specific feelings or sensations that may accompany these patterns. Opportunities can be provided for children to practice paying attention to and spotting any alterations in their behavior, and the accompanying changes in feelings and emotions. Some children may also need assistance in appreciating how behaviors and reactions can pass from one stage to another. Essentially, these children may have to become acquainted with the whole notion of an initial or an early warning stage, which can be followed by increasingly serious and painful stages. By gaining an appreciation of the steps or stages of behaviors or reactions in a crisis situation, a child can conceptually gain a better understanding of what it means to interrupt the sequence and catch an emerging problem early.

Some children in residential care seem capable of developing an increased awareness of the situations in which they are most vulnerable, and an increased capacity to anticipate and think ahead about these situations. Yet these abilities may not be enough to allow them to maintain control over their emotions in stressful situations that they could not anticipate beforehand. To effectively prevent themselves from becoming overwhelmed by their emotions, these children probably will have to call upon some mechanism that will allow them to interrupt their escalating emotional response. Thus, it can be critical to develop an appreciation of one's early warning signs, and the capacity to use them as signals to call upon some type of action or some type of strategy to interrupt or halt steps toward an even more disturbing experience.

Once the child is skilled in identifying these specific emotional or behavioral warning signs, the child and the child care worker can begin to develop ways for the child to reflect better upon the situation at hand, rather than to respond impulsively to feelings of stress. Sometimes simply providing a child with a mutually agreed upon safe place to take a time-out, and to think through a difficult situation, can serve to interrupt an otherwise out-of-control episode. It may even be possible to decide upon a mutually agreed upon sign, phrase, or gesture that the child and the child care worker can use to alert one another of the child's need to take a time-out to think through a specific situation or to handle an uncomfortable feeling. A child care worker can be very helpful in rewarding a child's effort to recognize early warning signs and to take some type of effective preventive action.

Like other critical skills, the ability to recognize and cope with emotional arousal can be strongly reinforced by the classroom teacher. An illustration is offered by Stone and Bernstein (1980) in their discussion of case management strategies of borderline children. The authors discuss how a teacher helped a child learn how to take a time-out and subsequently to go to a designated quiet corner, equipped with comforting furnishings, when the pressures of the day were piling up. The teacher initially had to sense when the child's anxiety appeared to be escalating and quietly encourage a time-out. Eventually, the child was able to develop his own internal signals, and subsequently he chose to go to the quiet corner on his own.

ASSISTING THE CHILD IN EFFORTS TO LABEL AND EXPRESS EMOTIONS AND EMOTIONAL EXPERIENCES VERBALLY

Whenever possible, the child care worker may also wish to assist and reinforce a child in efforts to verbally label and express his or her understanding of specific emotions, specific emotional experiences, and the specific triggering events or circumstances that might contribute to these emotional reactions. With practice, and with the support and direction of the child care worker, the child may grow more confident and more skilled in his or her ability to put into words some of the uncomfortable feelings engendered by a difficult situation or experience. Our hope is that by becoming more comfortable with the words and concepts that apply to particular emotional experiences, and more skilled in expressing to us in words, as well as possible, what these experiences and feelings are like, a child can have a means other than physical action for communicating difficult or painful emotions.

Some children in residential care seem quite unable to put their feelings into words. This may be especially true when they find themselves losing control. A child care worker who can appreciate the child's emotions at such a moment might be able to talk the situation through for the child. According to Hanson et al. (1983), this may afford the child who is experiencing a regression (in their discussion, the child with borderline symptoms) the chance to develop a cognitive handle on the situation. It may assist the child in understanding the situation, and his or her emotional response to it. At calmer moments, the child and child care worker can rethink the experience together; then the child, with the child care worker's support and guidance, might be allowed to practice verbally communicating what the actual experience was like.

ASSISTING A CHILD IN ATTEMPTS TO LEARN AND USE MORE EFFECTIVE RESPONSES TO EMOTIONALLY DIFFICULT SITUATIONS

As an alternative to a poorly controlled response to stress, we need to help the child with another, more effective course of action. This alternative will, in some way, be incompatible with out-of-control behavior; that is, the child probably will be unable to call upon this alternative action and to be out of control at the same time. Various treatment teams have found very creative ways to teach alternative behaviors. Some children respond quite well to various types of relaxation strategies; such children may be instructed in any number of different relaxation techniques, ranging from slow deep-breathing methods to specific muscle-relaxation exercises. The children are then encouraged to practice the relaxation or calming response in noncrisis situations, so that the response is well learned. Team members cooperate in trying to recognize and reinforce the children's subsequent efforts to use the newly learned skills in response to difficult emotional experiences.

Certain children respond well to alternatives that afford them the opportunity to discharge their energies in a more active and physical manner. One child seemed to respond well to taking a brief time-out and running a couple of laps around the campus when tensions began to build.

Another appeared to respond effectively to performing various quick exercises. Although these exercises might have seemed boring and repetitive to other children, for this child they were not; the activity proved very helpful in affording him the opportunity to refocus and redirect his energies when he otherwise would have been emotionally overwhelmed.

Still other children can learn certain specific statements and phrases that represent specific ways of thinking and responding when they begin to feel very stressed. These statements and phrases generally refer to thoughts about remaining calm, remaining in control, and not overreacting. They are intended to cue the child to such thoughts when he or she otherwise would react impulsively. One particular child seemed to respond best when he could say some of these phrases out loud when he felt himself growing increasingly out of control. Saying out loud "stay calm, don't overreact" seemed to be his way of breaking what had been a knee-jerk overreactive response to stress.

Regardless of the alternative behavior(s) selected, the hope is that the child will be afforded some new type of response option (whether cognitive, physical, or emotional) in the context of an otherwise overwhelming experience.

ASSISTING A CHILD TO MONITOR AND ASSESS ACCURATELY HIS OR HER OWN EFFORTS

We may wish to help children in residential care to develop their ability to monitor and assess their progress in some of the aforementioned areas. Here we are concerned with children's ability to pay close attention to their own effectiveness. As with the other skills they learn, children who are being encouraged to develop a self-monitoring skill will need to practice it, and to be reinforced by the child care worker for their efforts. Accurate self-assessment, and the willingness and desire to learn from one's own experience, receive the greatest staff attention, recognition, and reinforcement here; we are not necessarily concerned with how effective a child might have been in applying a particular problem-solving strategy. Our hope is that children will be able to accept their shortcomings and treat their efforts as learning experiences. Helping children to develop this capacity might reduce their feelings of defensiveness about their behavior.

CONCLUDING REMARKS

This chapter has attempted to highlight how we might gain a greater appreciation of a child's particular vulnerabilities by paying close attention to the situations, events, or experiences that may underlie or trigger crisis-related episodes. A checklist was provided to help team members identify specific precipitating or triggering events. Once we have this information at our disposal, we can take a closer look at the child's existing abilities, disabilities, and coping resources in order to determine whether we are expecting too much too soon. If such is the case, we may have to quickly alter our expectations.

The chapter also highlighted various skills that we may help the child to develop during the course of his day-to-day experience in residential care. These skills could prove critical in helping a child handle situations, events, or experiences that might otherwise eventuate in crises, and they might later be useful to the child in attempts to handle such situations, events, or experiences in the absence of the highly structured surroundings generally inherent in residential care. These skills may in effect serve the child well following discharge.

Central to the assessment and intervention process that was outlined here is a well-integrated treatment team that maintains a high commitment to the professional and emotional well-being of its individual members. Given the manner in which some of the children who find their way into residential care will communicate their desperation or rage, and the capacity these children may have in evoking in child care workers a range of potentially intense and powerful emotions, we may find ourselves in need of the help of other team members in our efforts to make sense of our feelings, and on occasion to replenish our energies. This simultaneous attention by the treatment team to the needs of both the child and child care worker is of such critical importance that it was mentioned here as a necessary foundation to all other assessment and intervention tasks that the team might embark upon in assisting the child in residential care.

REFERENCES

Hanson, G., Bemborad, J. R. and Smith, H. F. (1983). The day and residential treatment of the borderline child. In K. S. Robson, M.D. ed., *The Borderline Child: Approaches to Etiology, Diagnosis, and Treatment.* New York: McGraw-Hill, pp. 257–276.

National Organization of Child Care Workers Association. 1335 Eleventh Street, N.W., Washington, D.C. 20001.

Redl, F. and Wineman, D. (1957). *The Aggressive Child.* Glencoe, Ill.: The Free Press.

Stone, C. and Bernstein, L. (1980). Case management with borderline children: theory and practice. *Clinical Social Work Journal, 8*(3), 149–162.

Trieschman, A. E. (1969). Understanding the stages of a typical temper tantrum. In A. E. Trieschman, J. K. Whittaker, and L. K. Brendtro, eds., *The Other 23 Hours.* New York: Aldine Publishing Co., pp. 170–197.

RECOMMENDED READING

Budlong, M. J., Mooney, A., et al. (1983). *Training of Trainers and Therapeutic Crisis Intervention for the Child Care Worker.* Ithaca, N.Y.: Family Life Development Center.

Kendall, P. and Braswell, L. (1985). *Cognitive Behavioral Therapy for Impulsive Children.* New York: Guilford Press.

Lewis, M. and Brown, T. E. (Spring, 1980). Child care in the residential treatment of the borderline child. *Child Care Quarterly,* 41–49.

Meichenbaum, D. (1985). *Stress Inoculation Training.* Elmsford, N.Y.: Pergamon Press.

Schaefer, C. E. and Millman, H. L. (1981). *How to Help Children with Common Problems.* New York: Van Nostrand Reinhold.

4

Responding to Sexual Acting-Out

David A. Crenshaw

BRIEF OVERVIEW OF LITERATURE

One of the most vexing and anguishing problems direct care staff face in residential treatment centers serving emotionally disturbed children adolescents is to provide a therapeutic response to incidents of sexual acting-out behavior. Often direct care staff as well as seasoned clinicians are in a quandary as to how to respond therapeutically to overt manifestations of sexuality in disturbed children and adolescents.

This topic has received proportionately less attention than it deserves in the professional literature, given the frequency of these incidents and the urgent concern expressed by staff in responding to them. With the exception of a recent book on this topic (Shore and Gochros, 1981), it is necessary to refer to literature written on this subject in the sixties and seventies (McNeil and Morse, 1964; Redl, 1966; Easson, 1967; and Binder and Krohn, 1974). With few exceptions (McNeil and Morse, 1964; Redl, 1966; Iacona-Harris and Iacono-Harris, 1981), the available literature is geared more to guiding clinicians in treating these problems in psychotherapy than to issues of the practical, day-to-day handling of incidents of sexual acting-out that confront direct care staff.

This chapter is intended to address this void by emphasizing the kind of dilemmas often faced by direct care staff, child care workers and teachers, and the clinicians who provide guidance to them in residential treatment centers for emotionally disturbed children and adolescents.

RESPONDING TO SEXUAL ACTING-OUT IN THE THERAPEUTIC MILIEU: DEVELOPMENTAL ISSUES

One of Freud's major contributions was his view of the extent and importance of infantile sexuality. Before we focus on developmental considera-

*The author wishes to thank John B. Murdock, Ph.D. and George Mora, M.D. for their helpful suggestions in the preparation of this chapter.

tions regarding sexuality, it is important to look at some general developmental issues pertaining to children in residential treatment centers. Most contemporary investigators of child development agree that human infants begin life in an organized state (Lichtenberg, 1983; Sander, 1983; Stern, 1983, 1985; Levin, 1985). The constitutionally adaptive infant is capable of entering into an exchange with a responsive caretaker and through this dyadic interaction, given reasonably empathetic responses from the primary caretakers, the infant gradually acquires certain abilities. He learns to organize experience, regulate impulses, and discriminate between inner and outer reality, in a process that eventually leads to an integration of capacities and provides a stable sense of self and the ability to interact adaptively with one's interpersonal and physical world.

In the vast majority of children referred for residential treatment, various influences have combined to cause this normal developmental process to go awry at some point in the first three to four years of life. For these children, the empathic and sensitive attunement considered crucial for healthy development is often lacking in the preconceptual and preindividuated early period of life. In some cases, the problem may be due to a lack of responsive caregiving or even to extremely abusive and destructive caretaking. In other cases, it may be due to constitutionally maladaptive capacities in the infant that do not permit even responsive and empathic caregiving to favorably influence the course of development, as it ordinarily would with a constitutionally healthy infant. Often, a combination of these two factors causes the interactional sequences between infant and primary caretaker to result in a mismatch between the child's needs and the environmental provision (Balint, 1968). If the interactive exchanges between infant and primary caretakers do not permit the preconceptual child to organize and differentiate experiences because disruptive affect is not kept within tolerable limits, the child develops a defensive orientation of withdrawal that permits him to avoid a potential affective overload (Levin, 1985).

Thus, those experiences the child cannot master because of his limited adaptive organizational capabilities lead to a defensive orientation that is adaptive or at least self-preservative at that point in time. These early defensive orientations become indiscriminately generalized or transferred to others in their interpersonal environment.

The child's psychosexual development, like all other aspects of healthy personality development, depends upon reasonably empathic responding of primary caretakers to the child's sexual wishes, erotic feelings, fantasies, and behavior. Obviously many factors can interfere with the healthy integration and mastering of sexual drives and feelings. A seductive or overstimulating parent of the opposite sex, for example, may lead the child to withdraw and develop an avoidant attitude as an adaptive defensive response. This attitude may result in a rigid orientation characterized by inhibition and reticence that becomes generalized to all interactions with adults of the opposite sex (Levin, 1985).

Freud viewed the successful resolution of what he described as the oedipal conflict as imperative for healthy psychosexual development. Successful resolution of the conflict regarding oedipal wishes, that is, the feelings of erotic attraction to the parent of the opposite sex in early childhood, requires appropriate and empathic responding on the part of that parent. The three- or four-year-old child who proposes to marry the parent of the opposite sex needs for that parent to respond by setting a limit and indicating an alternative (Bacciagaluppi, 1984). A parental response that he/she is already married to the other parent and that the child will someday find a suitable partner outside the family meets the requirements. Parental responses are pathological when instead of directing the child's sexual feelings outside the family toward future alternatives, they exploit the child or keep the child bound sexually within the family in order to gratify the parent's own sexual strivings and/or preoedipal needs for power or affection (Bieber, 1962; Bacciagaluppi, 1984).

Children in residential treatment centers typically have experienced a lack of attunement or inappropriate responding at an even earlier period in development, in interactional sequences revolving around nurturing and feeding experiences and around beginning attempts at self-regulation such as bowel and bladder training. Freud (1905) described the developmental sequence of the dominant organ focus of tension and pleasure as proceeding from the oral to the anal and finally to the genital area, followed by a relatively dormant period of sexuality in latency where more investment is made in the intellect, and sublimation takes place through a variety of intellectual, athletic, and social activities.

Thus, many children and adolescents in residential treatment have suffered frustration in early interactional sequences around feeding and bowel training, as one part of a complex of massive failure of empathic relating between the child and primary caretakers. Sensitive attunement and empathic responding has been described as providing a core emotional connection essential for maturation at each phase of life (Kohut, 1977). Thus manifestation of developmentally disordered sexuality is only one feature of the developmental process going awry. Given the frequent disruptions and not uncommon abuse and destructive caretaking experienced by children and adolescents so ego-impaired as to require residential treatment, it is not surprising that the dominant organ focus of tension and pleasure for these youngsters often corresponds with that associated with early life.

Youngsters in residential treatment often are observed to be preoccupied with oral gratifications and exhibit such habits as licking, sucking, gum chewing, or even chewing on articles of clothing such as a shirt. In play therapy, they often regress to these very early-level gratifications by wanting to use baby bottles or center the play around some kind of eating or feeding play scenario. Excessive talking and chatter may reflect this primary organ of focus. Excessive sensual pleasure through the act of eating may also be observed, as well as much surplus emotional meaning associated with mealtime. As food is often equated symbolically with mother-love, mealtime in the living groups can be a source of either extreme pleasure or great tension and sometimes violent disruption.

Bettelheim (1986) has emphasized the need for residential treatment programs to create an environment of stability, consistency, and predictability whereby the child comes to feel safe, protected, and secure. When he realizes that his basic needs for food and safety are going to be amply met, he no longer needs to be preoccupied with these needs and thus is free to move to other issues reflecting a higher developmental progression.

Child care workers and teachers need to be sensitively attuned to the surplus meaning that food and other oral gratifications have for these children, who frequently have been deprived and frustrated with respect to their early nurturant needs. Making available ample supplies of both nutritious and satisfying food, as well as treats and snacks offered at predictable and consistent times, is an important aspect of providing these children with a developmentally corrective experience. Food fads should be tolerated, and sweets should be provided freely along with special dishes. Food preferences and favorite snacks should be taken into account in planning and providing meals. Given the intense affective meanings tied to food and feeding experiences, sometimes the slightest frustration regarding the food being served can lead to total disruption and chaos within a living group of such children.

During dinner, Michael's attitude was extremely hostile due to his wanting mashed potatoes instead of the corn and salad being served with the meal. He verbally spewed out insults and obscenities, which finally escalated into the need for physical restraint after he threw his plate at another child, resulting in a fight with several boys in the group exchanging punches.

Feelings of deprivation, anger, and frustration surrounding early feeding and nurturant experiences can also result in food being used as a weapon.

Rick and another child were involved in stealing eggs from the kitchen. A third child opened a window screen, and the three boys began throwing eggs out the window into the swimming pool behind the living group. A life space interview with the three boys following the incident indicated that one of the triggers of the acting-out was Mike's dislike for the dessert served during lunch.

The taking of medication dispensed by a nurse often is a focal point for intense disappointment and rage related to a lack of oral satisfaction early in life. Some youngsters in residential treatment require psychotropic medications to counteract psychotic or depressive tendencies, and in some cases to treat anxiety or hyperactivity associated with an attention deficit disorder. Given the intense oral preoccupations and often the hostility associated with their frustrated wishes, taking medication orally dispensed by a nurse-mother figure often produces a tense situation and sometimes a volatile moment.

Nicky gave the nurse a hard time about taking his medication. He splashed water in her face and also at another child. He started to kick the other child, and when the child care worker attempted to stop him, he proceeded to kick the worker in the leg several times. He had to be restrained in order to prevent possible injury, and when Nicky was thought to be calm, he was released only to kick the child care worker again, resulting in a cut on the worker's leg. A life space interview revealed that one of the underlying sources of rage contributing to this incident was missing out on a snack earlier in the day as a result of misbehavior in a group.

Any kind of withholding of food as a consequence for misbehavior may activate such basic feelings of rage and deprivation, which can explode in the intense fashion illustrated by the above incident with Nicky.

Of course, taking oral medication, in its own right, has much surplus meaning for youngsters, which needs to be explored in each individual case to permit effective work with the resistance involved. For some children, the taking of medication may be experienced as an attempt to *render impotent* the rage due to earlier deprivations. Thus, it may be experienced as an attempt to dampen or squash their intensely held feelings regarding the perceived injustices they have experienced. In this case, strong resentment and resistance would be expected, and would need to be handled and explored by the child's therapist in a sensitive manner.

Also evident in the above examples are the proclivities of children in residential treatment to sudden regressive eruptions of primitive feelings and impulses, owing to their lack of sophisticated defensive resources.

Frustrations around oral needs are unavoidable no matter how much attention and effort is devoted to satisfying these wishes through appealing and attractive meals, ample snacks, and treats. However, reliable and predictable provision of meals that reflect individual and group preferences, along with an attitude on the part of direct care staff that reveals an understanding of the importance of these needs to the child, will go a long way toward providing the needed developmentally corrective experiences.

Given the frequency of preoedipal disturbances in children in residential treatment, it is not uncommon to observe anal preoccupations as well. "Dirty (bathroom) talk" is quite common, as are long periods spent in the bathroom. Soiled underpants, messy rooms, personal uncleanliness, attempts to provoke spankings, flaunting buttocks, interest in odors, and nose picking are all fairly common occurrences.

Bowel training is one of the focal points for early attempts at self-regulation, and the quality of the interactional sequences revolving around this activity determines success. To provide corrective developmental experiences for children who have had unsatisfactory early experiences in self-regulation, the residential treatment program needs to offer a highly structured environment for external support, so that rules can be learned. Order and routine are important, as are simple directions and clearly defined tasks.

Maturity demands and requirements for self-regulation can be effectively pressed after earlier needs for nurturance, safety, and protection are met, and the child has at least an initial desire to internalize the values, rules, and regulations offered by adults with whom he is beginning to identify. These beginning attachments to caring adults are quite ambivalent, however. For some time, much testing of the reliability, consistency, and caring of the adults in the therapeutic milieu will continue.

Anal preoccupations arouse strong emotions in caretaking adults and often represent the most disagreeable situations that direct care workers are called upon to handle. Children in residential treatment whose tension and pleasure are primarily focused at the anal level may express this through fecal retention or soiling. More often such excitement and interest are shown in "dirty talk." Much pleasure is also taken in oppositional and stubborn behavior, which is a common derivative of the earlier dysfunctional interaction with early caretakers around self-regulation. Pleasure in teasing and provoking others is also common. The desire to handle things and to maintain strict control over material possessions is typical.

In older children, pleasure in manipulating others, and in exercising power and domination over them, is also a common derivative of unsatisfactory experiences revolving around early attempts at self-regulation. A persistent need to handle and manipulate things may be a factor in the inability of some older children to move from play to verbal therapy around the age of ten, as is normally expected (Klein and Mordock, 1975).

A crucial aspect of successful handling of incidents arising from anal preoccupations is to provide calm, firm, and consistent direction and to avoid responding to provocative gestures in a highly emotional manner, as this only intensifies the power struggle for the child around attempts to master self-regulation.

> During the evening routine, Jose entered the bathroom to take a shower. He complained to the child care worker about an obnoxious smell and upon entering the bathroom he found a face cloth packaging a large amount of human feces. After interviewing members of the group, it was discovered that Jose was the youngster who left the feces in the tub. A life space interview uncovered that Jose was still very angry about a loss of some group privileges following his angry tirade at another child care worker, who confronted him stealing a shirt from another child in the group.

Jose, feeling revengeful and refusing to comply with group rules and consequences, responded at a primitive level. His feelings of shame and humiliation at being caught stealing and the consequent punishment resonated with earlier feelings of rage and hurt stemming from unsatisfactory experiences with overcontrolling and intrusive caretakers—caretakers who could not establish in an empathetic way needed rules and regulations or values to be emulated. The amount of rage centered on such incidents is sometimes quite striking.

> Robert's underwear was found in a shower stall a few minutes after he had showered. The child care worker asked him to wash them out, and he refused. The child care worker walked to the back of the bathroom, filled a bucket with water to assist him in this task, and asked him again; again he refused. Then the child care worker asked him to go on to bed and said that he could clean them in the morning; again he refused. At this point the child physically attacked the child care worker and was restrained.

A variety of powerful affects often are expressed through such incidents, including shame, humiliation, and rage at earlier punitive, intrusive, and overcontrolling caretakers.

It should not be assumed that all of the intensive emotion expressed on occasions such as the above are strictly a result of transference from earlier figures with whom the child has had unsatisfactory experiences. Some of the rage and hostility may be intended directly for a child care worker or teacher who intervenes in a manner experienced by the child as punitive, hostile, or uncaring.When it comes to the unpleasant task of dealing with the child about soiled underwear, feces thrown against a wall, or "messes" of many kinds, staff often find it difficult to respond in an optimal way, providing needed firmness and boundary setting without the hostility and punitiveness the child has encountered in the past. In these situations, the support of fellow direct care workers and a supervisor can be critical in managing constructively the intense feelings that are stirred.

Brenda was walking back from gym when her teacher heard one of the other students yell out and complain that she was pulling down her shorts and exposing herself. The teacher did not see it, but she cautioned Brenda about disrupting the line. As they continued down the hall, the teacher was talking to another student but looked up just as Brenda pulled down the back of her shorts, exposing her entire buttocks to the same student. The student complained again, and at that point the teacher reprimanded her and demanded that she act like a young lady in the school. Brenda denied the entire incident even though her teacher had directly witnessed it.

The teacher in reporting the above incident described herself as feeling "thoroughly disgusted" upon observing Brenda flaunting her exposed buttocks. Such feelings are often aroused in direct care workers confronted with explicit sexual language and exhibitionistic behavior, which are quite often observed in emotionally disturbed children in the classroom and in the living groups in residential treatment (Morgan, 1984). These staff reactions are counterproductive. Consequently, considerable staff training and supervision need to be provided to help direct care workers respond in a calm and unemotional manner while establishing the needed boundaries and limits. Children need appropriate limits but not the punitive, angry, and rejecting responses they have received so often early in life.

Residential staff need ample opportunity to discuss their reactions and to role-play alternative ways of responding to such situations. They require guidance and support because they typically must respond quickly to these incidents without the benefit of consultation or time to think through a therapeutic response.

In the course of normal development, children ages three to six often find pleasures centered upon sensations in the genital area. Sexual fantasies may center on urinary and erective powers, and these fantasies typically develop toward the desire for genital contact with others. Competitiveness, envy, exhibitionism, and curiosity about sexual differences and functioning are strong in both sexes starting at about age three.

Older children in residential treatment who are developmentally functioning at this level with regard to sexuality, show many similar attitudes and behavior, which may range from frequent sex talk to general "horsing around." If shame has not developed, or if defiance of adults is still important to the child, he or she may engage in open masturbation (Klein, 1975). Thus, the phallic stage of sexual development leads to early centering on genital pleasures, which may include masturbation, exposure to others, sexual curiosity, sex play with peers involving genital play, organ and urinary comparison, early heterosexual interest, and sex talk. To the extent that these sexual behaviors are excessive, or an infringement on the rights and privacy of others, it will be necessary for staff to intervene.

In the case of excessive and compulsive masturbation, the direct care staff who become aware of it should consult with the child's therapist so it can be explored in therapy. Public masturbation is socially unacceptable and frequently infringes on the rights and privacy of others. It requires a firm and direct response on the part of direct care workers, who are calm and nonpunitive and can help the child learn to discriminate between private autoerotic activity and the public display of autoerotic activities and exhibitionism which are not socially accepted.

One of the most difficult judgments that the direct care worker is called upon to make is to what extent sexual behavior is reflective of a developmentally normal process, such as curiosity about sex or experimentation and sex play of a relatively innocent form; and to what degree is it reflective of developmental disturbance, characterized by excessiveness, compulsiveness, confusion with aggression, and fusion with drives for power and domination, and intertwined with attempts to manipulate, control, and/or dominate peers. And, they must decide to what extent the behavior is intended to taunt or provoke the staff to respond punitively. Some examples of acting-out behaviors centered on early genital pleasures appear below. They illustrate how provocative such behavior can be, and how difficult it is for direct care staff to respond in a calm and unemotional manner while setting appropriate limits.

The child care worker was in the living room for a minute and upon returning discovered Louise in the doorway lifting her nightgown to expose herself to a couple of boys in the hallway. The child care worker confronted her and brought her back into the living unit where she talked with Louise about the loss of some group privileges as a result of the socially inappropriate behavior and discussed the implications of her behavior at length in a life space interview.

Many residential treatment programs, in addition to providing formal therapies, also conduct various forms of behavioral modification programs in living groups and classrooms. Often these behavioral shaping programs are heavily geared to providing rewards and incentives for prosocial behavior and loss of various privileges for inappropriate or antisocial behavior. Various incentive programs provide immediate reinforcement or negative consequences to the child's behavior, and therefore can be powerful learning influences. They also provide direct care workers tools whereby expected and socially appropriate behaviors can be clearly delineated, and inappropriate behaviors spelled out.

These programs based upon learning theory principles can be effective in modifying sexually inappropriate behaviors when combined with life space interviews (Redl, 1966). But, it is important that the child *experience these attempts* at modifying behavior as nonpunitive expressions of concern and interest. It is valid to combine any such behavioral shaping program with a counseling follow-up. Even with a great deal of effort, and sensitive and empathic responding, some children still will respond as if the approach were punitive and hostilely intended. It may take many such experiences to modify this belief, a belief rooted in early caretaking experiences.

If used properly, the combination of behavioral modification principles and life space interviewing can be a constructive influence in enabling the child to integrate his sexual feelings and impulses and to develop socially acceptable ways of expressing these urges. What is critically important, as Bettelheim (1974) has pointed out, is the attitude, whether conscious or unconscious, held by the helping person. It will do little good for a child care worker to reassure the child that masturbation in private is a perfectly healthy expression of sexuality if secretly he feels disgusted, horrified, or anxious about this behavior.

For no apparent reason, Mike became verbally abusive toward the child care worker in his group. He was making explicit sexual statements regarding female genitalia. He then stood up and dropped his pants and started playing with his genitals. He continued to be verbally abusive toward staff for a while, and then he ran from the group.

In this instance the child clearly was very angry and used aggressive sexual language in addition to public masturbation to get back at staff members. One of the most common sexual behaviors encountered in the residential treatment setting is masturbation in public. This behavior is of concern to staff because frequently it infringes on the rights and privacy of other children, and also because of its stimulating effect on the group, which can lead to heightened sexual tensions and often group contagion. In this instance, a clear hostile intent is conveyed by the child, reflecting the frequent fusion of sexuality and aggression among children and adolescents in residential treatment. It may also reflect the proneness of children who are poorly integrated to respond with generalized excitation to stimuli that may not even be identified by others. It may be an internal prompting or some subtle cue within the environment that leads to a rather dramatic display of excitation, in this case combining both sexual and aggressive features. At other times, public masturbation would appear to be intended to excite the group and to unduly capture the attention of peers and staff.

> While the group was watching TV, Jerry began to rotate his hips and play with his genitals. When he had aroused himself somewhat, he called his roommate's attention to it. His roommate ignored him completely, but Jerry still had a very satisfied grin on his face.

Often such behavior as Jerry's is intended to shock and taunt the adult in charge as well as to capture the attention of peers. Jerry appeared to obtain gratification despite the lack of an overt response from his roommate.

Sexual curiosity and sexual play, between both same-sex and opposite-sex peers, is common during the phallic stage as well as during the so-called latency period, where sexuality is not so dormant as Freud and others once believed (see studies reviewed by Rutter, 1971). Certainly this is a fairly frequent occurrence within residential treatment. The following are examples of such play, which is often encountered and interrupted by child care workers:

> Michelle and Karen were in Karen's room playing. Periodic checks were made by the child care staff. The child care worker heard a belt smacking something. He went to check and found Michelle hitting Karen with a belt. Karen had her panties pulled down. Karen said Michelle made her do this. Michelle was laughing and stated that she was weird (meaning herself). Michelle said her parents do this.

> Roberta had been playing with a child from another group in the hallway. The child care worker was rotating through the group to check on the activities of the kids right after dinner. She was in the living room when she noticed that she didn't see or hear Roberta. She immediately walked down to the room where the door was closed and upon entering

she found Roberta on top of a boy, with her clothes on, rubbing her genitals against his. They immediately jumped apart and began making excuses.

A peer came to the child care worker and said that Jose was "peeing in the boy's butt." When staff walked into the room they found Jose and a peer behind a dresser. Jose was totally naked and had his penis up against the peer's buttocks. Another peer was watching and quite sexually excited and obviously ready to join in.

Roger was interrupted in the living room with his hand on a peer's penis while pretending to be watching TV.

The above examples were all actual occurrences in residential treatment, involving latency age children and early adolescents. They reflect the strong sexual curiosity and interest characteristic of the phallic stage of psychosexual development. They may also indicate that "latency" has not occurred because of excess sexual stimulation in early life.

Child care workers and teachers encountering such examples of sexual play among children in residential care are again faced with the difficult task of dealing with their own feelings in such a situation, along with the need to make a judgment about the developmental appropriateness of such behavior. They also need to consider the potential for group excitement and contagion, possible exploitation of one or more of the participants, and the nature of the relationship between the participants, among many other contextual and interactional variables, while they are faced with the need to respond immediately and hopefully therapeutically. This is a tall order indeed!

Religious, cultural, family, and personal beliefs and values, as well as the worker's own early developmental experiences regarding sexuality, can all influence the worker's response to the complex variables presented by the child or children engaged in sex play. Parents find it difficult within the typical family situation to respond in a calm and unemotional way when they interrupt five-year-old Johnny pulling down the pants of four-year-old Susie, the neighbor's child, in the backyard. Such behavior, though representing developmentally normal experimentation, arouses strong reactions that often confuse the child, and, depending on how punitive the response, may create shame, guilt, and inhibition of sexual expression.

Certainly boundaries and limits need to be established regarding sexual play among youngsters in residential treatment centers, but the manner in which this is done is crucial. If the worker's response is made in a highly emotional manner reflecting shock, disgust, or anger, it can be potentially damaging to the child's developing attempts to integrate his or her sexual feelings and impulses and to find socially appropriate means of expression.

This is another instance where formal staff training must be augmented by ample supervisory sessions and informal consultations with accessible clinicians. Such services enable direct care workers faced with the formidable task of responding appropriately to the sexual behavior of emotionally disturbed children to receive appropriate guidance and support. These services can enable them not only to respond therapeutically but to have a chance to work through the intense feelings often stirred as a result of the incidents.

Although the latency period was originally thought to be a relatively quiet and dormant period with respect to sexuality, it is now understood that a great deal of sexual interest, curiosity, and activity occurs during these years. Children in residential treatment, because they are developmentally functioning like younger children, show a great deal of interest and curiosity regarding sex during these years. All the preoccupations associated with earlier stages of development are seen frequently in latency age children in the treatment setting. Latency age children in residential treatment should be moving toward a greater investment in intellectual activities, and an interest in mastering games and sports and developing friendships; instead they frequently are still struggling with early developmental issues, often of a preoedipal nature.

These children, during their latency years, may exhibit a marked precocious or a perverse sexuality as a significant feature of their relationships and activities (Szur, 1983). These sexual activities may primarily express frustrated preoedipal longings for closeness, affection, physical comforting, and soothing. The more perverse expressions of sexuality may be intended to belittle and to devalue relationships, with the child turning to sensual excitement for relief from loneliness and anxiety. Szur (1983) also states, "The sexualization of interactions between children and adults imposes a fictitious peer-relationship that essentially denies or distorts the child's need to depend on adults for care and protection" (p. 47).

The child engaging in seductive and flirtatious behavior or making direct sexual advances or overtures to adults in the treatment setting thus may be expressing not only a devaluing of emotionally meaningful relationships but also an attempt to ward off the therapeutic influence of the treatment staff by reducing them simply to peers. These sexual advances or overtures from children in treatment should be responded to in a way very similar to the optimal parental response to the oedipal wishes of a child in the family. A limit needs to be set, and the child must be encouraged to anticipate future alternatives, as well as to substitute socially acceptable expressions of affection between children and adults.

Thus, the child can be told, "I am your child care worker or your teacher—I am not your boyfriend or girlfriend; therefore, it is not appropriate for you to grab my breasts or genitals, and I insist that you not do that. You will have a boyfriend or girlfriend when you are older, and you may wish to show your love by such touching. With your teacher or your child care worker, however, it is appropriate to give hugs if you wish or to shake hands." Alternative ways of expressing affection can be demonstrated and modeled at appropriate times. Often, repeated applications of both verbal explanations and modeling are needed to help the child come to terms with appropriate boundaries and alternative ways of expressing affection and closeness.

At times children may be responding largely to sexual arousal and excitation in an impulsive and inappropriate way, as in the following example:

Johnny came up from behind a new summer recreation staff member and grabbed her breasts. Johnny did not know the staff member as it was her first day. When confronted, Johnny denied that he had done anything even though these incidents had occurred before with other female staff.

In this example, the relationship was devalued because the child did not even know the worker, but approached her from behind and caught her totally off guard. This is also an example of fusion of sexual and aggressive impulses, as well as an impulsive reaction to excitation and arousal, typical of children who function at such a poorly integrated level. Such behavior requires a firm and direct response from the staff member, and consequences for violating the rights and private body zones of another person. A permissive attitude toward this kind of incident can only lead to further escalation, possibly drawing other members of the group into increasingly serious and possibly dangerous incidents of acting-out behavior.

During the normal course of psychosexual development, adolescents experience not only an intensification of sexual drives and interest at puberty but also a *reawakening* of *oedipal conflicts.* The increased urgency of sexual desires may cause considerable anxiety and conflict regarding any erotic feelings or wishes the child has about the parent of the opposite sex. These conflictual feelings are sometimes the underlying force behind emotionally charged interactions between adolescents and their parents, which provide the impetus for adolescents to move away from the family and develop a greater attachment with peers and adults outside the family, and ultimately to develop mature heterosexual relationships. This is the culmination of Freud's genital stage of psychosexual development.

A number of contemporary writers on adolescent sexuality have lamented the lack of love and meaningful emotional attachment associated with adolescent sexual encounters, especially during early and middle adolescence (Ashway, 1980; Duncan, 1982; Miller, 1983). The incapacity to form emotionally meaningful and caring relationships is even more typical of adolescents so ego-impaired as to require inpatient treatment (Easson, 1967). Easson maintained that staff should have no qualms in discouraging these often intense romantic relationships, which he viewed as potentially harmful.

Adolescents who lack the ego strength to function in the community and require continuing inpatient care are not capable of entering the kind of intimate relationship with the opposite sex that would promote emotional growth. Child care workers and teachers must make difficult judgments about the extent to which they should encourage or discourage a budding romantic attachment among early or middle adolescents in the institutional setting. In the context of such a relationship, adolescents may be expressing a mixture of healthy and developmentally appropriate needs and wishes and earlier unresolved developmental conflicts that can have a destructive impact on the participants. A common psychodynamic constellation underlying early heterosexual romances that are doomed to failure may be signaled by an abortive mourning process in response to the separation or loss of a valued staff member (Binder and Krohn, 1974).

Adolescents in residential treatment have experienced at the very least a sense of loss and separation associated with placement. Many have experienced repeated losses and disruptions of early attachments or discontinuities in caretaking that serve to resonate with any loss or separation arising during the course of placement. The loss may involve a valued staff member or still more losses associated with family or substitute caretakers such as foster families. Sometimes parental rights are surrendered or terminated during the course of placement. All of these experiences can produce a profound sense of loss; and instead of handling the loss through a healthy grieving and mourning process, the adolescent may respond by forming an intense romantic and possibly sexual involvement with a peer of the opposite sex. Such relationships inevitably lead to disappointment and the feeling of being further deprived, as needed mourning and grieving processes are avoided in misguided attempts to replace the lost relationship.

Another unresolved early developmental conflict underlying the formation of a sexual liaison between adolescents in care involves a flight from preoedipal ties (Binder and Krohn, 1974). Because of early losses, particularly of a parent or a parent figure, the adolescent struggle with separation–individuation often intensifies the regressive wish for reunion with the preoedipal mother. This wish threatens the developmental push toward autonomy and separation–individuation and stirs considerable anxiety. An urgent search for intense involvement with the opposite sex may result, as a way of defending against this anxiety. These early sexual experiences thus are misguided attempts to secure through passionate involvement with the opposite sex a solution to unresolved early developmental conflicts.

Direct care staff as well as clinicians sometimes encourage such relationships out of well-intended but misinformed concern. Explorations of these issues may arouse very powerful feelings. Many direct care staff are themselves young people, who have perhaps only recently resolved adolescent issues of their own, or are still struggling with them. They may advocate such liaisons as a way of fighting through their own battles with repressive forces they encountered in their own sexual development.

Other well-meaning and concerned staff may insist that these youngsters must learn to live in the real world. They forget that these youngsters were not able to live in the real world and were referred for corrective therapeutic experiences in a milieu especially designed to provide such experiences. These are vulnerable youngsters with severe ego disturbances in need of protection, considerable guidance, and firm boundaries in order to cope with their often intense and poorly integrated sexual feelings and impulses.

Thus, if it can be clinically ascertained that an adolescent in residential care is responding to compelling urges to form intense heterosexual relationships that are self-destructive because of unresolved early developmental conflicts, staff should discourage these relationships, and these adolescents should explore their feelings in life space interviews and in psychotherapy.

Other unresolved earlier and later developmental conflicts have been identified as underlying sexual acting-out in early adolescence. Early adolescent heterosexual relations are in some cases primarily motivated by counteroedipal defensive maneuvers (Offer and Offer, 1977). Thus, an adolescent feeling anxiety about erotic wishes toward the parent of the opposite sex or a parent substitute may become involved in a sexual liaison with an opposite sex peer as a way of defending against the anxiety of these wishes. In residential treatment, it may be observed that this anxiety is triggered by home visits or on vacations with the family, where oedipal strivings are awakened, or it may be stimulated by an attachment to the caretaking adult of the opposite sex that becomes eroticized in the treatment setting.

At a still higher developmental level, sexual liaisons between early and middle adolescents also sometimes serve to defend against homosexual strivings (Offer and Offer, 1977). Child development experts have identified a period in early adolescence when homosexual sex play and experimentation is fairly common and does not typically lead to homosexuality in adult life (Rutter, 1971). This is certainly not uncommon in institutional settings, given the extent to which these youngsters live in close proximity over a fairly long period of time. For the poorly integrated adolescent in residential treatment who is still struggling with earlier unresolved developmental conflicts, the experience of closeness via sexual play, even in milder forms such as horsing around, sometimes can lead to explosive protest reactions that seem to derive from a kind of homosexual panic. Thus, two girls rooming together who are suspected of having engaged in some sexual experimentation and play may be observed fighting bitterly for no apparent reason as a way of reasserting, in a primitive way, some distance in their relationship. Likewise adolescent and sometimes latency age youngsters in residential treatment will launch into a violent and highly emotionally charged battle with their "best friend," after their degree of closeness triggers panic about erotic feelings that arise.

> Melinda and her roommate were in their room prior to bedtime. They were constantly shutting the door. Every time the staff entered the room the two were engaged in some sort of sex play. They attempted to sit behind dressers and in out-of-sight areas. It became necessary to separate the girls into different rooms for the evening. The next day on the playground Melinda and her roommate became involved in a violent physical altercation involving hair pulling, hitting, kicking, and biting that required restraint of both girls to prevent injury, and it took a considerable period of time for both of them to calm down. The fight was triggered by no apparent reason.

Further follow-up with these girls in therapy and life space interviews by the child care staff revealed that Melinda was feeling significant conflict and panic about her feelings of closeness and affection with her roommate.

Sometimes these feelings can be triggered by horseplay; erotic feelings may be aroused that cause the adolescent boy to have to reassert his masculinity.

> James and several of his peers were involved in a sort of wrestling match. James became very hyperactive, picked up a belt, and hit one of the other boys. He then launched into a violent attack, swinging and kicking at the other boys and then the child care worker when he intervened to restrain James. Afterwards he accused the other boys of "humping him," and it took a very long time for him to calm down and regain his control.

Clearly erotic feelings were aroused in this youngster when he engaged in a wrestling match with other boys in his group. He projected these threatening feelings onto the others and accused them of "humping him." Also, by challenging his peers to a fight and in lashing out at the adult in charge, he made a primitive and urgent attempt to reassert his threatened masculinity.

Child care workers and teachers need to be aware that often even mild forms of horseplay, wrestling, and "fooling around" between same sex peers can trigger an affective storm that relates to the anxiety and sometimes virtual panic these youngsters feel when erotic feelings are stirred. Obviously, these same feelings can be stirred in interactions with a staff member of the same sex. Feelings of closeness or attachment become eroticized, particularly with those adolescents in care who in their early life experienced adults as seductive or sexually overstimulating.

Adolescent sexual acting-out sometimes reflects the unconscious wishes of parents or parent figures (Blos, 1963), who, while consciously and openly disapproving of sexual acting-out, may nevertheless experience some vicarious gratification as a result of these behaviors and unconsciously encourage and reinforce them.

The feelings and reactions about sexual issues stirred in direct care workers interacting with children and adolescents are a crucial element in residential treatment. The workers' own unresolved adolescent issues and conflicts about sexuality can easily be acted out through unrecognized signals to children and adolescents in care; so conscientious helping persons must be willing to look within themselves at these feelings to determine, sometimes with the help of a supervisor or a consultation with a clinician, whether their own issues are interfering with their responses to the child. One of the healthiest developments in psychotherapy in recent years has been the tremendous attention given to countertransference issues. This area needs constant attention and work in all residential treatment programs; for it is not a realistic expectation that all people working with troubled children and adolescents will have resolved beforehand all the issues pertaining to their own childhood and adolescence. Willingness to explore one's own reactions and to work toward a better understanding of one's own feelings is the key to successful therapeutic handling of these issues in residential treatment.

In addition to the strong instinctual gratifications it seeks, the sexual acting-out of adolescents toward others often expresses a sense of domination and power, and an imposition of their will on others, whereby sex is used as a frightening tool (Papanek, 1964). This issue has already been alluded to with respect to latency age children, and it frequently is seen with adolescents in residential care as well. The fusion of sexuality with issues of power, domination, and aggression undoubtedly reflects in most of these youngsters the extent to which they felt dominated, controlled, and sometimes abused in relation to early caretakers. Sex becomes a natural and powerful weapon in the hands of children whose early experiences have given them many reasons to hate adults (McNeil and Morse, 1964).

Adolescents in residential care sometimes make indiscriminate choices regarding sexual partners. Regressive needs for infantile love combined with hostility toward members of the opposite sex may lead adolescents to feel rejected, isolated, lonely, or empty, and to become involved in repeated loveless sexual relationships (Miller, 1983). These relationships provide some instinctual and regressive satisfaction, along with gratification of hostile and devaluing wishes toward the opposite sex. This pattern is difficult to change in outpatient therapy and can be dealt with effectively only in residential treatment settings by concerned and conscientious supervision, active attempts to discourage the relationships out of concern for the participants, and intensive therapeutic exploration to work toward resolution of the underlying sense of deprivation and rage.

Considerable anxiety and conflict can be engendered in direct care staff who try to intervene in such situations. A great deal of discussion between clinicians and direct care staff may be needed to delineate within any particular adolescent sexual relationship those elements that are healthy and need support, and those that are self-destructive and certain to lead to more hurt and frustration and ought to be discouraged.

The child care worker, not knowing how to respond to such incidents, can always decide to stop the activity and redirect the youngsters involved into other milieu activities, and either follow up later in a life space interview after consultation with a supervisor or clinician or refer the matter to a therapist for clinical exploration. It is perfectly permissible for direct care workers who think they have reached their personal limits of comfort in dealing with such issues to refer the adolescent to a therapist for a more thorough discussion of the issues, or to obtain consultation before making a follow-up response to a given youngster.

RESPONDING TO SEXUAL ACTING-OUT IN THE THERAPEUTIC MILIEU: SOME GENERAL ISSUES

The road to sexual maturity, even given favorable life experiences, is a long and often confusing journey. Children who for either constitutional or congenital reasons lack the adaptive capacities to be influenced by reasonably favorable environmental provisions, or whose environmental provisions are inadequate or destructive or both, face an especially arduous and difficult task.

A starting point for all direct care workers is an attitudinal one. We must try to intervene as calmly as possible, and nonjudgmentally. Direct care workers should be prepared to mark boundaries and set limits when sexual behavior is expressed in a socially unacceptable form or represents potential injury to one or more of the participants. Certainly this is the case when bigger and stronger or older children attempt to intimidate or force younger or weaker and more disturbed children to engage in some form of sexual behavior.

The direct care staff, teachers, and child care workers need training in dealing with sexual questions, language, and behavior. If the direct care staff responds with alarm, shock, or anxiety, this can only confuse and complicate the emotional reactions of the child. The direct care staff need to be desensitized to talking with children about sex, answering their questions, and dealing with examples of sexual behavior that are commonly manifested in residential treatment settings.

A comprehensive program of sex education for children and adolescents in care is another necessary building block. These programs need to provide basic information regarding not only the physiological aspects of sexuality but, more important, issues of personal choice, values, and responsibilities. Discussion of intimacy, meaningful attachments, loving, and caring for one another should be geared to the appropriate developmental levels of children and adolescents (Elsass, 1970; Sanctuary, 1971; Gochros, 1981).

For such a program to be effective, it needs a combination of inputs and approaches. It should include lectures along with informal group discussions, which can be led by direct care workers possibly in collaboration with a nurse or a therapist. In addition, plenty of one-to-one follow-up and informal discussion between direct care staff and individual children are required. Finally, children in residential treatment should explore many of these issues in individual therapy.

The direct care staff also need a great deal of support, guidance, and supervision to enable them to respond therapeutically to these issues. It is easy for an inexperienced child care worker to be manipulated into supplying vicarious sources of sexual excitement for children, by answering inquiries of a manipulative child who wishes to acquire information about the staff member's sex life (Lambert, 1976; Redl, 1966). In their eagerness to be of help and to dispel children's supposedly distorted ideas of sex, staff members may go overboard in sharing information about their private sexual lives, which can prove very stimulating and titillating to the manipulative child.

Direct care staff should also understand the extent to which their own use of language, gestures, and manner of expressing affection can be highly stimulating to a child and easily misinterpreted. Given the proclivity of children with early developmental disturbance to regress quickly and dramatically to more primitive modes of functioning, staff members need to appreciate the fact that an occasional swear word by a staff member may stimulate anal preoccupations in a child, which can quickly spread through the group in the form of a mud fight or some other messy type of play that gets totally out of hand.

The dress of staff members is also an important issue. Sexually provocative or suggestive clothing can reproduce for many of these children what was harmful in their early life—a parent figure who was overly seductive and excessively stimulating. Even the choice of toys and recreational activities can sometimes produce dramatic and unintended effects.

Terry and Frank were engaged in a water gun fight when Frank took Terry's water gun away. Terry proceeded to punch Frank in the head. Frank then swung at Terry and chased him. When the child care worker intervened, Frank turned his anger on the child care worker, swinging at her and pulling her hair. It was necessary to restrain Frank with the assistance of another child care worker. It took Frank at least 15 minutes to regain composure.

A water gun fight with its phallic implications obviously led to an escalating spiral of tension and excitement, which finally erupted in a violent episode.

The swimming pool, where the regressive pull of water combines with the sexual excitation arising from viewing scantily clad bodies and from the frequent bodily contact during horseplay in the water, often is a source of overstimulation.

Richard returned from the special evening swim making sexually explicit comments. Richard began to undress and then urinated on the floor. Soon Richard became physically aggressive to staff.

Upon returning from the swimming pool, Mickey began talking to one of the secretaries in the hallway. He followed her into the room with the soda machine. Once in the room he said, "You know what? I can tickle you if I want. I bet you're real ticklish." The secretary told him she wasn't ticklish and left the room. Once in the hall he began grabbing at her arms and side saying that he could tickle her if he wanted. She was able to physically remove his hands from her body and to obtain the help of a child care worker nearby who returned Richard to his group.

Given these children's impulsivity and tendencies toward generalized excitation as well as sexualized interactions with peers and adults, it is important for direct care staff to be sensitive to these issues and to engage in preventive planning to reduce the extent of such stimuli to manageable levels. Without such prior planning and thought, some activities are an invitation to disaster because of their regressive pull in response to sexual stimulation.

Lambert (1976) indicated that, in his experience, the greatest single error made by direct care staff in dealing with troubled children concerning sexual issues is to underestimate the amount of guilt and anxiety sexual thoughts and activity generate among the children. He also suggested that such sexual behavior has a frequent escalating quality, and the unchecked use of erotically charged language and gestures leads frequently to rapid escalation and to overt sexual acting-out. The ability of direct care workers to intervene early in the chain of these escalating erotic behaviors is crucial, particularly with highly disturbed children and adolescents whose impulse controls are tenuous, at best.

Finally, it is not uncommon for children and adolescents suffering from such guilt to engage in behavior intended to provoke punishment, to alleviate their guilt and anxiety (McNeil and Morse, 1964). It is also common for children experiencing such intolerable guilt to try to draw other children into acting-out behavior, to reduce the feeling of isolation and guilt by diluting it in the process of sharing it with others. Direct care workers who are aware of such predictable sequences may be able to intervene early in such a chain of behavior. By the use of life space interviews, staff may help a child or adolescent to verbalize such feelings of guilt and anxiety and thereby prevent a repetitious cycle of self-defeating acting-out behaviors.

RESPONDING TO THE SEXUAL ACTING-OUT
BEHAVIOR OF SEXUALLY ABUSED CHILDREN:
SPECIAL CONSIDERATIONS

In a recent survey conducted on the last one hundred admissions to The Astor Home for Children Residential Treatment Program, the case records of these children clearly documented that 56% of the children had suffered prior abuse, either physical or sexual, with 17% having experienced both physical and sexual abuse in their early years. These are probably conservative estimates because only clearly verified and documented incidents of abuse were included in the survey.

During the course of treatment, children may reveal in therapy, and sometimes to a trusted child care worker or teacher, that they experienced abuse that was never investigated or documented in case records. In dealing with the sexual acting-out behavior of these children, it is especially important to sensitize child care workers and teachers to some common defensive strategies these children employ so as not to add further to their sense of victimization.

Many children disclose their experience of sexual abuse only after they have resided in the treatment center long enough to feel safe and to develop trust. Threats of violent consequences if they ever told have kept them from unburdening sooner (Crenshaw et al., 1986b). When they finally can talk about these experiences, often they are flooded with the original painful affects, including terror, that accompanied the original experiences. Lister (1982) described this painful unburdening process with adult victims of trauma.

If the original trauma was compounded by threats to keep silent, child care workers and teachers need guidance on how to support the child in the painful and often frightening process of facing the reality of the abuse and the accompanying powerful affects, which frequently threaten to overwhelm the child's psychic equilibrium. These affects are especially strong because children in residential treatment often have not experienced a single isolated traumatic experience of abuse, but more typically have experienced repeated sexual abuse, frequently accompanied by violence (Crenshaw et al., 1986a).

De Young (1984) has described the counterphobic behaviors so often seen in multiply sexually abused children. These children often engage in seductive and flirtatious behavior that helping professionals and direct care staff can easily misinterpret as suggesting that the children are partially or even totally responsible for their own victimization. Delineation of the typical clinical features of sexually abused children enables direct care staff, to respond therapeutically to sexually provocative behavior of these children (Sgroi, 1982; Kempe and Kempe, 1984).

Van Ornum and Mordock (1983) and Lamb (1986) made the important point that when clinicians tell sexually abused children that the experience of abuse was "not their fault," it can have the unintended effect of diminishing the sense of power and control that the children may feel in addition to their guilt. Although it is crucial for helping professionals and direct care staff in the residential treatment center to believe and not blame children when they struggle to unburden themselves about abuse experiences, Lamb argued that their genuine feelings of guilt and responsibility need to be validated. If their feelings about participation in the abuse are refuted by well-meaning adults, anxious to relieve them of any sense of responsibility, it may very well leave these children feeling powerless and resigned to life as victims.

Borgman (1984) has also made some useful suggestions in planning milieu treatment for sexually abused adolescents. He recommended that abused children be encouraged to talk about their abusive experiences only if such sharing is in the service of mastering these experiences, rather than an attempt to avoid legitimate discipline or responsibility. Borgman recommended discouraging the child from talking about the abuse if it serves to perpetuate a deviant identity or is designed to provoke shock or rejection. Permitting children or adolescents to hide behind their victimization or to manipulate others to avoid responsibility further reinforces the deviant identity or maladaptive behavior, entrapping them further in a painful way of life whereby they repeatedly become victims. Borgman also described how sexually provocative behavior can be redirected into constructive outlets by encouraging such socially acceptable exhibitionistic behavior as talent shows, cheerleading, school plays, and other performing arts.

SUMMARY

As Miller (1983, p. 327) stated, "Nowhere is the interplay between environmental, interfamilial, and personal factors more evident than in the field of sexual behavior." In addition, sexual attitudes, feelings, and behavior are influenced by cultural and religious values and beliefs. Responding to the sexual acting-out behavior of children and adolescents in residential treatment centers is especially complicated because of the need to take into account not only developmental considerations and a host of environmental and cultural variables, but vulnerabilities of children and adolescents whose ego impairments are so severe as to preclude their living with their families or in family-type settings within the community. Indeed, a very large percentage of these youngsters have experienced physical or sexual abuse prior to placement, and through various defense and counterphobic maneuvers they may seek to provoke sexual encounters in the therapeutic setting. There is no easy or quick solution to developing a therapeutic strategy for dealing with these issues in a residential treatment center.

This chapter has identified the developmental issues and unresolved psychodynamic conflicts that frequently underlie sexual acting-out behavior of children and adolescents referred for inpatient care. A number of practical approaches dealing with these behaviors were discussed. Special considerations for dealing with the sexual acting-out behavior of sexually abused children were outlined to aid in planning milieu treatment for these youngsters.

While sexual acting-out behavior is multi-determined and the risk of oversimplification is great, certain common features emerge. Children and adolescents coming into residential treatment centers usually exhibit a degree of disturbance that has massively interfered with the developmental process. Most function emotionally and often socially as much younger children than their chronological age suggests. Their precocious and sometimes provocative sexual behavior is not just a reflection of their craving for physical contact to compensate for unmet infantile and early needs for nurturance, love, and protection, but is much more complex than that. These youngsters need considerable education, guidance, and protection as well as therapeutic intervention, as they undertake what is for any human being a difficult and sometimes anguishing task of finding appropriate and satisfying ways of meeting sexual needs.

Child care workers and teachers in residential treatment settings are called upon to guide and respond to various manifestations of the child's struggle to find appropriate expressions of their sexual needs. There is little practical guidance in the professional literature to assist them in this formidable task. It is hoped that the foregoing discussion will increase the dialogue regarding this complex and crucial management issue.

REFERENCES

Ashway, J. A. (1980). The changing needs of female adolescents. *Adolescent Psychiatry, 8,* 482–498.

Bacciagaluppi, M. (1984). Some remarks on the oedipus complex from an ethological point of view. *Journal of the American Academy of Psychoanalysis, 12,* 471–490.

Balint, M. (1968). *The Basic Fault: Therapeutic Aspects of Regression.* London: Tavistock.

Bettelheim, B. (1974). *A Home for the Heart.* New York: Knopf.

Bettelheim, B. (1986). Current issues in the treatment of the emotionally disturbed child. Presented at the Annual Conference at Rhinebeck Country School, Rhinebeck, N.Y., June 24, 1986.

Bieber, I. (1962). *Homosexuality—Psychoanalytic Study.* New York: Vintage Books.

Binder, J. and Krohn, A. (1974). Sexual acting-out as an abortive mourning process in female adolescent inpatients. *Psychiatric Quarterly, 48,* 193–208.

Blos, P. (1963). The concept of acting-out in relation to the adolescent process. *Journal of the American Academy of Child Psychiatry, 2,* 118–143.

Borgman, R. (1984). Problems of sexually abused girls and their treatment. *Social Casework, 65,* 182–186.

Crenshaw, D. A., Boswell, T., Guare, R., and Yingling, C. J. (1986a). Intensive psychotherapy of repeatedly and severely traumatized children. *Residential Group Care and Treatment, 3*(3), 17–36.

Crenshaw, D., Rudy, C., Treimer, D., and Zingaro, J. (1986b). Psychotherapy with abused children: breaking the silent bond. *Residential Group Care and Treatment, 3*(4), 25–38.

De Young, M. (1984). Counterphobic behavior in multiply molested children. *Child Welfare, 63,* 33–39.

Duncan, J. W. (1982). The problem(s) of the adolescent in the family. *Psychiatric Annals, 12,* 301–316.

Easson, W. M. (1967). Adolescent inpatients in love. *Archives of General Psychiatry, 16,* 758–763.

Elsass, N. C. (1970). Sex and sexuality presentations in emotionally disturbed children in a residential treatment center. *Child Welfare, 49,* 212–219.

Freud, S. (1905). Three essays on the theory of sexuality. *Standard Edition 7,* 130–243.

Gochros, J. S. (1981). Sex education programs for residents. In D. A. Shore and H. S. Gochros, eds., *Sexual Problems of Adolescents in Institutions.* Springfield, Ill.: Charles C. Thomas.

Iacono-Harris, D. and Iacona-Harris, D. A. (1981). In D. A. Shore and H. L. Gochros, eds., *Sexual Problems of Adolescents in Institutions.* Springfield, Ill.: Charles C. Thomas.

Kempe, R. and Kempe, C. (1984). *The Common Secret: Sexual Abuse of Children and Adolescents.* New York: W. H. Freeman.

Klein, B. (1975). The Klein–Astor clinicians guide. Unpublished manuscript, The Astor Home for Children, Rhinebeck, N.Y.

Klein, B. and Mordock, J. B. (1975). A guide to differentiated developmental diagnosis with a case demonstrating its use. *Child Psychiatry and Human Development, 5,* 242–253.

Kohut, H. (1977). *The Restoration of the Self.* New York: International Universities Press.

Lamb, S. (1986). Treating sexually abused children: issues of blame and responsibility. *American Journal of Orthopsychiatry, 56,* 303–307.

Lambert, P. (1976). Memo to child care workers: notes on the management of sex and stealing. *Child Welfare, 55,* 329–334.

Levin, D. S. (1985). *Developmental Experiences: Treatment of Developmental Disorders in Children.* New York: Jason Aronson.

Lichtenberg, J. D. (1983). *Psychoanalysis and Infant Research.* Hillsdale, N.J.: Analytic Press.

Lister, E. D. (1982). Forced silence: a neglected dimension of trauma. *American Journal of Psychiatry, 139,* 872–875.

McNeil, E. B. and Morse, W. C. (1964). The institutional management of sex in emotionally disturbed children. *American Journal of Orthopsychiatry, 34,* 115–124.

Miller, D. (1983). *The Age Between: Adolescents and Therapy.* New York: Jason Aronson.

Morgan, S. (1984). Counseling with teachers on the sexual acting-out of disturbed children. *Psychology in the Schools, 21,* 234–243.

Offer, J. B., and Offer, D. (1977). Sexuality in adolescent males. *Adolescent Psychiatry, 5,* 96–107.

Papanek, E. (1964). Management of the acting-out adolescent. *American Journal of Psychotherapy, 18,* 418–434.

Redl, F. (1966). *When We Deal with Children.* New York: The Free Press.

Rutter, M. (1971). Normal psychosexual development. *Journal of Child Psychology and Psychiatry, 11,* 259–283.

Sanctuary, G. P. (1971). Sex education for the child in foster care. *Child Welfare, 50,* 154–159.

Sander, L. W. (1983). Polarity, paradox, and the organizing process in development. In J. D. Call, E. Galenson, and R. L. Tyson, eds., *Frontiers of Infant Research.* New York: Basic Books.

Sgroi, S. M. (1982). *Handbook of Clinical Intervention in Child Sexual Abuse.* Lexington, Mass.: Lexington Books.

Shore, D. A. and Gochros, H. S. (1981). *Sexual Problems of Adolescents in Institutions.* Springfield, Ill.: Charles C. Thomas.

Stern, D. (1983). The early development of schemas of self, other, and "self with other." In J. D. Lichtenberg and S. Kaplan, eds., *Reflections on Self Psychology.* Hillsdale, N.J.: Analytic Press.

Stern, D. N. (1985). *The Interpersonal World of the Infant: A View from Psychoanalysis and Developmental Psychology.* New York: Basic Books.

Szur, R. (1983). Sexuality and aggression as related themes. In M. Boston and R. Szur, eds., *Psychotherapy with Severely Deprived Children.* London: Routledge and Kegan Paul.

Van Ornum, W. and Mordock, J. B. (1983). *Crisis Counseling with Children and Adolescents: A Guide for Nonprofessional Counselors.* New York: Continuum.

5

Discipline and Child Behavior Management in Group Care

Arthur J. Swanson
and
Beverly A. Richard

Clinicians and child care workers in residential treatment are faced with the task of providing a therapeutic environment 24 hours a day. Staff are responsible not only for addressing the clinical problems that led to each child's placement, but also for ensuring that each child's daily needs are met, establishing and maintaining daily routines (mealtime, bedtime, etc.), providing a stable, secure environment, and providing an opportunity for positive interactions among staff, children, and their peers. In order to accomplish this Herculean task, it is essential that staff establish clear, consistent guidelines for maintaining discipline and for controlling the behavior of children who often have had a history of behavior problems.

The focus of this chapter is on the application of social learning theory and behavior therapy principles to the problem of discipline and behavior management. We will briefly review these basic principles, and then provide specific suggestions for dealing with both positive and negative behaviors. Although many of these techniques are most relevant for direct care staff, they have implications for other members of the treatment team as well.

The techniques being offered are derived mainly from the authors' work with emotionally disturbed boys in residential treatment. In most situations, however, there are more similarities between the behaviors of "normal" and emotionally disturbed children than there are differences. These techniques, therefore, are effective in working with both "normal" and emotionally disturbed boys and girls. In dealing with certain populations of children (i.e., abused, aggressive, and isolated children), some of these techniques may be more effective than others. In that light, we will discuss special considerations involved in dealing with these populations of children.

BASIC PRINCIPLES OF BEHAVIOR MANAGEMENT

The foundation of behavior management techniques can be found in social learning theory and the principles of behavioral psychology (Bandura, 1969, 1977). The basic premise of this approach is that both positive and negative behaviors are learned and maintained through similar processes. Furthermore, modification of negative behavior can be accomplished through the application of learning principles and the manipulation of environmental contingencies that serve to maintain the negative behavior. These basic principles are as follows:

1. *Behavior that is reinforced, or rewarded, tends to be repeated.* This process can apply to the learning of both socially appropriate and socially inappropriate behavior. For example, a child who is rewarded with a desired object (candy, a toy, etc.) almost every time he or she says "please" will repeat this behavior and say "please" when making a request. A similar process takes place when a child throws a temper tantrum and the parents or other caretakers "give in" in order to stop the temper outburst. A child who learns that a temper tantrum will be rewarded will repeat this behavior whenever he or she is frustrated or denied a desired object.

2. *Reinforcement is most effective when it is clearly linked to the behavior being reinforced.* For example, if a child is praised for completing his or her chores and then given the privilege of going outside to play, that child will quickly learn that the privilege of extra playtime is related to completion of the chores. That child will be more likely to repeat the desired behavior (chore completion) than the child who is neither praised for the behavior nor told that task completion results in extra playtime.

3. *Attention, even negative attention, can be reinforcing.* Children find adult attention especially reinforcing and will tend to repeat any behavior that is rewarded with attention. When that attention takes the form of praise for positive behavior, the child will repeat the positive behavior. Yet, even negative attention, in the form of reprimands for inappropriate behavior, can be reinforcing, particularly if the child is not receiving attention for positive behavior. Children can learn these negative behaviors by observing the response of adults to a peer's inappropriate behavior. Frequently, if the behavior is reinforced by adult attention, other children in the group will begin to exhibit the negative behavior. Parents, teachers, and child care staff are all familiar with the "contagiousness" of such behavior.

4. *Reinforcement and punishment are most effective when they immediately follow the target behavior.* Children are better able to learn to control their behavior in response to rewards and punishment if these contingencies closely follow the occurrence of the behavior. Short-term goals, easily attained by the child, can be established to aid a child in

learning to set and reach long-term goals. For example, the child who receives daily praise for completing his or her homework will be more likely to repeat this behavior and to do well in school than the child who is only rewarded for earning good grades at the end of the semester. Similarly, the child who is punished for acting-out in a group meeting by being asked to leave the group will be more likely to avoid this behavior in the future than the child who is told that he or she cannot join the next group meeting because of his or her previous behavior.

5. *Rewards tend to be more powerful than punishment.* The reason for this is twofold: first, rewards teach the child what behaviors are expected of him or her, whereas punishments, by teaching the child what not to do, provide little clue about what to do in a given situation; second, children will often engage in negative behavior for its immediate reward, despite the possibility of punishment. An example of this is the child who acts out in a group to gain the attention of peers while being fully aware that a punishment for such behavior is forthcoming.

APPROACHES TO INCREASING POSITIVE BEHAVIOR

It is the premise of this chapter that every child is capable of exhibiting positive behavior. Frequently, children in residential treatment have also learned a set of negative behaviors that are severe and, at times, chronic in nature. Given the disruptive quality of these behaviors, it becomes difficult for staff involved with these children to identify and then act upon their strengths. Yet, the act of "catching a child being good" is an extremely effective way of improving a child's self-esteem and of increasing desirable behaviors. The following strategies are particularly effective in this regard.

Using Praise

Praise involves noticing and commenting upon a child's positive behavior. Such attention tends to affirm a child's sense of self-worth and to make the child more likely to repeat the behavior that was praised. Praise can be given in response to a variety of behaviors including cooperativeness, thoughtfulness toward others, remembering to do a chore, and so on. Some adults feel uncomfortable praising a child for behavior that is expected. Behaviors that are taken for granted, however, tend to occur less often.

There is some belief that praise should be directed not at a child's personality but rather at specific behaviors that he or she exhibits. Haim Ginott, a noted psychologist, once observed that "Direct praise of personality, like direct sunlight, is uncomfortable and blinding." Comments such as "You're a great kid" may make a child feel uneasy because either such comments do not correspond with the child's self-perception, or because the child may fear being thought of as a "bad kid" if he or she misbehaves. Instead, it is recommended that the child's specific behavior, rather than the whole child, be praised. For example, one might say, "I see you made your bed very neatly today"; or "It was nice of you to help Pedro with his homework." In administering praise, the following guidelines should be kept in mind.

Guidelines:

1. *Make eye contact.* With small children, it helps to get down on your knees or to lean over so that you are face to face with them to accomplish this. The trip will be well worth it.
2. *Be sincere.* Do not make up things to praise or give false praise. If the child's behavior is not praiseworthy, consider praising his or her efforts. For example, if a child attempts to make his or her own bed, but, finds the task too difficult, do not praise the sloppy bed, but praise the child's fledgling efforts. You might also encourage him or her to keep practicing the task.
3. *Praise the specific behavior.* Do not use global praise for the reasons stated above. Also, such praise often fails to tell the child what specific behavior you are praising. For example, "Susan, you're such a nice girl" is not nearly so specific or effective as "Susan, it was very nice of you to share your toys with Jennifer."
4. *Give praise immediately.* Although it is never too late to give praise, it is most effective when it immediately follows the behavior being praised.
5. *Gradually increase praise.* If you are unaccustomed to praising, increase the praise gradually, lest you and the child feel uncomfortable with your new behavior.
6. *Do not contaminate praise.* Do not praise the child and then say "That's better than you usually act," or "Why didn't you do that before?" Under such circumstances the child probably will remember your criticism of past behavior better than your praise of present behavior.
7. *Vary the wording.* Use different words and terms each time to describe the child's positive behavior, or the phrase you use will become repetitious and meaningless to both you and the child.

More subtle forms of praise are communicated to children through showing them respect and treating them courteously; for example, by saying "please" and "thank you." Finally, one may praise a child through one's actions. For example, remembering to ask a child about a math test or framing an award for the child are ways of showing that he or she is important, and that his or her positive behaviors have been recognized.

Using Rewards

While praise may be considered a "social" reward, children also respond to more primary rewards such as food, money, toys, and attendance at special events. Primary reinforcers are particularly effective with younger children, who will frequently work hard to attain even the simplest such rewards.

Guidelines:

1. *Vary the reinforcer.* Use a variety of reinforcers so that no one reinforcer loses it value. Staff may wish to administer a children's reinforcement schedule to the children to determine which rewards are of particularly high value to the individual child. When selecting the reinforcers, remember that it is important to consider the developmental level of each child. For example, younger children tend to find concrete rewards (i.e., food, toys, or other material objects) more reinforcing, whereas a more mature child may prefer more social rewards (i.e., increased responsibilities or privileges).
2. *Reinforce frequently.* Particularly when a child is learning a new behavior, it is more desirable to give small rewards on a frequent basis than a large reward at a later time.
3. *Administer rewards immediately.* Much like praise, primary reinforcers are most effective when administered immediately after the performance of the desired behavior. When this is not possible, a token can be used to help bridge the gap between the behavior and its ultimate reward.
4. *Choose a reinforcer that is under your control and is compatible with the treatment program.* It is preferable to choose a reinforcer to which a child does not usually have access. For example, it is more effective to have children work toward a trip to a special sports event than to use television as a reinforcer because the former reward would be seen as an addition to regular programming, whereas the latter would not. Reinforcers such as television are often too readily available to children to be used contingently. In addition, the withdrawal of such reinforcers would more likely be perceived as punishment by the child than would the withdrawal of noncustomary reinforcers. Using reinforcers that are compatible with the treat-

ment program refers to the need to select reinforcers that are not detrimental to the treatment goals of the child. For example, you might not want to reward an aggressive child with a toy gun, or an overweight child with a snack.

The same argument used against praise could be lodged against the use of primary reinforcers. That is, why reinforce children for something they should be doing anyway? It is true that some behaviors might be expected of a child; but if such behaviors have not been developed, some method must be employed to help the child enter a more positive cycle of behavior. Administering rewards contingent on behavior is clearly a more effective way of motivating children than either nagging or using punishment for noncompliance. Ultimately, the goal is not that the child will become dependent on material rewards, but that he or she will become more responsive to the social praise that often accompanies such improved behavior. Finally, the praise of others may result in self-praise, in which the child comes to appreciate and acknowledge his own strengths, thus developing an internal sense of self-worth and self-efficacy.

Modeling Positive Behaviors

Research indicates that a substantial portion of the behavior a child exhibits is learned through watching others (Bandura, 1969). Children are constantly observing and then mimicking significant others in their lives, particularly adults. In fact, children are more likely to behave consistently with what adults do than with what they say. A parent who lies is likely to produce a child who lies even if that parent emphasizes the wrongfulness of such behavior. Therefore, modeling the behavior you want to see, whether it be honesty, expressing feelings, working hard, or whatever, will greatly increase the chances of its occurrence in the children who are in your charge. This modeling effect is further strengthened through praising a child whom you observe imitating such prosocial behavior.

APPROACHES TO DECREASING NEGATIVE BEHAVIOR

Even if significant emphasis is placed on the value of increasing positive behavior, children sometimes exhibit negative behaviors that must be confronted directly. Such negative behaviors might include a child's having an uncontrollable temper tantrum, stealing, noncompliance with a staff member's request, and so on. Responses to such negative behaviors can range from ignoring the behavior to punishing the child through the imposition of appropriate consequences. The selection of an appropriate means of discipline depends on a variety of factors, including the age of the child, the type of problem, and the child's response to previous forms of discipline. The following techniques are offered as effective means of decreasing negative behavior in children.

Using Ignoring

Some behavior that children exhibit is not normal childishness but rather immature behavior intended to gain adult attention. Such behaviors as whining, inappropriate crying, and temper tantrums are examples of such attention-getting acts. Typically, adults respond to such behavior by repeatedly telling the child to stop. Paradoxically, the attention given the child in the reprimand reinforces the behavior and makes it more likely to reoccur. If staff wish to decrease the frequency of these behaviors, it becomes important that they *pay absolutely no attention* to them when they occur. At first, the child will increase the frequency of the behavior in an attempt to gain your attention. However, if you persist in ignoring the unwanted behavior, the child will learn that another behavior is needed to get your attention. It is crucial that you respond immediately and in a positive way to the new behavior if it is more appropriate than the earlier one.

Guidelines:

1. Only ignore behavior that is not dangerous to the child or others.
2. Ignoring the behavior involves pretending that it is not even occurring. No response, either verbal or physical, can be given to the child.
3. Ignoring is sometimes difficult to use effectively in group settings where the child's behavior might be ignored by you but reinforced by peers.
4. Ignoring is effective only if it is paired with praise for behavior that is the opposite of the undesired act, (i.e., being pleasant rather than whiny).

Using Redirecting

Some negative attention-getting behavior can be dealt with by redirecting the child's energies into a more constructive behavior or activity. For example, children who are needlessly quarreling with one another might be encouraged to go outside to play or to spend some quiet time reading. The concept here is that it is not always necessary to repond to the behavior the child presents, as it may merely be the child's way of gaining attention. Instead, it is desirable to redirect the child's attention to a more constructive activity and then to lend your full support and attention to it.

Using Soft Reprimands

Sometimes children exhibit behavior that can be neither ignored nor redirected. This is particularly true in a group setting where the attention of other children may be maintaining the behavior you are trying to change. Most often, loud reprimands are given to the child, ones that are audible to the rest of the group. However, soft reprimands, ones that only the child can hear, are more effective in reducing disruptive behavior (O'Leary et al., 1970). Although soft reprimands initially require more work, they usually "pay off" in terms of the child's showing more positive behavior and the staff's having to reprimand less. Another advantage of using soft reprimands regularly is that when a staff member needs to use a loud reprimand, it will have considerably more effect it if has been used infrequently.

Using Time Out

At times, a child's behavior is so out of control that he or she needs to be removed from the situation in which it is occurring. For example, a youngster who is kicking another child would need to be separated from the victim and placed in a less reinforcing environment. You might tell the child to sit in a chair placed away from other children, or, in extreme cases, to accompany you to a room that, though comfortable, offers no external stimulation (games, dolls, pictures, etc.). The child would then be instructed to sit quietly for a designated period of time, after which he would be allowed to return to his regular activities. This procedure works particularly well with young children because their placement in a non-reinforcing environment is mildly discomforting to them. By contrast, older children, (age twelve and above) often respond better to other approaches, and if given time out, might even like the time away from other children. In any case, Hall and Hall (1980) claim that time out always results in a decrease in the negative behavior if used correctly and with young children. The following guidelines, however, need to be followed to ensure the success of this technique.

Guidelines:

1. *Give a warning.* If you see a child exhibiting disruptive behavior, calmly warn the child to stop the behavior, or he or she will be placed in time out.
2. *Follow through.* If the behavior continues, remove the child immediately from the group, first by asking the child to leave, but, failing that, by physically leading him or her to the time-out area.

3. *Make time out an appropriate length.* Time out is most effective when administered immediately and for a short duration of time (three to five minutes). Inform the child that the time spent in time out does not start until he or she settles down. That is, a child serving three minutes who become disruptive during the second minute must start again to serve the three minutes of quiet time. Except for informing the child of the time remaining in time out, it is essential not to interact with him or her during the time out because such interactions are reinforcing and likely will increase the child's disruptive behavior.

Using Loss of Privilege

Loss of privilege offers another way of disciplining children. In this case, a child who fails to perform a requested behavior or misbehaves may lose a privilege that is important to him or her. Privileges might include the opportunity to go outside, to watch TV, or to play some game. It is especially helpful if the privilege that is lost is somehow "linked" to the misbehavior. For example, a child's failure to come in on time might result in his or her having to come in an hour earlier the following evening. The loss of privilege should not be too great (e.g., not leaving the cottage for one week), or the child is likely to get discouraged and rebel even more. If the "punishment fits the crime," the child will learn from the experience and will be more likely to conform to adult requests in the future.

Loss of privilege can be a very effective technique if: (1) you use it only once in a while; (2) when you use it, you follow through with denying the child the privilege. It is very important that the child receive the punishment you warned of so that he or she knows that in the future you "mean business." If you do not follow through, the child will not believe any future warnings you give him.

Guidelines:

1. *Ask the child to stop.* If the child is misbehaving, quietly ask him to stop.
2. *Give a warning.* If the behavior persists, inform the child that he or she will lose a privilege unless the behavior stops immediately.
3. *Follow through.* If the child fails to respond to the warning, inform him that he has lost a privilege that is appropriate to the transgression.

In using this technique with adolescents, it is important to emphasize the issue of choice in their behavior. That is, an adolescent child might *choose* not to do a chore with the understanding that, by failing to do it, he or she will forfeit that week's allowance. Rather than attempting to make an adolescent conform to cottage rules, it is often more useful to carefully explain the rules and the consequences for breaking them. To the extent that adolescents need to become more responsible for their behavior, they need to be given greater opportunity to choose either to disobey rules and suffer the consequences or to obey them and retain their privileges.

Using Physical Restraint

In those cases where a child's behavior is a serious threat, either to him- or herself or to others, or could result in significant property damage, the use of physical restraint is often warranted. In these instances, minimal force should be used to hold the child because the intent should never be to cause bodily harm. Similarly, corporal punishment involving slapping, pinching, squeezing, hitting, kicking, or any other acts that cause physical discomfort to the child should not be used. If a child is consistently in need of physical restraint, either the treatment team needs to explore the reasons for it and attempt alternative methods of discipline, or the case needs to be reevaluated as to the appropriateness of placement. In some instances, a child might be better served in a more restrictive setting than that offered in residential care.

SPECIAL CONSIDERATION FOR SELECTED POPULATIONS

The Abused Child

Many of the children currently in residential treatment have a history of physical abuse. These children often enter placement with an extremely low self-image, thinking of themselves as "bad kids" who in some way deserved the punishment inflicted upon them. The primary goal with these children is to provide a safe and secure environment where they can feel free to be themselves and not fear being beaten for their misbehavior. At the same time, abused children have often learned a set of behaviors that can elicit anger and frustration from those involved with them. Hence, it becomes important to state clearly the consequences for certain misbehaviors and to follow through with them in a direct but nonpunitive way. Particularly in the case of abused children, the message must be communicated that it is the behavior that is being punished, not the child.

The vicious cycle must be modified in which some abused children exhibit behavior that invites abuse. Using physical restraint with these children can be particularly problematic. Although use of this technique sometimes is unavoidable, it should be used sparingly because of the possibility that the child's provocative behavior is being reinforced by the physical contact that follows it. One solution is to help children find other ways to gain the physical contact they so often crave. Modeling by staff of positive social interactions (handshakes, hugs, etc.) can often help a child learn more appropriate ways to achieve such contact. When necessary, the use of time out is also an excellent technique for such children.

The Aggressive Child

The aggressive child has learned that "aggression pays." That is, such children have learned that they can satisfy their needs through aggressiveness toward their peers and in some cases, toward adults. With this type of child, it is crucial to create a milieu that does not reinforce aggressive behavior. Specifically, rules for appropriate behavior need to be stated explicitly, along with the consequences for violating the rules. When a child has violated a rule, the consequence needs to be administered immediately and in a consistent manner. Along with punishment for antisocial behavior, aggressive children need to be given praise and rewards for prosocial behavior. Token economies, in which children are rewarded for positive behaviors, are particularly effective in decreasing aggressive behavior (Patterson and Reid, 1973).

Of equal importance in reinforcing prosocial behavior exhibited by an aggressive child is staff modeling of nonaggressive ways of handling conflict. Aggressive children need to learn that adults whom they admire are capable of getting their needs met without acting aggressively.

The Isolated Child

The isolated or withdrawn child, who causes few problems for others, is often neglected in treatment programming. Yet, such children can have needs as pressing as those of the acting-out child. The isolated child frequently lacks the skills required to make friends or to achieve any sense of mastery over his or her environment. Isolated from others, this child is denied opportunities for learning more advanced social skills, such as resolving conflicts with peers or establishing and maintaining interpersonal relationships. This type of child may prefer to interact with adults as a way of avoiding peer interactions.

With the isolated child, it is important to praise any effort toward greater involvement with peers. Often, it is necessary to reinforce successive approximations toward a goal. For example, one might first need to solicit a response and then to reinforce a child for offering a comment in a group meeting. Once the child has reached minimal levels of involvement, it is possible to increase the demands slowly. Eventually, a child might be rewarded for playing a game with peers or for going on an off-campus trip with a selected friend. The use of a more socially skilled peer as a model and a "buddy" for the isolated child can be particularly effective in helping such children overcome their asocial tendencies.

SUMMARY

In this chapter, principles of social learning theory and behavior therapy have been applied to the problem of discipline and the behavior management of children. The techniques that have been described are effective with both emotionally disturbed and "normal" populations of children. In both cases, interventions that emphasize the reinforcement of positive behaviors are preferable to those that rely on the punishment of negative ones. Residential treatment programs should combine both reinforcement and punishment strategies while maintaining sensitivity to children with special needs, in order best to meet the needs of all children in care.

REFERENCES

Bandura, A. (1969). *Principles of Behavior Modification*. New York: Holt, Rinehart and Winston.

Bandura, A. (1977). *Social Learning Theory*. Englewood Cliffs, N.J.: Prentice-Hall.

Hall, R. V. and Hall, M. C. (1980). *How to Use Time Out*. Lawrence, Kans.: H & H Enterprises.

O'Leary, K. D., Kaufman, K. F., Kass, R. E., and Drabman, R. S. (1970). The effects of loud and soft reprimands on the behavior of disruptive students. *Exceptional Children, 37,* 145-155.

Patterson, G. R. and Reid, J. B. (1973). Interventions for families of aggressive boys: a replication study. *Behavior Research and Therapy, 11,* 383-394.

6

Special and Unusual Events in Residential Treatment: Theoretical and Clinical Perspectives

Peter H. Cormack

In the ongoing life of a residential treatment center, a number of events, some occurring regularly, some occasionally, have a tremendous impact on the flow of energy and on patient perceptions of the availability of security anchors in the milieu. Anticipating and planning for these events make it possible for a program to use these occurrences as tools to further the treatment process.

Residential treatment involves meticulous attention to detail. A residential treatment center must become a psychologically safe arena for each patient if it is to be the setting where meaningful personality change is stimulated, nurtured, and managed. The task of the residential treatment center is to aid each patient and his or her family in the process of creating order out of the inner and systemic chaos that are the hallmarks of their lives when they enter treatment (American Association of Children's Residential Centers, 1972). It is in attending to detail, tying and retying the many threads created by patient and program needs, that the fabric of psychological safety is woven. The guide to how these threads should be tied is the philosophical and conceptual framework of the residential treatment program. Programs that are effective as treatment agents are those that have a clearly specified philosophical and conceptual foundation and have developed methods of operation that consistently translate these ideas into daily practice (American Association of Psychiatric Services for Children, 1985).

Many philosophical and conceptual frameworks have proved useful in managing residential treatment programs. In the author's experience, several factors combine to determine program success, with the specific theoretical framework employed being of secondary importance. There appear to be two critical elements: the degree of consistency the program achieves in the translation of ideas into practice, and the awareness of program managers of the practical realities that confront those who live with and treat severely disturbed patients. This awareness of practical realities dictates areas where philosophy and theory must be translated into specific modes of operation. Staff of effective programs understand what they are doing, why they are doing it, and whom they are doing it with—and they do it well.

The special events referred to in the opening paragraph of this chapter fall into two broad categories: (1) those whose occurrence we know about in advance; and (2) those events whose occurrence we can anticipate in advance although we do not know who will be involved and when the actual event will happen. Events in the latter category are often referred to as crises, the common element being that they serve to disrupt the flow of the ongoing process of the milieu. Events in the first category, on the other hand, occur naturally in the lives of patients and the life of the program, with the common element being that they relate to times of transition and passage, times of celebration as well as events that cause current painful realities to stand out in stark contrast to hopes, desires, and ideals. Events in this category include the celebration of Christmas, St. Valentine's Day, and other significant holidays; the celebration of patient birthdays; patient admissions and discharges; shifts in program focus and structure (e.g., school ending for a summer break, with the living area thus becoming the primary focus and locus of activity); and alterations in a patient's life pattern because of major shifts in the treatment plan. In the second category are patient assaults on staff and/or property; elopements from the program; sudden eruptions of frustration or other painful emotions; termination of relationships with departing staff; patients suffering injuries and patients being temporarily removed from the program for hospitalization due to physical health needs.

These events and some of the issues that surround them will be discussed in this chapter, and recommendations for utilizing these events as tools in an overall therapeutic process will be offered. The list of events in each category is not exhaustive; however, it is hoped that the following discussion will demonstrate an approach to and way of thinking about these problems that readers will find helpful in dealing with issues unique to their own programs. The ideas presented here are based on the author's experience in residential treatment with children (primarily ages six to twelve), as well as concepts drawn from theoretical approaches that stress the importance of both the internal life of each patient, including the emotional and cognitive spheres, and the patient's familial sociocultural system. Many of these suggestions can be applied to work with adolescents, but they should first be reviewed and modified appropriately in light of the developmental and clinical issues associated with the adolescent period.

It was noted above that a residential treatment center must become a psychologically safe arena for patients if significant personality change is to occur. August Aichorn, Fritz Redl, David Wineman, Bruno Bettelheim, Albert Trieschman, Melvin Lewis and Joseph Noshpitz, to name a few, have all written extensively about the nature of a therapeutic milieu and how this milieu forms the axis around which all other therapeutic activities in the residential treatment center revolve. (See references for some of their works.) These discussions will not be recapitulated in the present context, but several concepts introduced in these writings are basic to handling special events and will be discussed.

Children in residential treatment centers are keenly aware of the sub-rosa social order that exists within living units and within the program generally (Polsky, 1965). The most powerful individuals are clearly defined, and so are the most vulnerable. It often may appear that patients are at odds with staff, and/or view what staff do as irrelevant as long as it does not affect them directly. Clearly this is not the case. Staff, through their ongoing patterns of actions, interactions, and reactions, are constantly sending powerful messages to patients about how safe and secure the place is. The most potent messages establish the patients' perceptions of how staff deal with individuals whom the other residents view as the most weak and vulnerable. Apparently the strong can feel safe if they believe that the weak will always be protected. Remember this point when dealing with the various special and unusual events that are the subject matter of this chapter. It suggests that ongoing attention to the treatment milieu will help ensure that the patient and staff are in the best possible position to cope with eruptions of impulse and pain when reality, social system, and/or intrapsychic issues strain a patient's control system beyond endurance. The emotional climate of the setting where help is delivered is as crucial as the specific interventions offered, in stimulating therapeutic growth (Redl and Wineman, 1957).

The essential task that milieu therapists confront in trying to maintain an environment that will be both curative and supportive of others' therapeutic work is to organize and individualize that environment in such a way that it provides for patients externally those things that they do not have available to them internally. For example, what must be done to help particular patients to maintain their trust that they will be cared for and accepted for themselves during times of emotional upheaval? What must be done to help a child contain angry impulses and learn to deal with them effectively, when expression of these emotions drastically undermines the child's fragile sense of self-esteem? There are as many of these questions as there are patients. The point is that the issues of any one patient impact upon and affect all other patients in a living group such as a cottage in a residential treatment center. Special or unusual events, even though they may center around one or two patients, are also issues for the larger group; and this awareness must help guide the program's response to what is occurring.

CHRISTMAS, ST. VALENTINE'S DAY, AND OTHER SPECIAL HOLIDAYS

Our society has been described by sociologists as a highly mobile one whose ongoing process has served to weaken the nuclear family and loosen kinship ties. However, at times our society appears temporarily to reverse this trend, and the energies of the mass media and commerce flow in the direction of reminding us of the way things once were, and of what we should strive to achieve in terms of family and a satisfying life. These events are the major holidays, with the messages being most clear in relation to Christmas and the Christmas season. No one can escape the message that Christmas is a time for reuniting with family and loved ones, for submerging old hurts and conflicts, and for looking toward the future with renewed hope. It is a time when relationships are renewed and sometimes intensified, when existing commitments between people are highlighted, and when being separated or estranged from others may become extraordinarily painful. It is also a time when, even in the well-functioning family system, relationships can be strained and old hurts reactivated and intensified. Dysfunctional families and emotionally disturbed individuals often experience holidays as unsettling, even regressive, times.

Children living in residential treatment centers, and their families, are often particularly impacted by Christmas. Feelings of separation, abandonment, and rejection may become even more painful, giving rise to increasingly fragile control systems. This may result in acting-out toward others, toward previously accepted rules and expectations, or toward property, often the symbols of the season. An idealization of the absent parents or child may also occur, with the negative side of ambivalent feelings seeming to disappear. Even though these are generally temporary phenomena, it may appear on the surface that some hard-won therapeutic gains have been lost.

The giving and receiving of gifts may reactivate many past feelings of deprivation and neglect in residential treatment children, so that at times they cannot accept and may even need to destroy or at least devalue what they receive. The inevitable comparison of gifts that occurs when a child sees what other children have received may lead those children who measure their worth by material possessions to experience very painful feelings of rejection; and it may serve to activate old tensions around sibling rivalry, resulting in fear, panic, or depression.

The handling of the Christmas season with children in residential treatment and their families should flow from an understanding of the dynamics of the season, of the therapeutic process, and of the way our society in general copes with these kinds of events. In terms of the larger society, times of transition and times of great emotional significance are often draped in ritual. Some Christmas rituals have significant religious content, whereas others suggest a holiday spirit. The rituals of Christmas, particularly those that are devoid of specific religious content, can be helpful supports in therapeutically managing the season. They can become the backdrops against which the emotional issues of individual patients emerge. The purchase and decoration of a Christmas tree, preparation of special foods, making or shopping for gifts for loved ones, communication of wants and desires to those who will be purchasing gifts, and sending and receiving of greeting cards are all examples of these kinds of ritualized events. A second benefit of participation in these ritualized activities is that, once activities are scheduled, they become anchor points and give some additional organization to the celebration of the season.

It is recommended that residential treatment programs avoid group-based participation in the frankly religious rituals of the Christmas season. Religion has a very significant place in family life and plays an important role in the lives of many children placed in residential treatment. Patient populations are diverse, with many religious orientations and patterns of belief represented in in the patient mix. Some patients or their families may find religious observances counter to their beliefs, and some may even feel demeaned and emotionally assaulted if they are required to participate in such ceremonies. The addition of conflict around religion, with all of its personalized meanings, to a time that is already emotionally complex serves to obfuscate clinical issues and create additional Gordian knots for staff to unravel. This is both a perversion of religion and a block to clinical effectiveness.

A Christmas ritual that can have particular meaning and be a valuable treatment tool is the giving and receiving of holiday greetings. Children in residential treatment can be characterized by the chronic nature of their emotional distress and their great difficulties in maintaining a realistic perspective on themselves. Low levels of self-esteem and self-images hallmarked by numerous negative elements are often the mode in patient groups. When such children receive numerous cards from treatment staff and other patients—cards that are noncontingently given, and wish happiness and good will—the cards bring the powerful message that those children are cared for. This is particularly true when the cards are all delivered at once, at an event such as a cottage party specially planned for the distribution of these cards. Some children will receive the message of the cards more directly than others. In fact, some patients' reaction to the experience may be only to note the volume of paper that comes their way and then to pay little attention to the nature of the greetings or who sent them. Other children will study each card, pondering the message and carefully noting who sent it. Some cards are even displayed in bedrooms, and may be found decorating the walls many months after they were received. Whether children read or weigh their cards, many glean a further sense that they are worthwhile human beings from the experience of receiving these greetings. This kind of milieu-based message helps serve as a counterpoint to the regressive pull that the stress of the season may create for some patients, and it may also contribute to their becoming more invested in their treatment. The receiving of cards may also be initially painful for some patients, as the event provokes either painful memories or active anxieties. The value of the cards and card parties in these cases lies in the fact that they highlight issues in need of therapeutic attention and create a background for dealing with those issues.

It is also important that the overall treatment program be maintained in its basic form during the Christmas holiday season. This is necessary so that familiar patterns and routines, which have become sources of security and anchor points for the children, continue to be available. The handling of the issues that the season stimulates in individual patients can also proceed most effectively within the guidelines of their individual treatment plans, when the usual pattern of program structure and organization is maintained.

It is not only patients and their families who are influenced by the special meanings of the Christmas holiday season. It is quite important that treatment staff also make an extra effort during the Christmas season to be aware of their own emotions and retain their clinical objectivity.

The rituals associated with other special holidays can also be incorporated into ongoing programs and become valuable treatment tools. The discussion of Christmas cards also applies to Valentine cards. The giving of candy or other special treats traditionally associated with the Easter season, and the festivities of Thanksgiving with their emphasis on comradery and the sating of appetites, all provide stimuli that can provoke the emergence of important treatment issues at a time when usual defenses are weakened, and the possibilities of a patient moving toward a healthier, more stable pattern of personality organization can be maximized. The point is that special holidays should be viewed as opportunities for furthering treatment, not an intrusion into ongoing therapeutic processes that must be tolerated even though the real work of the program is disrupted.

BIRTHDAYS

Christmas and the various special holidays are events surrounded by society-wide celebrations. Birthdays, on the other hand, are of great importance to the individual child and his or her family, but do not receive this broader notice. The celebration of a birthday is thus a more personal and individualized experience than Christmas or Thanksgiving in most families. This should also be true in a residential treatment center, with close attention being paid to the emotional impact of the celebration on the celebrant, his or her family, and the other patients in the treatment program.

The issues that pertain to Christmas and the other special holidays are also relevant to understanding the emotional impact of birthdays. Being separated from family at a time when he or she feels drawn toward them may be particularly distressing for the child. The separation, with its constant reminder of reduced involvement in an important phase of their child's life, stimulates uneasiness in parents. Their children's birthdays may aso stimulate a host of issues related to growing old in some parents, which may also be distressing to them. Birthdays thus may become times of increased stress and vulnerability even though they are meant to be times of joy and celebration.

The handling of birthdays should proceed along lines similar to the handling of other special events. The rituals should be attended to; that is, the holiday party attended by cottage mates and selected others invited by the child, the giving of gifts, and the ensuring of some contact with the family, even if only by telephone. It is the sensitivity of staff to the needs and issues manifested around these events by patients and families that determines how much therapeutic mileage can be made around them. A birthday celebration can occasion the emergence of fear, anxiety, and old rivalries with siblings, or serve to confirm, in a patient's mind, that he or she really is alone. A sense of failure as a parent or anger generated from old deprivations may emerge in parents who see the residential treatment center providing more for their child than they ever received as children, or could provide for them in the present. The birthday celebration, like other celebrations, thus is both background and stimulus for the continued delivery of therapeutic services.

PROGRAM ALTERATIONS AND SHIFTS

This section presents a series of events having the common denominator of being consequences of decisions made by program staff concerning the clinical needs of individual patients or groups of patients. These events include patient admissions and discharges, alterations in individual treatment plans that impose new or revised definitions of reality on patients, and, finally, planned shifts in program focus such as school vacations, trips into the community, and so forth.

Each of these events requires some sort of accommodation on the part of patients, based on a giving-up of relationships, routines, or structures of the immediate past, and investing in an altered reality, even if it is only temporary. Some patients are able to accomplish these accommodations with relative ease, and eagerly look forward to something new or different. Other patients are profoundly affected when they recognize that another patient is ready to leave, or when they must deal with someone new, who may be experienced as a competitor for staff time and affection or as an intruder in a place that finally feels safe. These various events are clearly most unsettling to those patients who are highly vulnerable to stress.

Anticipation and planning are the keys to ensuring that these events are utilized in a therapeutic manner. Discharges involve preparing patients for the new things they will confront (a public school, living at home on a full-time basis, etc.); facilitating their farewells; and dealing with the separation issues involved. Those who remain must be helped with their feelings of separation, abandonment, and at times discouragement over their own progress. The patients who are left, as well as those newly admitted, must also deal with revisions in the social system of the living area and the larger program, shifts in the status and power hierarchies, and the conflicts between patients that accompany these changes. Preparation and planning for discharge should begin even before a patient is admitted. The setting of treatment goals, which define what should happen before a patient is ready to leave, is the initial step in this process; and the events that occur throughout the patient's residential treatment experience contribute to the achievement of these goals.

Two sets of treatment process events deserve mention here. One of these has to do with programmatic responses to plateaus or impasses with individual patients, the second with the need to alter program periodically because of staff needs for vacations.

On some occasion a patient's forward progress in the treatment process simply seems to stop. The patient appears comfortable; he or she is functioning well within the structure and organization of the program; there is little conflict with staff and/or other patients; parental visits are going well—in fact, almost everything seems right. Another "no noticeable forward progress" pattern is seen in the patient who appears to be at war with the entire program, expending considerable energy on undermining and/or defeating program goals. The common denominator is that both of these patient types are using the program to avoid treatment issues that they must resolve in order to make real progress.

The clinical handling of these plateaued cases often needs to be sufficiently dramatic to bring the patient back on course. This typically involves strategies that directly confront the patient's avoidance mechanisms and focus on the emotions behind them. There are a variety of ways of accomplishing these types of goals, but discussion of specific strategies is beyond the scope of this presentation. The point of our discussion is that a certain amount of confusion ensues for the general patient population when there is a significant shift in focus in the care of a single patient. In addition to the impact that a significantly revised approach has on the patient in question, some other patients may react to what they see happening in ways reflecting the nature of their disturbances. The balance of the milieu is disrupted, a sense of insecurity is stimulated in some patients, and capacities for self-control may be challenged. It is crucial that plans for dealing with these plateaued cases consider total milieu impact of the intervention strategies employed, so that the clinical needs of all affected patients may be addressed.

The pattern and structure of a residential treatment program shift from time to time because of staff vacations. School ends, and the living unit becomes the primary locus of activities for a while; there may be an influx of temporary staff at these times, whose presence makes it possible for living area staff to take vacations. These are unsettling times for many patients. These events often stimulate a retesting of the intent and capacity of the milieu to provide care and refuge, as well as feelings of abandonment and sadness that a favorite adult or activity is temporarily unavailable. The change in the structure may precipitate grief reactions in some children, who mourn the loss of what they had come to count on while actively testing the mettle of their new reality. The situation is often the most tense when these events are first occurring, as the first round of staff depart. The newness of the changes is compounded by the fact that many of the permanent staff who remain are also ready for vacation. Many are emotionally fatigued, and so are somewhat less sensitive to the nuances of patient need than usual. When they are confronted with escalating displays of pathological functioning, concerns about maintaining physical control may take precedence over concerns about maintaining therapeutic control, and the overall tenseness of the situation is compounded even more.

Programs should recognize that these phenomena occur, and build in additional supports as necessary. One solution is a very tightly organized program that tries to help the patients have as much fun as possible. It is also helpful to solicit and utilize patient imput into the planning of various activities as a way of maximizing investment. Special attention should be given to the orientation and training of temporary staff. Regular program staff should try to communicate to patients a message of confidence in new staff. The regular staff can serve as relationship bridges between new staff and patients, and this should be encouraged. Active and ongoing supervision of temporary staff is also highly important, and probably does more than any one thing to ensure continuity in treatment when program focus is in a period of natural transition.

* * * * * * * * * *

The remainder of this chapter will focus on events whose common element is that they can all be regarded as therapeutic crises. By definition, a crisis is a critical period that has an impact on the course of future events. Crises are thus opportunities for therapeutic growth if they are managed effectively. The manner in which these kinds of events are experienced by patients, those directly involved and those who observe, is influenced by a combination of the individual personality dynamics of the participants and the overall culture of the treatment milieu.

The culture of a treatment milieu consists of all those shared definitions of what constitutes the actual reality of the therapeutic environment. The real place of and concern about patients in the treatment center, as viewed by patients, is one parameter of this culture. Which forms of impulse expression are permitted, and which are not, is another dimension. The routes patients must take in order for a problem between themselves and other patients, or themselves and staff, to be addressed is also defined by program culture. Ways to obtain an increase in autonomy, status, or privileges are also elements of the culture. Staff should be keenly aware of the culture that has evolved in their program and actively seek to shape and direct that culture in ways that allow it to contribute maximally to the therapeutic mission of the residential treatment center. This discussion will focus on several types of crises: patient assaults on other patients, staff, and property; patient elopements from the program; departures of staff from the program; and injuries and/or significant illnesses affecting patients.

PATIENT ASSAULTS ON OTHER PATIENTS, STAFF, AND PROPERTY

Several characteristics are common to many patients in a residential treatment center:

- Great difficulties in coping with aggressive feelings and in the area of impulse control.
- A propensity to view persons or events external to themselves as at fault when they feel emotionally distressed.

- A propensity to convert experienced distress into action, often pre-cipitating in others the distress that they cannot tolerate in themselves.

When a group of such patients share all aspects of their lives, some assaultive behavior directed toward persons or objects is inevitable. Recognizing this fact and making advance provision for dealing with these occasional events greatly facilitate using them in a therapeutic fashion.

Each program should incorporate a set of safety valves that permit the draining off of accumulated stress and frustration on a regular basis. In addition to devices built into the pattern of scheduled activities (such as periodically involving patients in activities that require strong physical exertion and providing for nurturance needs through snacks and the like), it is also very helpful to develop specific program structures that allow patients to escape from stressful situations to a place where individual attention is available to facilitate conflict resolution. These structures must be built in such a way that they are easily accessible at patient request or when staff see a need for them. It is also important that the culture of the program validate these program structures so that a loss of status does not accompany their use, and they should be constructed and perceived as helpful rather than punishing. For example, crisis intervention stations that are a part of the overall living area and/or school area programs are such structures. These crisis stations should be staffed by an experienced staff member who can help individual patients deal with their immediate issues, and then reconnect the patients with the staff who were originally involved with their difficulties, to further work out the issue(s). These crisis stations also provide patients a chance to cool off and take time out from a stressful area. If the patient has lost control of his or her behavior in the context of the crisis, step one is to regain that control; then the issues can be resolved. The regaining of control may involve dealing with the patient in a variety of ways (increasing structure, decreasing autonomy, restraint, etc.). In the author's experience, this process is most facilitated if the adults involved focus on helping the child regain self-control and become reintegrated into the ongoing program. Do not try to understand the meaning of the disturbed patient's behavior and then address the issues at this time, as such efforts only serve to compound, intensify, and, in the patient's eyes, justify his or her distress and behavior. First reestablish control; then deal with why it was lost.

Another type of built-in safety valve is to allow patients easy access to the program head whenever necessary. The program director should be quite visible to all patients, with patients being allowed, even encouraged, to share their joys, frustrations, and concerns with this person. This may create some difficulties for a program administrator, and at times may seem to encourage efforts by the more manipulative patients to play line staff and administration against each other; but many benefits accrue as well. A primary advantage is the feeling among patients that what they say is taken seriously, and that they can have some influence over what happens to them. A second benefit is that patients come to perceive a solidarity and consistency between line staff and program decision makers, and can benefit from the sense of security that this brings. Third, the program head sometimes must play an important mediational role involving patients and staff; and credibility with patients is necessary for this to be done effectively.

Consider, for example, what happens when a patient assaults a staff member. In a residential treatment center, life goes on in spite of such occurrences. A patient who assaults a staff member at 11:00 A.M. still has to eat lunch, and may have to deal with that same staff member at mealtime. The program keeps patients and staff in close contact with each other, and they must interact with each other constantly. On-scene staff must quickly and thoroughly deal with patients' losses of control so that they do not continue and escalate. An additional set of issues is generated when the loss of control involves an assault on a caretaker. These events must be brought to closure with both the patient and the staff member as soon as possible, in an atmosphere that is minimally compounded by fears of retaliation and retribution. The program administrator plays a key role here. This individual can intervene, work to reestablish limits, and integrate the patient back into the ongoing program structure, freeing the line staff member to work with the patient about why he or she lost control and the issues related to this. This type of intervention is typically done in the form of an interview held as soon as clinically feasible after the assault occurs, with both the patient and the involved staff member participating. There is almost a ritualistic aspect to this; these interviews may come to be defined in the program culture as the end point in the sequence of events that included the assault. If properly carried out, these interviews also serve to "clear the air" so that affected staff can continue to treat the children, and disruption to the ongoing process of the milieu is minimized.

By quickly dealing with losses of control and bringing them to closure, we help the patient who has lost control as well as the other patients in the program. The histories of many residential treatment patients contain numerous reminders of their problems and failures, with minimal acknowledgment of successes and accomplishments. It is therapeutically beneficial for patients to live in an environment where they are not haunted by the aftermath of the impulsive expression of their psychopathology. Staff actions make a significant contribution to patients' being able to leave their problems behind them.

Some aspects of the physical environment contribute to crisis management. Draperies attached to curtain rods by snaps rather than hooks may be replaced quickly, with no apparent damage, should they be torn down by an upset child; likewise, it may help to use chests of drawers whose drawers can be removed to reveal functional shelves for patients who attack property when upset. Thus we may tailor the environment to the functional levels of patients. If the environment is built to absorb acting-out without appearing partially destroyed in the process, patients living in it can be helped to move toward more effective ways of coping with inner distress.

THE RUNAWAY PATIENT

Patient runaways can be roughly subdivided into two groups: attempts to escape something unpleasant, and attempts to reach something that has become important for any of a variety of reasons. If ongoing efforts are made to address patient needs for safety and security, and if the program culture values dealing with problems as they arise, then patient escapes from the program will be extremely rare phenomena. Also patients will run away to something infrequently, although the runaways that do occur will generally fall in this category.

Each program should develop protocols and procedures to observe if a patient elopes from the program, with these procedures including at least a search of program facilities, notification of family, notification of local police authorities, and program staff making some efforts to locate the runaway(s) in the larger community. A runaway should be viewed as a behavioral expression of a patient's disturbance, with the clinical handling of the patient flowing from this perspective once he or she has returned to the program. This involves welcoming the runaway patient back, adjusting program form and structure to aid the patient in maintaining more effective self-control, and then dealing with the clinical issues behind the behavior in a manner consistent with the patient's overall treatment plan. In some "running to" incidents, families may also need to be actively involved in this process, and one or more focused family interviews may be helpful in bringing out and working on the issues that impelled the patient to leave the program. These types of interventions can dramatically illustrate family support of the treatment program, as well as contribute to resolution of specific clinical problems. This type of approach also sends a message to the program at large that running away accomplishes little, that it does not confer any additional prestige or status, and that impulse expressions will be dealt with in a therapeutic manner rather than through punishment. This latter message must be sent repeatedly to maintain a therapeutic milieu, as it will most often be met with disbelief due to the intense, often conflicting emotions that many patients have about their losses of control.

STAFF DEPARTURES

In the life of every residential treatment program, staff who have highly significant relationships with some or all of the patients leave the program to follow other pursuits. These departures can be used to further treatment goals with some preplanning. It is of major importance that ample time be allowed for patients to express their emotional reactions about the pending departure of a staff member, and to work those issues out with that staff member or through other staff if possible. The goal here is to help the patient to experience whatever emotions the situation stimulates and ultimately to understand the situation accurately. That is, the patient realizes that the departing staff member is doing something to get on with the business of his or her own life, not abandoning the patient or the program. Patients should also understand that it is acceptable to experience a wide range of emotions about the event, that angry feelings do not in any way invalidate positive ones, and that saying good-bye is difficult.

Patients should realize that staff may also feel ambivalent about departing even though they have made the decision to move on. In terms of program functioning, once staff members depart, they should be discouraged from maintaining contact with patients. The primary reason for this is that patients must grapple with the meanings that relationship losses have for them, and this process can be undermined if some of the losses patients encounter during their treatment experience are not real.

THE INJURED AND PHYSICALLY ILL PATIENT

Injuries and physical illness in residential treatment patients stimulate the reemergence or intensification of feelings of vulnerability and issues around dependency. An appreciation of this reality should influence how required medical care is provided to patients. The vast majority of injuries and illnesses seen in a residential treatment center are relatively minor, including cuts, scrapes, colds or flu, gastrointestinal disturbances, and so on. Occasionally a patient breaks a limb, needs emergency surgery, or is found to have a catastrophic disease.

Minor injuries are typically dealt with directly by program staff, with consultation and backup from medical personnel as necessary. On such occasions other patients view the sick or injured patient as quite vulnerable; so staff handling of the situation has many implications for defining the safety and responsiveness of the milieu for the patient group at large.

When a residential treatment patient must be taken to a general hospital, one guiding concept should be that, insofar as possible, the treatment program should accompany the patient. Treatment center staff should be available to provide as much direct care and support to the patient as possible during the hospitalization. A liaison should be established between treatment center medical staff and hospital medical staff to facilitate communication and joint planning. Patients also should be as involved as is clinically feasible.

Remember too that the patients at the treatment center need to be kept informed of what is occurring at the hospital, at least in a general way. Then staff can deal realistically with the reactions of these patients to their peer's hospitalization and its associated events.

The return of the hospitalized patient to the therapeutic milieu also deserves special consideration, particularly if the patient has been away for an extended period of time. The suggestions given above regarding program admissions apply here, and staff should incorporate them into the planning process while making whatever adjustments the patient's medical condition necessitates.

The above discussion has touched on a wide range of events that are part of the ongoing stream of life in a residential treatment center. The comments and recommendations are offered to illustrate a way of thinking about these and related issues that staff of residential treatment programs can apply to problems unique to their own setting and patient population.

REFERENCES

Accreditation Standards for Psychiatric Services for Children and Youth (1985). Washington, D.C.: American Association of Psychiatric Services for Children.

Aichorn, A. (1935). *Wayward Youth*. New York: Viking Press.

American Association of Children's Residential Centers, ed. (1972). *From Chaos to Order: A Collective View of the Residential Treatment of Children*. New York: Child Welfare League of America.

Bettelheim, B. (1974). *A Home for the Heart*. New York: Knopf.

Lewis, M. (1980). Residential treatment, in Kaplan, H., Freedman, A. and Sadoek, B. (eds.), *Comprehensive Textbook of Psychiatry/III*, Third Edition, Volume 3, pp. 2685–2692. Baltimore: Williams and Wilkins.

Noshpitz, J. D. (1962). Notes of the theory of residential treatment. *Journal of the American Academy of Child Psychiatry*, 1(2), 284, 296.

Polsky, H. (1965). *Cottage Six, the Social System of Delinquent Boys*. New York: Wiley Interscience.

Redl, F. and Wineman, D. (1957). *The Aggressive Child*. New York: Free Press.

Trieschman, A. E., Whittaker, J. K., and Brendtro, L. K. (1969). *The Other 23 Hours: Child Care Work in a Therapeutic Milieu*. Chicago: Aldine.

Whittaker, J. (1979). *Caring for Troubled Children*. San Francisco: Jossey-Bass.

7

The Influence of the Peer Culture in Residential Treatment

Carol Gwynn,
Rebecca Meyer,
and
Charles Schaefer

It is in some way ironic that emotionally disturbed children who have had enormous difficulties interacting with others live in a peer group as a major part of their rehabilitation in residential treatment centers. In fact, some observers believe that the adjustment to group living is one of the hardest tasks these children face (Mayer et al., 1978). Although parents sometimes seek group living experiences to enrich a child's life (e.g., summer camp, boarding school, travel tours), this is far from the reason for residential placement. Placing a child in a residential center/facility is generally a last resort from an untenable family situation. The child's need for coordinated therapeutic programs that are part of residential treatment centers does not necessarily include the need to live with fourteen other emotionally disturbed peers (Mayer et al., 1978).

In any case, this intense and total group living experience has a profound impact on the child's socialization, rehabilitation, and daily activities. Although the peer group can contribute to positive social development, the interpersonal problems of emotionally disturbed children may make group living a barrier to treatment. These children typically suffer from significant social skill deficits, overaggressive and antisocial behaviors, fears of groups, distortions in reality assessment, hyperactivity, impulsiveness, and other ego weaknesses. Thus, the peer culture influence in residential centers is generally negative, one in which antisocial values are reinforced while prosocial values are undermined, negatively reinforced, or punished.

INFLUENCE OF THE PEER CULTURE ON THE SOCIALIZATION OF CHILDREN

In American society, two primary groups responsible for the socialization of children are the family and peers. Ideally, the roles of these groups are complementary and mutually supportive. Parents provide love, security, and indoctrination in established cultural values, whereas peers provide friendship, normalizing influences, opportunities for reality testing, and a context in which rules may be negotiated. In general, the peer group has a significant influence on a variety of behaviors, at times promoting healthy development and at other times undermining adaptive socialization.

How Pervasive Is the Influence?

A child's self-concept is affected by and partially formed in peer relationships. Acceptance increases self-esteem, whereas rejection has the opposite effect. The peer group also provides information about one's strengths and weaknesses. Children continually compare themselves with their agemates on various characteristics such as intelligence, attractiveness, popularity, honesty, dependability, and aggressivity, as they search for their place in the world (Mussen et al., 1979). Although these perceptions may be realistic or distorted, they are taken into account in the formation of the child's self-concept.

Parents rely on the child's peer group to help in socializing the expression of aggression. Research has shown that overt aggression occurs about three times more often with peers than with family members (Mussen et al., 1979). In groups with others of equal size and developmental status, children learn effective aggression skills of defending themselves against attack, making others angry, and controlling aggressive behaviors (Bandura et al., 1967; Beller, 1972).

In addition, the peer group supports and extends parental efforts in socializing gender-appropriate behavior. Sex-typed behaviors are reinforced, while inappropriate responses are punished. In fact Mussen et al. (1979) believe that in some cases peer influences may counteract the effects of cross-gender training and identification learned in the home. For example, feminized boys may begin to exhibit more masculine behaviors in nursery school due to peer pressure. This statement has received some empirical support from a series of studies in which sex-inappropriate behaviors decreased following exposure to a peer model who demonstrated alternate activities or explicitly inhibited gender-inappropriate play (Kobasigawa, 1968).

The peer group also can have a positive influence in increasing prosocial behaviors. Results from laboratory and naturalistic studies have shown that children are likely to emulate peer models who exhibit constructive and cooperative social behaviors such as donating to charity, expressing sympathy, or helping someone in distress (Bryan and Walbek, 1970; Elliot and Vasta, 1970; Hartup and Coates, 1967). Other research has demonstrated the effectiveness of peer models in reducing timidity and promoting social participation (Bandura et al., 1967). Furthermore, in countries where there is a strong ideology related to nationalism and social responsibility [Israel (in the kibbutzim), the Soviet Union, and China], the peer group provides the main source of socialization. Finally, for children who have experienced parental deprivation, the peer group has been found to offer basic nurture and love in addition to normalizing experiences (Freud and Dann, 1951; Harlow, 1958). Thus, it seems that the peer group can augment the role of parents and function as a positive socializing force if the group has been taught high moral and altruistic values by adults.

On the other hand, the peer group sometimes may serve to increase undesirable antisocial behaviors. For example, peers provide massive support for the maintenance of already existing aggressive behavior (Devereux, 1965; Patterson et al., 1967). As early as the nursery school years, peers frequently reinforce the bodily attack of a child, attack with an object, or invasion of territory. The victims of the aggression may also reward these behaviors by yielding to the aggressor's wishes, withdrawing from the conflict, or crying. Thus, the nursery school setting is believed to be a highly unlikely place for the extinction of aggressive behavior for children who enter with these behaviors at high strength (Devereux, 1965; Patterson et al., 1967). In addition, children who are initially passive or only moderately aggressive become more aggressive as they learn to counterattack. These counterattacks sometimes are successful in warding off further attacks or in defeating the aggressor. Hence, as these children are victims less often, their own aggressive behavior is reinforced, with a subsequent increase in the initiation of aggressive acts (Patterson et al., 1967).

The situation does not improve as children grow older. Even normal preadolescents tend inadvertently to reinforce deviant behavior in their peers. Solomon and Wahler (1973), for example, studied peer reinforcement of the problem behavior of disruptive children (e.g., out of seat, talking out, rule violations). They found that social attention (looking at, verbally commenting on, etc.) provided by all the sixth grade students in the classroom was directed exclusively to the disruptive behavior of five problem students. It is this social attention that reinforces behaviors and makes them more likely to be repeated. Also it was significant that the prosocial behavior of these five children was completely ignored by their twenty-five classmates. However, when the peers were trained to ignore others' deviant behavior and to reinforce appropriate behavior, the deviant acts of the problem children were substantially reduced, and prosocial behaviors increased in frequency. This study demonstrates the tremendous value of peer social attention.

Peers' aggressive behavior also can serve as a role model. Children who merely watch other children aggress, against other children or even against inanimate objects, will acquire more aggressive behavior (Bandura and Walters, 1963). For example, in one experiment nursery school children were shown a film of a child model making many aggressive responses — hitting a plastic doll with a bat, striking it with a mallet, throwing balls at the doll, or punching it in the nose (Hicks, 1965). Another group of children saw the same film except that the aggressive responses were modeled by an adult instead of a child. After viewing the film, each child was subjected to some mild frustration and then taken to an experimental room containing a variety of materials, some of which could be used to replicate the model's aggression. It was found that the peer models were particularly effective in evoking imitative aggression; their responses were copied more frequently than those of the adult model. Equally important, at six-month follow-up the effects of exposure to the models were still discernible. Although the total amount of imitative aggressive behavior decreased appreciably over time, those exposed to an aggressive model still exhibited many of the responses they had observed. Thus, the influence of the peer group on the socialization of children can be powerful. Peers can function as a positive prosocial force in helping children develop and grow, or they can function in ways that reinforce and increase deviant antisocial behaviors.

When Will a Child Conform to His Peers?

Several factors determine the extent to which a child will conform to the values and attitudes of his peers, among them developmental stage, personality attributes, cultural norms, and historical era.

Research has generally supported Piaget's theory of early childhood as being presocial and egocentric. Thus, although preschool children may form close attachments to children their age, they are largely unaffected by normative pressure (Hartup, 1970). By age five, only 12% of children show any shift in the direction of conforming to group norms (Hunt and Synnerdale, 1959). However, peer influences on behavior becomes more significant as the child grows older and develops more intimate and sustained relationships with others of his age. By middle childhood, the tendency to conform to peers' values and attitudes increases substantially

(Costanza and Shaw, 1966; Iscoe et al., 1963; McConnell, 1963; Patterson and Anderson, 1964). The shift from parents to peers as the child's main source of influence appears most typically to occur during the sixth grade, although some believe that peers currently exert an earlier and greater impact than in previous times (Condry and Simon, 1968; Floyd and South, 1972). The peer group of preadolescent and adolescent children has been found to have more influence over their behavior than either parents (Davis, et al., 1941) or teachers (Berenda, 1950).

One result of this is that now a large number of the juvenile delinquents referred to court are in the seventh and eighth grades. In addition, "mousepack" gangs of preadolescent boys (eight to twelve years old) are on the increase in the United States (Peterson, 1974). These youthful delinquents espouse a violent, destructive, and thrill-seeking lifestyle, trying to prove they're the "baddest" by vandalizing schools, assaulting old ladies, killing rival gang members in knife fights, pushing dope, and gang-raping young girls. A further and especially alarming characteristic of this trend is that the most serious criminal offenses have recently shown substantially greater proportionate increases among juvenile delinquents than among older adults (Stephens, 1964). For example, in 1957 the rate of delinquency cases (per 1000 children ages ten through seventeen) disposed of by the U.S. juvenile courts was 19.8, whereas in 1971 the rate was 34.1 (U.S. DHEW, 1972).

Other factors that determine the extent to which a child will conform to the values and attitudes of his peers are individual personality characteristics and family dynamics. Research has shown that conforming children in middle childhood and adolescence tend to have low self-esteem, low ego strength, and high social sensitivity, and to repress impulses (Hartup, 1970). In comparing "peer-oriented" children with "adult-oriented" children, Bronfenbrenner (1970) found that the former were more influenced by a lack of attention at home than by the attractiveness of the peer group. Peer-oriented children generally held negative views of themselves and the peer group. They rated their parents lower in the expression of affection and in the exercise of discipline and control than did the adult-oriented children. Peer-oriented children also reported engaging in more antisocial behaviors such as lying, truancy, teasing, and "doing something illegal." Not surprisingly, children from large families tended to be more peer-oriented than family-oriented (Johnson and Medinnus, 1969).

The power of peers to act as socializers has been found to vary in different cultures and historical eras. Contemporary American children are probably with peers now more than ever before and beginning at a younger age. The increased percentage of women in the work force and increased geographical mobility have meant that children are spending large portions of time with other children in daycare centers, after-school activities, or unsupervised "hanging out." In a study of over 700 sixth grade American children, Bronfenbrenner (1970) reported that they spent an average of only two to three hours on a weekend day with their parents, while they spent twice as much time with their peers. On the other hand, Chinese children and Mexican children living in small villages spend more time in the family and less time with peers (Campbell, 1964). French parents traditionally teach their children to stay close to the family and do not encourage play with other children (Mussen et al., 1978). In some cultures (e.g., the Soviet Union), the peer group norms are more support- ive of and consistent with adult social values than in the United States (Bronfenbrenner, 1967).

Thus, American children are spending an increasing amount of time with their peers. The degree of parental involvement in child-rearing has declined in recent years so that the peer group is exerting an earlier and more powerful influence on the socialization of our youth. When family influence is minimal and children rely on their peers for their upbringing, the influence tends to be in an antisocial direction. This is borne out by the fact that delinquency in the United States is increasing, and delin- quent acts are becoming more violent. As a result, residential treatment centers of all types (hospital wards, group homes, state training schools) are faced with the problem of coping with a large number of delinquent and predelinquent children who have a long history of parental deprivation.

INSTITUTIONAL PEER CULTURE

A key aspect of residential treatment for children is "milieu therapy" (Cumming and Cumming, 1970), which can be defined as a scientific or systematic manipulation of the environment aimed at producing changes in the deviant behavior of patients. Milieu therapy takes an ecological or social systems approach to treatment (Hobbs, 1975). The fundamental premise of this approach is that manipulation of the milieu variable influences the child in the direction of modification toward a clinically desirable goal (Redl and Wineman, 1952).

A basic difficulty with the milieu approach is that the peer group subcultures within the total milieu operate to undermine the prosocial values of the treatment staff (Rapaport, 1960). As a result, aggressive and unethical behaviors (e.g., lying, stealing, and fighting) have been found particularly difficult to extinguish in a residential setting (Schaefer and Millman, 1973). A basic dilemma is posed by group care versus group contagion, and group members may act to hinder each other's socializa- tion (Mayer et al., 1978).

Empirical studies of institutionalized youth have verified the negative impact of the peer culture. In one study with institutionalized delinquents, for example, it was found that the peer group positively reinforced antisocial talk and actions (e.g., rule-breaking, criticisms of adults, and aggressive behaviors), whereas it negatively reinforced or punished socially conforming behavior (e.g., saying they liked someone on staff, expressing cooperation with the treatment program, etc.) (Buehler et al., 1966). Peer groups expressed disapproval when behavior deviated from the delinquent norms. Nonverbal modes of communication (looking, nodding, smiling, winking) were employed by the peer group to reinforce delinquent behavior 82% of the time, whereas verbal reinforcement was used in only 18% of the responses. The following example illustrates how the delinquent adolescents reinforced antisocial behavior:

Roberta: "She is sickening" (referring to housemother).
Steve: "Not very smart either."
Karen: Laughs.

In this exchange, criticism of an adult authority figure is both verbally and nonverbally reinforced. The authors concluded that, regardless of the institutional size, the peer group communication patterns tend to maintain the very attitudes and behavior that originally led to institutionalization. Group settings that provide extended interactions among delinquent adolescents may help to maintain existing deviant behavior as well as afford the "novice" an opportunity to acquire new deviant behavior through discriminant peer reinforcement.

Other investigators have similarly concluded that institutions for delinquent youth function as "teaching machines" for the acquisition, maintenance, and strengthening of deviant behavior (Duncan, 1974; Lement, 1967; Newberg, 1966). Moreover, it has been well documented in the field of adult corrections that the main influences on institutionalized offenders are other offenders (Grosser et al., 1969). Inmate social systems have been found to negate the treatment programs at correctional facilities (Ohlin and Lawrence, 1959). In reviewing these findings, one is reminded of the observation of the theologian Reinhold Niebuhr, in his book *Moral Man and Immoral Society*, that man cannot be moral when the society he lives in is immoral.

How does a delinquent subculture function in a residential treatment center? Polsky (1959) and Cohen (1955) have graphically described its inner dynamics. In the first place, there is a strong, authoritarian power structure with the brighter and stronger youths exploiting and tyrannizing the weaker ones. Status, masculine identification, and social acceptance are the rewards for delinquent acts. Antisocial norms and values prevail; that is, "an eye for an eye" justice, materialistic values, and a "take what you can get away with" orientation. There is also an avoidance of constructive activities and a lack of real involvement in school, personal relationships, jobs, or community.

Hostility is so prevalent in this culture that after a while it becomes an automatic response, readily displaced upon any available target. Redl and Wineman (1952) describe hate in residential treatment center children as a primary, basic striving and as a secondary reaction to task failure. The children are unable to acknowledge fear, anxiety, or insecurity of any kind without breakdown into disorganized aggression. The aggressive acts, in turn, lead to intolerable feelings of guilt and anxiety. The result is a repetition of the same aggressive acts that initiated the guilt.

Delinquent gang leaders serve as the chief source of models for superego or conscience development. These leaders view social authorities as persecutory and punishing. For example, any attempt to talk with a child about a residential treatment center infraction is viewed as an accusation. As a result, the relationship between counselors and children is a deadly game, and the main rule is "beat them or they'll beat you" (Fisher, 1972). Going over to the "enemy" is punishable by social death. Those who reform are ruthlessly ostracized by the group. Thus, gang leaders are sought not only as sources of "delinquency support" in maintaining familiar behavior patterns (Redl and Wineman, 1952), but also to help avoid the inevitable group exile should an individual's behavior shift in the socially acceptable direction.

Wariness and caution in interpersonal relationships are the norm rather than the exception. Hostility often is employed as the children's only known method of relating to another, as well as a temporary reprieve from anxiety-producing feelings of sadness and loneliness (Bettelheim, 1955). No one trusts in this setting, and everyone is hungry for love, acceptance, and affection (Fisher, 1972). In addition to affect hunger, delinquent children exhibit a constant stimulus hunger. Turned off to school, reading, and other constructive activities, they attempt to relieve their intense feelings of boredom by a quest for excitement and adventure, usually antisocial in nature.

In short, the predominant behavior of delinquent youth has been aptly described by Cohen (1955) as malicious (enjoyment of the discomfort of others), negativistic (defined by its negative polarity to society's norms), hedonistic (pursuit of immediate pleasure rather than of rational, long-term goals), and nonutilitarian (no rhyme or reason to much of the behavior).

TREATMENT IMPLICATIONS

In light of the previous findings, it seems reasonable to assume that the peer culture within residential treatment centers operates to undermine the milieu therapy approach devised by staff. Indeed, in a number of institutions—particularly those primarily custodial in nature—the children may leave the institution even more delinquent than when they entered. What can be done about a peer culture influence that appears so powerful and sinister? The following approaches appear to hold the most promise for effective intervention.

Family-Style Treatment

Rather than making treatment extremely difficult, if not impossible, by placing a large number of antisocial youth together in a living unit, residential treatment centers might try placing a greater number of deviant youth in foster homes staffed by professional surrogate parents. A professional foster parent is one who has received intense training in mental health and child development. The role of foster parents would be to function as surrogate parents who offer "personal genuineness, intellectual and affective sympathy, and a warm unconditionally positive regard even while restructuring certain behavioral consequences" (Rieger, 1972, p. 108). As a supplement to these satellite foster homes, residential treatment centers could offer "family-style," group-home treatment units both on-grounds and in the local community. Family-style treatment means placing no more than six to eight children (males and females) of varying ages together under the stable, long-term care of professional houseparents.

In education today the practice of "mainstreaming" is frequently employed; that is, placing a few exceptional children in regular classrooms with normal children. This reduces the stigma of being segregated and labeled, and increases positive interactions between exceptional and nonexceptional children. A major impetus for mainstreaming children has been our experience with segregated societal institutions (e.g., jails, Indian reservations, and racially segregated schools), which has shown them to be among our most cruel and dehumanizing practices (Masters, 1974). In terms of residential treatment then, rather than placing all delinquent or disturbed children together in a cottage, consideration should be given to placing only one or two maladjusted children in each home. The other children could be either neglected–dependent children or youth who have been in treatment for an extended period and who seem able to exert a prosocial influence on the deviant ones. This practice would make the homes more family-style in that most of the children in a home would have internalized society's norms.

In lieu of short-term, "revolving-door" treatment then, family-style homes would offer long-term care (permanent whenever possible) and real "psychological parenting" (Schaefer, 1977). They would provide the continuity of relationships, surroundings, and environmental influences that a number of child welfare experts deem essential for a child's normal development (Goldstein et al., 1973). Family-style homes such as these have proved successful in producing "adult-oriented" rather than "peer-oriented" children (Wolins, 1974). They also seem to reduce the harmful effect of stigmatizing a child by sending him away to a home for wayward children or disturbed youth (Tappan, 1949).

Family-style grouping also affords the opportunity to develop the helping role of the peer group. It recognizes the support function that children themselves provide each other when they are in heterogeneous age groupings, and when they stay together in a small family group for a number of years (Ridgway and Lawton, 1969). The older and more mature children in the family group can be taught to help the younger ones with many social, emotional, and educational tasks. Mutual support and cooperation can be the keynote of an extended-care family group setting such as this.

Although the family-style approach appears both simple and sensible in theory, there are many problems in its implementation. Among the difficulties that must be recognized are the typically high turnover rate of child care counselors in residential treatment centers, the relatively high cost involved in placing only a few children in a living unit, resistance by natural parents to extended family-style placement and/or mainstreaming, and the possibility of one or two antisocial children contaminating the behavior of the prosocial children (i.e., the "rotten apple" effect).

Strengthening the Family

It is widely agreed that parents are important contributors to the development of both antisocial and prosocial behavior in their children. For example, Block (1963), in studying character development longitudinally, found "an unequivocal relationship between the family atmosphere in which a child grew up and his later character structure" (p. 258). Monahan (1957) advocated that "A strengthening and preserving of family life . . . could probably accomplish more in the amelioration and prevention of delinquency and other problems than any other single program yet devised" (p. 258).

Cross-sectional studies link delinquency to familial rejection, conflict, and inconsistent discipline practices. For example, Gluek and Gluek (1950) found that male delinquents were more often rejected by their parents, and received less supervision than their matched nondelinquent peers.

Longitudinal studies also lend convincing evidence to a view of families as prime targets for intervention strategies. Positive associations have been found between parental discord and behavior disturbances in children (Werner and Smith, 1982; Rutter, 1971). Families that produce delinquent children are repeatedly characterized by parental disharmony, harshly punitive and rejecting attitudes, overpermissiveness, inadequate supervision, and erratic discipline (Farrington and West, 1980; Olweus, 1980; McCord, 1986).

In McCord's (1986) "criminogenic" families, parents were also likely to be aggressive, insecure, and unable to provide high expectations for their sons' behavior; "No one provides supervision or attempts to direct the children's behavior" (p. 352). On a more positive note, the father's esteem for the mother, the mother's self-confidence, and maternal affection served to insulate children from criminogenic stresses. In the absence of maternal affection, a mother's self-confidence and consistent discipline continued to mitigate negative outcomes. These data suggest that interventions that seek to improve family relationships and discipline practices can have a positive impact on these children's problem behavior. Rather than the drastic intervention of removing a child from his home, which tends to make him even more vulnerable to the counterculture of his peers, an alternative is to keep the child in the home by offering extra services and support to the family. Among the techniques employed are structured parent training (e.g., Patterson, 1976) and family counseling and therapy (e.g., Ackerman et al., 1970), as well as the use of subprofessionals (B.A. degree or less) trained in counseling, homemaking, or utilization of community resources, who provide direct services to the family (Tharp and Wetzel, 1969). A fourth technique is to give the families of deviant youth a really intensive therapeutic experience by requiring them to live together for a week or more on the grounds of the residential treatment center (Catanzaro et al., 1973). During this period, their interaction patterns are closely observed by trained professionals. The goal of all these procedures is to minimize the negative influence of the peer group in the local community by augmenting a child's ties to his family rather than to his peers.

A main difficulty of this approach is that because residential treatment is used only as a last resort, many families of children in residence are largely unmotivated for treatment. In addition, residing separately from the child may be desirable for some families because of reduced emotional intensity. Furthermore, as children enter adolescence, the power of the family tends to decline while the peer group influences grow stronger.

Treatment Group Technique

One way for institutionalized children to maintain contact with the normal peer group is the treatment group technique (Feuerstein and Krasilowsky, 1974), which involves placing a small number of troubled youth in regular group contact with a much larger number of normal, well-adjusted youth. The two groups interact freely while engaging in structured activities such as arts and crafts, games, and work. These activities are supervised by a relatively large number of staff who prevent and intervene in distressing situations.

The basic assumption of the treatment group technique is that through social learning and imitation the prosocial values of the adjusted youth will permeate the thinking of deviant youth. The danger, of course, is that the opposite will occur—that the antisocial children will contaminate the behavior of the normal children. However, some research has shown that this approach does teach prosocial behavior, and that the "rotten apple" contamination does not necessarily occur (e.g., Feuerstein and Krasilowsky, 1974).

For example, Feldman et al. (1975) placed five nine- to twelve-year-old antisocial boys in a residential summer camp populated by a large number of prosocial children (eighty-one boys and seventy-five girls). Each antisocial boy was placed in a group of about a dozen prosocial children, with whom he lived, ate, and played with for a twenty-day experimental period. Trained observers discreetly kept records of the behavior of both the antisocial and prosocial children. It was found that living with the prosocial children seemed to have an immediate and strong taming effect on the antisocial boys. In fact, the behavior of the two types of children was so similar that staff had difficulty identifying the antisocial boys. Importantly, although the prosocial children did experience some initial stress, the antisocial boys did not prove a bad influence on the other children at the camp. Because the number of children studied thus far is small, the authors cautioned against drawing firm conclusions. Nevertheless, because the camp staff had no special training in dealing with antisocial children, the researchers speculated that such an integration program with trained personnel might show significant and lasting improvement for deviant youth.

Peer Therapies

The technique of peer therapy involves one adult therapist treating two, usually latency age, children together (Mueller and Cohen, 1986). Two examples of this technique, duo therapy and pairs therapy, may hold promise in altering the antisocial impact of the peer culture in residential treatment centers. Both therapies involve providing an environment that facilitates appropriate and healthy peer interaction, in which problems can be addressed and resolved (Mueller and Cohen, 1986).

In duo therapy, first instituted by Jennie Fuller of the Framingham Youth Guidance Center (Massachusetts) in 1972, two children are paired with one therapist. The child pairs are matched on sex, age or developmental level, and some shared problem or concern. In addition, however, they are matched on compatible differences in either symptomatology or personality style. Thus, a child who deals with problems largely by acting-out may be paired with a child who tends to withdraw from others. The hope is that children will learn there are alternative ways to respond to pain, rather than their characteristic ones.

Duo therapy techniques are based in part on psychodynamic thought, and it has been suggested that a more intensive transference situation is created than in individual therapy (Fuller, 1977). Early in treatment, the duo partners are wary of each other and engage in competition for the therapist's attention, similar to the way they vied for parental affection. However, the therapist frustrates the children in their attempts to be in the number one position. The partners join together in their frustration and form an alliance. This alliance is fostered by the therapist so that the children can help each other (Mueller and Cohen, 1986). Thus, duo therapy may help children improve peer relations and social skills, share common problems and solutions, and learn new more prosocial behaviors through modeling and vicarious reinforcement (Mitchell, 1976).

Pairs therapy is being conducted by Selman and colleagues at Judge Baker Guidance Clinic (Boston), specifically with emotionally troubled and learning-disabled children (Mueller and Cohen, 1986). Each child is assigned a pairs partner, and they meet one hour per week with a specially assigned pairs therapist. The goal is to help children learn to negotiate their own needs effectively with their agemates. This is especially important for emotionally troubled children, who are frequently unable to do this. For example, if one child wanted to play one game and the pairs partner another, the therapist would help them think about how they could both have their needs met. The children are encouraged to drop rigid adherence to either dominating–controlling or submissive–withdrawn styles. In addition to developing negotiating skills, pairs therapy often creates a situation in which friendships are formed. It seems that sharing intense emotional experiences leads to feelings of mutual liking among very troubled children (Mueller and Cohen, 1986).

Teaching Values

The positive peer culture (PPC) technique (Vorrath and Brendtro, 1974) represents an innovative approach to directly intervening in the delinquent peer culture of residential treatment centers. Recognizing that negative, harmful behavior is typical of this peer group, PPC seeks to teach the basic value of loving and caring for one another, that is, wanting what is best for another. The basic technique of PPC involves small discussion groups wherein both staff and peers pressure individual boys to change their attitudes and behavior. Specific procedures involve modeling prosocial behavior and the use of "relabeling" and "reversing" techniques. Relabeling refers to attempts to teach youth the concept that helping behavior is "strong," "mature," and "powerful," whereas aggressive, hurting behavior is "weak," "immature," and "ineffective." This involves attempting to reverse the way delinquent youth typically label these behaviors. Reversing is defined as the process of helping a child assume responsibility for his actions rather than allowing him to project blame onto others. This technique is very similar to that employed by Glasser (1965) in his reality therapy approach for delinquent youth. PPC departs from the Glasser approach primarily in its emphasis on the peer group rather than staff as the prime agent for changing delinquent behavior. The adult in charge of a group of children in PPC establishes the nature of the behaviors to be discussed and reinforced, but exerts influence primarily through the group and on the basis of the group process. Every child in the group is encouraged to assume the role of "child helper" and to see it as both a challenge and an opportunity for self-growth—particularly the growth of social interest and responsibility.

The Essexfield program (Pilnick et al., 1966) has similarly attempted to rehabilitate young delinquents by designing a social system to alter deviant "street norms" and to create, through group experiences, new norms that are prosocial in nature. In recognition of the group nature of a number of delinquent behaviors, the program's key elements include group-shared work experiences and guided group interaction sessions under professional guidance. Through these experiences the boys are helped to develop new prosocial norms, traditions, language, and conceptions of deviancy. Boys who have been in the program for an extended period then transmit the new value system to newcomers. The same pressure to conform that afflicts delinquents in the community through an antisocial peer group is applied at Essexfield by a peer group ascribing to conventional norms. The authors describe the techniques used to initiate such a culture, including a variety of relabeling and reversing-oriented procedures. At first, they found it helpful to "seed" a group by transferring in a core of prosocial boys from other treatment programs.

In a very directive, authoritarian approach, Hendrickson and Holmes (1959) reported success with a highly structured program at a psychiatric service of a university hospital that relentlessly applied psychological pressure to adolescents—both individually and as a group. Keynotes of this program were as follows: (1) Very definite, almost Victorian standards of social behavior were established at the beginning and were stringently enforced thereafter. For example, patients were expected to be obedient and respectful to all staff members and to attend all required activities. Strong taboos were set up against profane and obscene language, fighting, and sex play. (2) The adolescents were expected to respond at all times to the verbal controls of staff, who took care to exercise their authority as diplomatically and effectively as possible. All staff members supported one another in insisting on the absolute authority of each and every one. Although each patient was held responsible for controlling his own behavior, he was given unlimited psychological support in his attempts to do this. (3) The entire program was conditioned to establish all these requirements as an inevitable and permanent part of the entire social organization. Everywhere the adolescent was exposed to the same central adult attitude: that these behavioral norms were an unavoidable reality.

Deliberate attempts also were made to exploit the tendency of adolescents to form groups, by promoting group identification with adult social values. Through insistent staff expectation in this regard, the adolescents developed such a personal investment in these norms that any individual defying them found that he defied his peer group standards as well. Thus the hallmark of this program was the provision of rigid, moralistic standards of behavior and the expectation and demand that each adolescent be successful in subscribing to the high standards. Other investigators have similarly reported that high expectations by staff of normal behavior in emotionally disturbed children is a crucial aspect of a therapeutic environment (Hobbs, 1975, p. 220).

A major question about such an authoritarian approach is, how much does one internalize the prosocial values when there is such strong pressure to conform? When the external controls are renounced, will the child revert to his antisocial ways?

Other programs are available that provide curricula for teachers and parent-surrogates to directly teach the process of making moral judgments to youth. These planned learning experiences seem effective in assisting children to decide for themselves the basis for the rightness or wrongness of their values (Ojemann, 1967), and to clarify their existing values (Simon et al., 1972).

In general, there seems to be growing awareness of the value of treatment programs that attempt to alter the attitudes, beliefs, and values of delinquent youth and then to employ peer group pressure to bring about lasting behavioral changes. Van Dusen and Sherman (1974) advocate even greater use of what they term the "cultural therapy" approach to treatment. They are convinced that this approach, using larger social forces (i.e., the peer culture), is at least as effective as conventional individual, group, and family treatments.

Behavior Modification

Behavior modification refers to the use of learning principles (e.g., classical and operant conditioning, shaping, modeling) to modify the overt behavior of others. For example, Phillips (1968) and Bardill (1972) used a token procedure to eliminate the use of aggressive verbalizations in a rehabilitation setting for predelinquent boys. A token procedure is an individually oriented system that provides a child points or tokens exchangeable for concrete rewards or privileges for engaging in a variety of prosocial acts and/or avoiding "symptomatic" behaviors (Krasner, 1965). In a token program the child is individually reinforced if his behavior meets the specified goals.

An alternate approach is to involve the peer group in the determination of whether a child is rewarded or not. The goal here is to teach group members that they are all responsible for each other's behavior. For example, Patterson (1965) taught members of a classroom group that a particular child's "good" behavior was to some extent contingent upon their own reactions to the child. They were further instructed that it was to their advantage to do what they could to avoid attending to or otherwise reinforcing this child's deviant behavior because of a group-contingent reward initiated by the experimenter. Patterson found that it was possible to reinforce social responsibility in group members and thereby reduce the maladaptive behavior of individual members. Other investigators (Fairweather, 1959; Carlin and Armstrong, 1968) have similarly reported successful attempts to inculcate social responsibility in group members; that is, teaching children that the behavior of other group members is partially their own responsibility. After reviewing a number of studies, Michaels (1974) concluded that group reward structures (group reward contingencies and competition) generally have been more effective than individual reward structures (individual reward contingencies and competition) in strengthening such group processes as cooperation, peer tutoring, peer rewards and punishment, and mutual concern. Other investigators (Lott and Lott, 1960) have noted that just providing children in a group with rewards of any type (individual or group) increases group cohesiveness more than a no-reward situation.

Structure and Controls

Working with delinquent boys in a residential treatment center, Matsushima (1962) found that the coercive power of the peer group to produce antisocial behavior in its members is inversely related to the effectiveness of consistent group controls as exercised by staff. Controls involve not only clearly stated rules, regulations, and routines, but also the careful development of a variety of constructive activities (e.g., recreational programs, dramatics, art-crafts projects, indoor games, and frequent outings). Team and group cooperation rather than individual competition should be the focus of many of these activities. Furthermore, not only must staff provide positive reinforcement for signs of prosocial values and behaviors, but they must consistently confront and enforce limits on deviant behaviors—particularly peer pressures toward deviancy. The foundation for these controls should be a close, affectionate relationship with staff members. Within such a close relationship the youngsters will be likely to identify with staff members and their values.

When staff controls are uncertain or lax, Matsushima (1962) reports that chaos prevails in an institution (e.g., frequent runaways, fire setting, fighting, excitement and thrill seeking, and the destruction of property). Polsky (1959) further confirms that when the residential treatment center program is boring and monotonous, delinquent boys are likely to seek excitement of an antisocial nature. Polsky states that a major task of the professional cottage worker is to motivate the boys toward constructive activities that are realistic in terms of individual and group achievement, and that are meaningful to them. The delinquent culture must be "invaded" by the cottage worker, who attempts to supplant the aggressive, vicious cycles in the cottage with positive relationships, activities, values, and goals. Boys are remotivated by confronting them with constructive alternatives for achieving satisfaction and competence.

Intervening to Prevent Escalation

Two concepts that have been emphasized in recent research literature—reciprocity and escalation—help explain how antisocial behaviors are perpetuated. The notion of reciprocity means that, in an interchange, the behavior of one child toward another is characterized by acts of the same type in return. Smile and the world smiles back. Escalation, a specific kind of reciprocity, occurs when the reciprocity goes beyond "tit-for-tat" and involves a perceived or actual increase in the intensity of the action (Cairns and Cairns, 1986). Escalation involves negative acts eliciting counter negative acts of a similar type, where the intensity of the responses matches or exceeds the intensity of the original acts that elicited them. It is important to note that entrapment in escalating interchanges, which may arise either from faulty perception or from intention, will have increasingly severe consequences for one or all of the persons involved (Cairns and Cairns, 1986). Accounts of aggressive escalation have involved peer relations (Hall and Cairns, 1984), police brutality (Toch, 1969), coercive families (Patterson, 1986; Patterson and Cobb, 1971), and violent mice (Cairns and Nakelski, 1971).

Many of the children in residential treatment seem to have aggressive interchanges characterized by increasingly higher levels of mutual hurtfulness. What begins as mild, somewhat playful teasing frequently turns into serious name-calling, often escalating into defamations about the other child's family. About half of these aggressive conflicts seem to occur with explosive abruptness, both in incarcerated youth (Perrin, 1981) and in normal junior high school adolescents (Cairns et al., 1985). Furthermore, there is meager evidence that the termination of conflicts involves any remediation of the difficulty. Perrin (1981) found that 95% of the conflicts among incarcerated youth that ended, did so abruptly and without effort on either person's part to remedy or ameliorate the interpersonal rift. Thus, it seems that defining the concept of escalation to the immediate, present episode may be too narrow (Cairns and Cairns, 1986). Rather, there may be a buildup of hostile feelings, and escalation may occur across episodes and over time. Some empirical support for escalation across aggressive incidents comes from a study that found that the probability of new conflicts arising was greatest in the brief period immediately following a previous conflict (Cairns et al., 1985). In fact, Cairns et al. believe that the failure to resolve old conflicts is responsible for the most "serious" ongoing recurrent episodes.

The treatment implications of this line of research are that active interventions by cottage and clinical staff are necessary to prevent aggressive escalation across episodes. These could include techniques such as group therapy sessions and on-the-spot discussions (e.g., life space interviewing), where the children, together with an adult, talk out their conflicts, correct misperceptions, learn to accept the perspective of another, and resolve or accept differences.

PARTICIPATION IN PROSOCIAL ACTIVITIES

In family life there usually are numerous expectations and opportunities for positive, other-oriented behaviors. Examples include taking care of a younger sibling, helping a parent or a neighbor, aiding someone who is unhappy or is being treated unjustly, and so on. There is some evidence that children's participation in prosocial activities that are an integral part of a family's functioning increases the likelihood of prosocial behavior (e.g., Bathurst, 1933; Rosenhan, 1969; Staub, 1970; Whiting and Whiting, 1973, 1975).

In an often-cited research study, Whiting and Whiting (1973, 1975) observed children and family practices in six cultures. Altruistic and egoistic acts were recorded. They found that those cultures in which children were responsible for tasks helpful to family maintenance, and, in particular, tasks of caring for younger siblings, were cultures in which children were significantly more altruistic. In addition, this finding held true when comparing individual children and family practices within a culture.

Staub (1970) studied this relationship in the laboratory. The results were similar: children who were responsible for "taking care of things" while the experimenter was out of the room showed a greater tendency to respond to the cries of a child in an adjoining room than children who were not given this responsibility.

In a similar vein, Bathurst (1933) compared children who had a pet with those who did not. Children who had a pet were found to have higher levels of sympathetic behaviors with their peers than children without pets. This was interpreted as deriving from a sense of responsibility for the pet. However, it may result from experiencing reciprocal affectionate contact or may reflect initial differences in people who choose to have a pet (Radke-Yarrow and Zahn-Waxler, 1986).

Finally, other research has shown that children who participate with parents in responding to the needs of others have an increased likelihood of prosocial behavior. For example, Rosenhan (1969) found that youth deeply involved in the civil rights movement had childhood memories of participating with their parents in prosocial activities.

The general treatment implications of this line of research would be for staff of residential centers to expect, require, and structure positive other-oriented behaviors into the program. Children may participate in such prosocial activities as sharing cottage tasks, being rewarded for helping when a person is unhappy or distressed, and taking part in an organized program to help those in the community in need of some service. Older children may have some area of responsibility for the youngest or for those recently admitted.

Therapeutic Cottage Groupings

Instead of assigning children to residential treatment center cottages randomly, groupings within each cottage should be planned. For instance, in the selection of children for therapy groups, it is generally accepted that too great a variation in age, developmental level, or degree of disturbance can interfere with effective group functioning (Schaefer et al., 1982). The group process is facilitated by a balance of active/passive and verbal/nonverbal participants. Similarly, if cottages contain too many acting-out aggressive children, frequent chaos and disruption mar their daily structured routines. In addition, children's initial responses to residential placement may differ greatly from their behavior after the "honeymoon" period. A transitional cottage might be used for observing children until a clinical decision can be made about appropriate cottage placement.

Creating Opportunities for Success

Sociological theory holds that groups who feel deprived of true opportunities to succeed, and who perceive existing means of achievement as illegitimate, may then use other means, often criminal ones, to overcome failure (Silver, 1981). Delinquent subcultures develop when people who "fail" begin to question societal means for attainments of goals. Delinquent group members often feel they are legitimately qualified, but denied opportunities for illegitimate reasons such as race.

It follows that acceptance of societal norms could be fostered by providing opportunities for success. One way to do this would be a work program. Work provides a milieu in which the social skills of relating to authority figures and fellow workers can be learned (Cumming and Cumming, 1970). Work that is carried out under pleasant, realistic, unambiguous conditions and requires small graduated steps for improvements can lead to monetary rewards, as well as esteem, approval, and a sense of achievement. These activities may then be expected to foster positive rather than negative group behavior.

Monitoring TV Viewing

The impact of TV viewing on the socialization of children is well documented (e.g., Eron and Huesmann, 1986). Field and laboratory studies have concluded that TV viewing and subsequent behavior are causally related, and that both aggression and prosocial behavior can be induced by watching TV (Lefkowtiz and Husemann, 1981; Huesmann, 1982).

Taking a developmental perspective, studies have shown that some children are already attentive to television at six to nine months of age

(Hollenbeck and Slaby, 1979). Imitation of television behaviors has been observed in two-year-old children (McCall et al., 1977). Increases in viewing violent TV programs and subsequent aggressive behavior in children occur from grades one through three, and third grade is considered an especially susceptible period for the viewing of TV violence to affect children's behavior (Eron et al., 1983). The most convincing relationships between television violence and aggression are shown for children at this age (Chaffee, 1972; Lefkowitz et al., 1977).

On a more positive note, studies that relate television viewing and prosocial behavior have shown promising results. These studies indicate that aggressive behavior can be decreased (Pitkanen-Pulkkinen, 1979) and prosocial behavior, including self-control (Friedrich and Stein, 1972) and altruistic behavior (Ahammer and Murray, 1979), increased in children exposed to films containing prosocial content. Children presumably use TV actors and actresses as models for their behavior (Bandura et al., 1963). Thus, increased viewing of TV programs that offer cooperative, helping models, who verbalize feelings, show empathic concern for others, use self-control, and demonstrate adaptive, positive methods of problem-solving, would seem to have a significant positive influence on children.

These findings may be particularly cogent for children in residential treatment. Many of these youngsters have histories of school failure and poor social relationships, two variables that lead to increased TV viewing (Eron and Huesmann, 1986). Exposure to either aggressive or prosocial behavior is likely to influence children toward responding to life situations in a corresponding manner. Institutionalized youngsters who repeatedly observe prosocial behavior would be more likely to emulate that behavior and less likely to emit aggressive responses when problem-solving situations arise. This preventive strategy may serve to modulate the potentially antisocial influence of their peers.

Volunteers

In recent years, there has been increasing recognition that mental health services cannot adequately be provided by a small, specially trained group of professionals (Schaefer, 1981). There are simply too many people needing help and too few therapists. The goal of group care for children is expected to move away from residential treatment toward more preventive interventions (Haeuser and Schwartz, 1980). One proposed solution is to use nonprofessionals for certain tasks that do not require highly specialized training or experience (Grosser et al., 1969). In this way, mental health specialists can multiply their effectiveness by working through less well-trained people (Hobbs, 1964). There seems to be a vast reservoir of human talent among individuals who want to contribute their time and efforts to a meaningful enterprise. A number of successful programs (e.g., Big Brothers–Big Sisters) have demonstrated to a previously skeptical public that high-level, dependable service can be provided by volunteers.

A "new age" of volunteering seems to be emerging as volunteers are used in more varied and innovative functions. Volunteers who were once used as "party givers" and "friendly visitors" are now becoming respected members of interdisciplinary treatment teams and viewed as "therapists with the human touch." These helping individuals are no longer seen as people with "time on their hands," but are regarded as persons influential in promoting cross-disciplinary communication, providing a sense of community concern, and preventing the tendency of residential treatment centers to "pass the buck" (Haeuser and Schwartz, 1980).

The role of the volunteer in the residential setting has typically been to spend time with the children, with a view toward providing them with a supportive and caring relationship. Evaluative studies of the volunteers' performance have shown that nonprofessional volunteers have been more effective with some groups than professionals have been (Blau, 1969). The close one-to-one relationship that the volunteer establishes with the person seems to account for his success (Nichtern et al., 1963). Within this supportive, inspiring relationship, the volunteer seems able to convince patients that someone believes in them, is able to guide them, and stands for a new set of standards. Volunteers serve as alternative identification figures that some patients seem to respond to better than to professional therapists, because patients see volunteers as more equal to themselves in social status (Goodman, 1972; Rioch et al., 1963). In the residential treatment center, direct-service volunteers may be able to form relationships that are less easily established by caseworkers. The volunteer simply does not have the authority and control over the child's life inherent in the casework role. Thus, the volunteer is less likely to be perceived as threatening and can become a safe person to whom a child can express feelings about the workers, the residential center, and his placement in residential care (Haeuser and Schwartz, 1980).

The use of volunteers appears to be a promising intervention to counteract the antisocial influence of the residential treatment center peer culture. By identifying with an individual volunteer through a positive relationship, children may be less susceptible to the negative influence of their peers. Volunteers could act as prosocial role models whom children seek to emulate, and help children develop their own individual personalities and standards.

SUMMARY AND CONCLUSION

Out of their need to achieve some independence from their parents yet to "belong" and avoid isolation, youth create their own subculture. This culture is complete with its own values, norms, language, and symbols. In our present society, parental influence over children seems to have declined, while peer influence has increased. When children become peer-oriented at too early an age, they tend to form gangs that engage in antisocial behaviors. There is evidence that violent crimes by youth are becoming more prevalent and occurring at earlier ages. Placing these delinquency-prone youth together in a residential setting may augment the negative impact of their counterculture. In any event, the peer-group culture seems to have a pervasive, subtle, and powerful influence in residential centers. Many experts believe it is the predominant force in the center. To be most successful, the residential treatment center must acknowledge, monitor, and channel the powerful force of the peer subculture, both within the institution and in the community. In certain institutions staff probably should take stronger measures than this to counteract the sinister power of the delinquent subculture. A number of the more promising countermeasures have been summarized in this chapter.

This chapter's description of possible treatment strategies for youth with group-oriented, delinquent tendencies is frankly speculative in nature. Rather than presenting a critical review of reported treatment approaches, we have attempted to heuristically suggest some promising alternatives. In fact, we sorely lack solid research evidence upon which to base firm conclusions about the differential effectiveness of treatment approaches. Clearly there are no easy solutions to the delinquent subculture problem that exists in many of our correctional and treatment institutions. We hope this chapter will make the reader more aware of the difficulty, and stimulate well-controlled experimentation with innovative approaches.

REFERENCES

Ackerman, N. W., Papp, P., and Prosky, P. (1970). Disorders and interlocking pathology in family relationships. In E. J. Anthony and C. Kaupernik, eds., *The Child in His Family.* New York: Wiley.

Ahammer, I. and Murray, J. (1979). Kindness in the kindergarten: the relative influence of role-playing and prosocial television in facilitating altruism. *International Journal of Behavioral Development, 2*(2), 133-157.

Bandura, A. R. and Walters, E. (1963). *Social Learning and Personality Development.* New York: Holt, Rinehart, and Winston.

Bandura, A., Ross, D., and Ross, S. A. (1963). Imitation of film-mediated aggressive models. *Journal of Abnormal and Social Psychology, 66,* 3-11.

Bandura, A., Grusec, J. E., and Menlove, F. L. (1967). Vicarious extinction of avoidance behavior. *Journal of Personality and Social Psychology, 5,* 16–23.

Bardill, D. R. (1972). Behavior contracting and group therapy with preadolescent males in a residential treatment setting. *International Journal of Group Psychotherapy, 22,* 333–342.

Bathurst, J. E. (1933). A study of sympathy and resistance (negativism) among children. *Psychological Bulletin, 30,* 625–626.

Beller, E. K. (1972). Research in teaching: organized programs in early education. In R. Travers, ed., *Handbook for Research on Teaching.* New York: Rand-McNally.

Berenda, R. W. (1950). *The Influence of the Group on the Judgments of Children.* New York: King's Crown Press.

Bettelheim, B. (1955). *Truants from Life.* Glencoe, Ill.: The Free Press.

Blau, T. H. (1969). Psychologist views the helper. In C. Grosser, W. E. Henry, and J. G. Kelly, eds., *Nonprofessionals in the Human Services.* San Francisco: Jossey-Bass.

Block, J. (1963). *Lives through Time.* Berkeley, Calif.: Bancroft.

Bronfenbrenner, U. (1967). Response to pressure from peers versus adults among Soviet and American school children. *International Journal of Psychology, 2,* 199–207.

Bronfenbrenner, U. (1970). *Two Worlds of Childhood.* New York: Russell Sage Foundation.

Bryan, J. H. and Walbek, N. (1970). The impact of words and deeds concerning altruism upon children. *Child Development, 41,* 747–759.

Buehler, R. E., Patterson, G. R., and Furniss, J. M. (1966). The reinforcement of behavior in institutional settings. *Behavior, Research and Therapy, 4,* 157–167.

Cairns, R. B. and Cairns, B. D. (1986). The developmental–interactional view of social behavior: four issues of adolescent aggression. In D. Olweus, J. Block, and M. Padke-Yarrow, eds., *Development of Antisocial and Prosocial Behavior, Research, Theories, and Issues.* New York: Academic Press, pp. 315–342.

Cairns, R. B. and Nakelski, J. S. (1971). On fighting in mice: ontogenetic and experiential determinants. *Journal of Comparative and Physiological Psychology, 71,* 354–364.

Cairns, R. B., Perrin, J. E., and Cairns, B. D. (1985). Social structure and social cognition in early adolescence: affiliative patterns. *Journal of Early Adolescence,* 339–355.

Campbell, J. D. (1964). Peer relations in childhood. In M. L. Hoffman and L. W. Hoffman, eds., *Review of Child Development Research,* Vol. 1. New York: Russell Sage Foundation, pp. 289–322.

Carlin, A. S. and Armstrong, H. E. (1968). Rewarding social responsibility in disturbed children. *Psychotherapy: Theory, Research and Practice, 5,* 169–174.

Catanzaro, R. J., Psani, V. D., Fox, R., and Kennedy, E. R. (1973). Familization therapy, an alternative to traditional mental care. *Diseases of the Nervous System, 34,* 212–218.

Chaffee, S. H. (1972). Television and adolescent aggressiveness (overview). In G. A. Comstock and E. A. Rubinstein, eds., *Television and Social Behavior,* Vol. 3:

Television and Adolescent Aggressiveness. Washington, D.C.: U.S. Government Printing Office.

Cohen, A. K. (1955). *Delinquent Boys: The Culture of the Gang.* Glencoe, Ill.: The Free Press.

Condry, J. C. and Simon, M. L. (1968). An experimental study of adult vs. peer orientation. Unpublished manuscript, Department of Child Development, Cornell University.

Costanza, P. R. and Shaw, M. E. (1966). Conformity as a function of age level. *Child Development, 37,* 967–975.

Cumming, J. and Cumming, E. (1970). *Ego and Milieu.* New York: Atherton Press.

Davis, A., Gardner, B. B., and Gardner, M. R. (1941). *Deep South.* Chicago, Ill.: University of Chicago Press.

Devereux, E. C. (1965). Socialization in cross-cultural perspective: a comparative study of England, Germany and the United States. Unpublished manuscript, Cornell University.

Duncan, D. F. (1974). Verbal behavior in a detention home. *Corrective and Social Psychiatry, 20,* 38–42.

Elliot, R. and Vasta, R. (1970). The modeling of sharing: effects associated with vicarious reinforcement, symbolization, age, and generalization. *Journal of Experimental Child Psychology, 10,* 8–15.

Eron, L. D. and Huesmann, L. R. (1986). The role of television in the development of prosocial and antisocial behavior. In D. Olweus, J. Block, and M. Radke-Yarrow, eds., *Development of Antisocial and Prosocial Behavior.* New York: Academic Press.

Eron, L. D., Huesmann, L. R., Brice, P., Fischer, P., and Mermelstein, R. (1983). Age trends in the development of aggression, sex typing, and related television habits. *Developmental Psychology, 19,* 71–77.

Fairweather, G. W. (1959). *Social Psychology in the Treatment of Mental Illness: An Experimental Approach.* New York: Wiley.

Farrington, D. P. and West, D. J. (1980). The Cambridge study in delinquent development (United Kingdom). In S. A. Mednick and A. E. Baert, eds., *Prospective Longitudinal Research: An Empirical Basis for Primary Prevention.* Oxford: Oxford University Press.

Feldman, R. A., Wodarski, J. S., and Flax, N. (1975). Antisocial children in a summer camp environment, a time-sampling study. *Community Mental Health Journal, 11,* 10–13.

Feuerstein, R. and Krasilowsky, D. (1974). The treatment group technique. In M. Wolins, ed., *Successful Group Care.* Chicago: Aldine.

Fisher, S. M. (1972). Life in a children's detention center: strategies of survival. *American Journal of Orthopsychiatry, 42,* 368–374.

Floyd, H. H. and South, D. R. (1972). Dilemma of youth: the choice of parents or peers as a train of reference in behavior. *Journal of Marriage and the Family, 34,* 627–634.

Freud, A. and Dann, S. (1951). An experiment in group upbringing. *The Psychoanalytic Study of the Child.* New York: International Universities Press.

Friedrich, L. K. and Stein, A. H. (1975). Prosocial television and young children. The effects of verbal labelling and role playing on learning and behavior. *Child Development, 46,* 27-38.

Fuller, J. S. (1977). Duo therapy: A potential treatment of choice for latency children. *Journal of the American Academic of Child Psychiatry, 16,* 469-477.

Glasser, W. (1965). *Reality Therapy: A New Approach to Psychiatry.* New York: Harper and Row.

Gluek, S. and Gluek, E. T. (1950). *Unraveling Juvenile Delinquency.* Cambridge, Mass.: Harvard University Press.

Goldstein, J., Freud, A., and Solnit, A. (1973). *Beyond the Best Interests of the Child.* New York: The Free Press.

Goodman, G. (1972). *Companionship Therapy.* San Francisco: Jossey-Bass.

Grosser, C., Henry, W. E., and Kelly, J. G. (1969). *Nonprofessionals in the Human Services.* San Francisco: Jossey-Bass.

Haeuser, A. A. and Schwartz, F. S. (1980). Developing social work skills for work with volunteers. *Social Casework, 48,* 595-601.

Hall, W. M. and Cairns, R. B. (1984). Aggressive behavior in children: an outcome of modeling or reciprocity? *Developmental Psychology, 20,* 739-745.

Harlow, H. F. (1958). The nature of love. *American Psychologist, 13,* 673-685.

Hartup, W. W. (1970). Peer interaction and social organization. In P. H. Mussen, ed., *Carmichael's Manual of Child Psychology,* Vol. 2. New York: Wiley, pp. 457-558.

Hartup, W. W. and Coates, B. (1967). Imitation of a peer as a function of reinforcement from the peer group and rewardingness of the model. *Child Development, 38,* 1003-1016.

Hendrickson, W. J. and Holmes, D. J. (1959). Control of behavior as a crucial factor in intensive psychiatric treatment in an all adolescent ward. *American Journal of Psychiatry, 115,* 969-973.

Hicks, D. (1965). Imitation and retention of film mediated aggressive peer and adult models. *Journal of Personality and Social Psychology, 2,* 97-100.

Hobbs, N. (1964). Mental health: third revolution. *The American Journal of Orthopsychiatry, 34,* 822-833.

Hobbs, N. (1975). *The Futures of Children.* San Francisco: Jossey-Bass.

Hollenbeck, A. R. and Slaby, R. G. (1979). Infant visual and vocal responses to television. *Child Development, 50,* 41-45.

Huesmann, L. R. (1982). Television violence and aggressive behavior. In D. Pearl, L. Bouthilet, and J. Lazar, eds., *Television and Behavior: Ten Years of Scientific Progress and Implications for the 80's.* Washington, D.C.: U.S. Government Printing Office.

Hunt, R. G. and Synnerdale, V. (1959). Social influences among kindergarten children. *Sociology and Social Research, 43,* 171-174.

Iscoe, I., Williams, M., and Harvey, J. (1963). Modification of children's judgments by a simulated group technique. A normative developmental study. *Child Development, 34,* 963-978.

Johnson, R. L. and Medinnus, G. R. (1969). *Child Psychiatry.* New York: Wiley.

Kobasigawa, A. (1968). Inhibitory and disinhibiting effects of models on sex-inappropriate behavior in children. *Psychologia, 11,* 86–96.

Krasner, L. (1965). The token economy. Colloquium at the Department of Psychiatry, University of Washington School of Medicine.

Lefkowitz, M. M. and Huesmann, L. R. (1981). Concomitants of television violence viewing in children. In E. L. Palmer and A. Dorr, eds., *Children and the Faces of Television: Teaching, Violence, Selling.* New York: Academic Press.

Lefkowitz, M. M., Eron, L. D., Walder, L. O., and Huesmann, L. R. (1977). *Growing Up to Be Violent: A Longitudinal Study of the Development of Aggression.* New York: Pergamon.

Lement, E. M. (1967). The juvenile court: quest and realities. *Task Force Report: Juvenile Delinquency and Youth Crime.* Washington, D.C.: U.S. Government Printing Office.

Lott, B. E. and Lott, A. J. (1960). The formation of positive attitudes toward group members. *Journal of Abnormal and Social Psychology, 61,* 297–300.

Masters, E. W. (1974). Some thoughts on mainstreaming. *Exceptional Children, 41,* 150–153.

Matsushima, J. (1962). Group work with emotionally disturbed children in residential treatment. *Social Work, 7,* 62–70.

Mayer, M. F., Richman, L. H., and Balcerzak, E. A. (1978). *Group Care of Children.* New York: Child Welfare League of America.

McCall, R. B., Parke, R. D., and Kavanaugh, R. D. (1977). Imitation of live and televised models by children one to three years of age. *Monographs of the Society for Research in Child Development, 42*(5), 95.

McConnell, T. R. (1963). Suggestibility in children as a function of chronological age. *Journal of Abnormal and Social Psychology, 67,* 286–289.

McCord, J. (1986). Instigation and insulation: how families affect antisocial aggression. In D. Olweus, J. Block, and M. Radke-Yarrow, eds., *Development of Antisocial and Prosocial Behavior.* New York: Academic Press.

Michaels, J. W. (1974). Classroom reward structures and academic performance. *Center for Social Organization of Schools, Report No. 186.* Baltimore, Md.: The John Hopkins University.

Mitchell, C. A. (1976). Duo therapy: An innovative approach to the treatment of children. *Smith College Studies in Social Work, 45,* 236–247.

Monahan, T. (1957). Family status and the delinquent child: a reappraisal and some new findings. *Social Forces, 35,* 251–258.

Mueller, E. C. and Cohen, D. (1986). Peer therapies and the little latency: a clinical perspective. In E. C. Mueller and D. Cohen, eds., *Process and Outcome in Peer Relationships.* New York: Academic Press, pp. 161–183.

Mussen, P. H., Conger, J. J., and Kagan, J. (1979). *Child Development and Personality,* New York: Harper and Row.

Newberg, P. M. (1966). A study of how the concept of self is affected by incarceration. *Corrective Psychiatry and Journal of Social Therapy, 12,* 258–263.

Nichtern, S., Donahue, G. T., O'Shea, J., Marans, M., Curtis, M., and Brody, C. (1963). A community educational program for the emotionally-disturbed child. *American Journal of Orthopsychiatry, 34,* 705–713.

Ohlin, L. E. and Lawrence, W. (1959). Social interaction among clients as a treatment problem. *Social Work, 3,* 4.

Ojemann, R. H. (1967). Incorporating psychological concepts in the school curriculum. *Journal of School Psychology, 5,* 195–204.

Olweus, D. (1980). Familial and temperamental determinants of aggressive behavior in adolescent boys: a causal analysis. *Developmental Psychology, 16,* 644–660.

Patterson, G. (1965). An application of conditioning techniques to the control of a hyperactive child. In L. Ullman and L. Krasner, eds., *Case Studies in Behavior Modification.* New York: Holt, Rinehart and Winston.

Patterson, G. R. (1976). The aggressive child: victim and architect of a coercive system. In E. Mash, L. Hamerlynck, and L. Handy, eds., *Behavior Modification and Families.* New York: Brunner/Mazel.

Patterson, G. R. (1986). The contribution of siblings to training for fighting: a microsocial analysis. In D. Olweus, J. Block, and M. Radke-Yarrow, eds., *Development of Antisocial and Prosocial Behavior.* New York: Academic Press, pp. 235–261.

Patterson, G. R. and Anderson, P. (1964). Peers as social reinforcers. *Child Development, 35,* 951–960.

Patterson, G. R. and Cobb, J. A. (1971). A dyadic analysis of "aggressive" behaviors. In J. P. Hill, ed., *Minnesota Symposium on Child Psychology,* Vol. 5. Minneapolis: University of Minnesota Press.

Patterson, G. R., Littman, R. A., and Bricker, W. (1967). Assertive behavior in children: a step toward a theory of aggression, *Monographs of the Society for Research in Child Development, 32*(5), 1–43.

Perrin, J. (1981). Reciprocity of aggression in youthful offenders. Paper presented at the annual meeting of the American Psychological Association, Los Angeles.

Peterson, J. (Feb. 1974). Mousepack mayhem. *Youth Reporter,* 5–7.

Phillips, E. L. (1968). Achievement place: token reinforcement procedures in a home-style rehabilitation setting for predelinquent boys. *Journal of Applied Behavior Analysis, 1,* 213–223.

Pilnick, S., Elias, A., and Clapp, N. W. (1966). The Essexfields concept: a new approach to the social treatment of juvenile delinquents. *Journal of Applied Behavioral Science, 2,* 109–125.

Pitkanen-Pulkkinen, L. (1979). Self-control as a prerequisite for constructive behavior. In S. Feshbach and A. Fraczek, eds., *Aggression and Behavior Change.* New York: Praeger.

Polsky, H. W. (1959). Changing delinquent subcultures: a social psychological approach. *Social Work, 4,* 3–15.

Radke-Yarrow, M. and Zahn-Waxler, C. (1986). The role of familial factors in the development of prosocial behavior: research findings and questions. In D. Olweus, J. Block, and M. Radke-Yarrow, eds., *Development of Antisocial and Prosocial Behavior.* New York: Academic Press, pp. 207–233.

Rapaport, R. N. (1960). *Community as Doctor.* New York: Tavistock Publications.

Redl, F. and Wineman, D. (1952). *Controls from Within.* New York: The Free Press.

Ridgway, R. and Lawton, P. (1969). *Family Grouping in the Primary School.* New York: Aganthon Press.

Rieger, N. I. (1972). Changing concepts in treating children in a state mental hospital. *International Journal of Child Psychotherapy, 4,* 89–114.

Rioch, M. J., Elkes, C., Flint, A. A., Usdausky, B. S., Newman, R. G., and Silber, E. (1963). National institute of mental health pilot study in training mental health counselors. *American Journal of Orthopsychiatry, 33,* 678–689.

Rosenhan, D. (1969). Some origins of concern for others. In P. H. Mussen, J. Laanger, and M. Covington, eds., *Trends and Issues in Developmental Psychology,* New York: Holt, Rinehart, and Winston.

Rutter, M. (1971). Parent–child separation: Psychological effects on the children. *Journal of Child Psychology and Psychiatry, 12,* 233–260.

Schaefer, C. E. (1977). The need for psychological parents by children in residential treatment. *Child Care Quarterly, 6,* 288–299.

Schaefer, C. E. (1980). The impact of the peer culture in the residential treatment of youth. *Adolescence, 15*(60), 831–845.

Schaefer, C. E. (1981). Relationship therapy for troubled boys. *Adolescence, 16,* 727–742.

Schaefer, C. E. and Millman, H. L. (1973). The use of behavior ratings in assessing the effect of residential treatment with latency age children. *Child Psychiatry and Human Development, 3,* 157–164.

Schaefer, C. E., Johnson, L., and Wherry, J. N. (1982). *Group Therapies for Children and Youth.* San Francisco: Jossey-Bass.

Silver, I. (1981). *Criminology.* New York: Harper and Row.

Simon, S. B., Howe, L. W., and Kirshenbaum, H. (1972). *Values Clarification.* New York: Hart.

Solomon, R. W. and Wahler, R. G. (1973). Peer reinforcement control of classroom problem behaviors. *Journal of Applied Behavior Analysis, 6,* 49–56.

Staub, E. (1970). A child in distress: the effects of focusing responsibility on children on their attempts to help. *Developmental Psychology, 2,* 152–154.

Stephens, T. M. (1964). Using reinforcement and social modeling with delinquent youth. *Review of Educational Research, 43,* 323–340.

Tappan, P. W. (1949). *Juvenile Delinquency.* New York: McGraw-Hill.

Tharp, R. G. and Wetzel, R. J. (1969). *Behavior Modification in the Natural Environment.* New York: Academic Press.

Toch, H. (1969). *Violent Men: An Inquiry into the Psychology of Violence.* Chicago: Aldine.

U.S. Department of Health, Education and Welfare. (1972). National Center for Social Statistics, Juvenile Court Statistics, 1971. Washington National Center for Social Statistics.

Van Dusen, W. and Sherman, S. L. (1974). Cultural therapy: a new conception of treatment. *Drug Forum, 4,* 65–72.

Vorrath, H. H. and Brendtro, L. K. (1974). *Positive Peer Culture.* Chicago: Aldine.

Werner, E. E. and Smith, R. S. (1982). *Vulnerable but Invincible.* New York: McGraw-Hill.

Whiting, B. and Whiting, J. W. M. (1975). *Children of Six Cultures*. Cambridge, Mass.: Harvard University Press.

Whiting, J. W. M. and Whiting, B. B. (1973). Altruistic and egoistic behavior in six cultures. In L. Nader and T. W. Maretzki, eds., *Cultural Illness and Health: Essays in Human Adaptation*. Washington, D.C.: American Anthropological Association.

Wolins, M. (1974). Young children in institutions: some additional evidence. In M. Wolins, ed., *Successful Group Care*. Chicago: Aldine.

8

Family Work in Residential Treatment

John Van Hagen

To the extent that family therapy is a way of thinking about problems, it can be helpful to providers of residential care. It can help them understand the larger context of the permanency planning continuum, adapt and modify the agency to interact within that continuum, and work with families served by that continuum. This chapter argues that if the larger context is understood, an agency may develop a strategy that not only guides the clinician in working with families, but helps the agency in its own growth.

Any discussion of family work when a child is placed outside the home tends to be idiosyncratic. The author not only has a particular theoretical orientation, but is usually describing a particular treatment approach or research design. Two recent books on family work when a child is placed (Maluccio and Sinanoglu, 1981; Sinanoglu and Maluccio, 1981) are really collections of articles by various authors who cover certain aspects of the topic. One conclusion is that family work in residential treatment is not a univocal concept. It is regulated by such factors as research emphasis, population, financial resources, public–private cooperation, legislative requirements, and theoretical approaches, as well as the time when the work was done. The following example from my own experience underscores the difficulty in writing about this topic.

A residential treatment center conducted a grant-sponsored study in 1980 with special funding to include both service to families of children placed at the agency and research that could later be published. The results of the project soon appeared in journals (Van Hagen, 1982, 1983). Yet, at the same time, changes were occurring that would dramatically alter the agency's work with families. State legislation was passed in 1982 that emphasized the need for placement prevention services. The children referred to the agency showed an increased history of psychiatric hospitalization and less likelihood of returning home. Loss of special funding and usual turnover in clinical staff also had some impact. In short, two years after the articles appeared, family work at the agency was quite different from its published descriptions.

We will not go over the ground covered by the Maluccio and Sinanoglu books; instead, this chapter is a more personal essay on the relevance of family therapy to agencies that provide family work when a child is placed. The basic assumption is that family therapy provides not only helpful techniques in working with some families but, more important, a valuable lens for the agency to view itself and its work. In fact, the major part of the chapter will focus on the valuable lens rather than the helpful techniques.

CONTEXT

Schultz (1984) reminds us that family therapy is not so much about families as it is about individual persons in the context of their families. He goes on to say that the hallmark of family systems thinking is attention to context (p. 319). Minuchin (1974) had made this same point earlier when he described structural family therapy as approaching man in his social context. This ecological view of the individual interacting with his environment is contrasted with the psychodynamic view of the individual acting upon his environment (pp. 4-5). The point here is not to argue about the relative merits of individual and family therapy but to underscore the importance of context for agencies that work with families where a child is in placement or at risk of placement.

Many elements go into the creation of a context, and an agency can be more or less dependent upon that context; however, one major contextual element is the federal legislation passed in 1980, Public Law 96-272. In brief, that legislation calls for prevention services when a child is at risk for placement; reunification services and return home as soon as possible for those who are placed; and long-term care leading to guardianship or adoption for those who are placed but cannot return home. This legislation also provides procedural safeguards during the decision-making process. One goal of PL 96-272 is to provide permanent plans for children at risk so that they do not drift in the welfare system. Although the impact of this permanency planning legislation is not fully known, it supports on legal grounds a range of services for at-risk children and their families. Legal support for such a range or continuum of services has also been established by a number of court cases. Knitzer (1982) gives an example of such a continuum established in North Carolina, in part because of a lawsuit on behalf of children in need of mental health services (pp. 140-143).

Whittaker (1979) has long championed such a continuum from a clinical perspective. He holds that the American social, health, and welfare services have failed to develop a continuum of care that would provide adequate services to troubled children and their families. He sees that failure as being at the root of problems with children's services in the United States, and offers as a major first goal the development of such a continuum. He would see a range of programs and services from placement prevention through various residential options, all of them linked, not only to each other but to the other community-based systems in which a child or family participates (pp. 3–6).

What emerges, then, is a convergence from both legal and clinical perspectives that supports and defines a range of services for children and families that can be called the permanency planning continuum. This continuum, to use the language of family therapy, is the basic context in which residential care agencies interact. Although a particular agency's interaction may be limited by a number of factors, it cannot not interact (to paraphrase some early family therapists). When a child is placed, there should have been reasonable efforts at preventing that placement, efforts that need to be evaluated in developing a treatment plan. There should be clearly defined case plans that would lead to reunification or long-term care, and that would involve other agencies and services, as well as require specific court reports from the residential agency.

The above is not to imply that residential centers only can react passively to the permanency planning continuum. On the contrary, residential programs have much to offer. As Whittaker (1979) points out, residential programs have an excellent structure for moving into home-based, placement-prevention programs. In fact, many have already done so. Most residential programs offer some form of aftercare or reunification service at the time of a youngster's discharge. Lawder et al. (1984) described a project that offered similar home-based services to two groups of families, one where there was a child at risk for placement, and one where there was a risk for re-placement (i.e., the child was returning from out-of-home care). Initial results suggested that the same service was helpful for both groups.

Another important service that speaks to both prevention and reunification needs is day treatment. A child may be maintained at home, with day treatment offering services to both child and family. Likewise, a child may be able to leave a residential program with day treatment as an appropriate form of aftercare. Although prevention and reunification services are challenging programs, PL 96-272 reminds us that a third group of children requires our attention: children who will not return home. For this group, necessary services would include long-term foster care, perhaps leading to guardianship or adoption, and community-based group care leading to emancipation. While these latter services may not appear as exciting or innovative as some placement prevention services, they remain critically important for children referred to residential care. It may be that as the permanency planning continuum develops, referrals to residential programs will be comprised mainly of clients from failed prevention and reunification efforts. Another possibility is that there will be fewer referrals to out-of-home care.

As the permanency planning continuum continues to evolve, it remains a powerful context that will shape and be shaped by residential centers. These centers are uniquely positioned to contribute to that continuum. They have worked with the client population in substitute care and increasingly are working with that population in such settings as home-based services, day treatment, and foster care. They interact with the public and private agencies that also work with this population: social services, probation, schools, family service agencies, mental health departments, and psychiatric hospitals. They are sensitive to case management issues and are accustomed to developing, in a timely fashion, information that is crucial to the resolution of permanency planning issues.

STRATEGIES FOR CHANGE

As residential agencies interact within the context of the permanency planning continuum, they will change and be changed. Family therapy theory can help in this evolutionary process. Fisch et al. (1982) have argued that strategic therapy can be applied to the problems of larger systems, which they label as metaclinical problems. From their perspective, the agency itself would be the client, and the theory would provide techniques to assist in the process of change. These ideas have been tested at a residential center where the author is clinical director. What follows is a brief description of several years of evolution framed in the language of strategic therapy.

Several years ago, the agency was a single-service provider, offering residential treatment to latency age boys. The first metaclinical problem was concerned with how the agency would evolve; the first question was to determine the most advantageous starting point for change. An aftercare program for children who graduated from the agency emerged as having certain advantages. Staff were genuinely interested in what happened to graduates. A working relationship had developed with child and family during the course of placement. Finally, it was thought that looking at what happened to a child after he left would give staff ideas for changes in the campus program that would better prepare other students for discharge.

After a grant was secured to start up such services, graduate students from a family therapy training program were recruited to staff the aftercare program. Agency social workers were offered consultations on family therapy techniques. Parents were encouraged to participate in predischarge planning, including the development of service agreements. Aftercare services were provided for a six-month period and would take place in the parents' homes. This increased parental involvement led to the development of a parents association that made specific requests about the agency's weekend programming, as well as served as a support group to parents. In this way, some responsibility for treatment was being taken from the residential staff and placed with parents.

In retrospect, the agency was undergoing dramatic changes. It was not only becoming more family-oriented; it was becoming more than a one-service agency. As could be expected, tension developed, and complaints needed to be addressed. Staff meetings proved to be a helpful forum, although a few staff left the agency, in part because of the changes.

Working through one change seemed to help the agency become more open to future changes. To use family therapy terminology, a change brought a different view of self (i.e., insight). The development of aftercare set the stage for another evolutionary step: the formation of a multi-service agency. Over the next few years, foster care, day treatment, and home-based placement prevention services were begun with the help of grants. While foster care could be used by some graduates from the residential program, day treatment and home-based services were primarily offered to clients who were at risk for residential placement. In short, the agency had become something more than a residential program. Again, the changes caused some tension. Staff in one program felt in competition with staff from others. These and similar feelings tended to complicate efforts at collaboration across programs. Senior administrators were chagrined because they believed the different programs should see themselves as part of one happy family.

It became clear over time that a multi-service agency was not necessarily an integrated agency. Forums and procedures were needed to promote that integration. Most valuable was a weekly forum for administrators from the different programs, where problems could be addressed. Also, efforts were made to provide in-service training across programs. This allowed staff to work together in a neutral setting, as well as develop some basis for identity as members of a single agency. Personnel guidelines were developed for staff wishing to move from one program to another. Although tension was resolved, it may be that the process of integration will always be unfinished business, requiring the attention and commitment of all staff. Yet the greatest challenge was found in attempting to integrate the agency with others that were part of the permanency planning continuum. The agency became part of a network of residential agencies, public providers, and schools from one particular county that hoped to develop a continuum of services for at-risk children and their families. Over a two-year period, representatives met to plan a unique system, tailor-made for that particular county. Although the agency representatives faced serious problems in developing a network, cooperation was fostered by a facilitator, who stressed the urgency of a collaborative effort. In fact, it was presented as a way of surviving in the face of more needy children and limited resources.

Another way of bonding the network members together was to develop a common language based on PL 96-272. That legislation outlined a comprehensive approach for working with at-risk children, and suggested some of the case management and procedural efforts necessary to safeguard the parents' rights to due process. On the other hand, PL 96-272 is an effort to reform the entire child welfare system by preventing placement whenever possible through the introduction of specialized services. Given the immense tasks of developing new resources as well as reforming the system, our guiding strategic principle has been to go slow and look for small changes.

Although the network suffered a setback recently when it lost funds for the facilitator, the vision of an integrated permanency planning continuum is still alive. Efforts to make the vision a reality are ongoing. The following chart is a summary of the evolutionary changes and the strategic principles that have guided these efforts. One critical element was common to all stages, the infusion of additional resources such as grant funded positions and start-up costs. It is difficult to imagine how a residential agency could perform its required tasks and devote time and energy to change and growth without those additional resources.

CHANGE	STRATEGY FOR CHANGE
From child-centered to family-oriented.	Take one down position; put some responsibility for treatment on parents. Work for compliance from staff vs. hope for spontaneous support for change.
From single-service to (nonintegrated) multi-service agency.	Do something different, and through changed behavior, see self differently (behavior brings insight).
From nonintegrated to integrated multi-service agency.	Success brings its own problems; go slow.

From single agency to part of a network of services.

Reframe effort as necessary for survival; develop common language and frame of reference (PL 96-272). Acknowledge immense difficulties; go slow.

TECHNIQUES FOR FAMILY WORK

Family therapy is both a way of thinking about problems and a series of techniques. This chapter has tried to emphasize the value of this way of thinking for the agency itself as it interacts with the overall context of the permanency planning continuum. However, a by-product of this thinking would be for the agency to become more open to family work by developing services and programs for families served by that continuum. Also, staff from those other programs would be available to the residential staff in what may be becoming an extremely problematic area: offering specific services to families when a child is placed.

Given that the agency itself can become a powerful resource for family work, the next step would be to describe how an agency might work with particular families. The following types of family problems, with suggested interventions, are offered as models for family work. Obviously these types do not exist in a pure form, and they are complicated by such extenuating circumstances as age of child, family resources, chronicity of problems, and court involvement. On the other hand, these examples are arranged in a spectrum that attempts to cover the range of family work when a child is placed.

Absent Parent

In this situation, the parents are not available because they are chronically mentally ill or incarcerated, or simply do not visit. Fanshel (1975) has pointed out the high correlation between number of parental visits and successful reunification. The absence of parental visits then, in itself, becomes an argument for long-term care. On the other hand, the child may still be quite attached to parents through fantasy ("They will rescue me from this place") or guilt ("I need to go home and take care of my parents").

The task for the agency is to protect the child from the noxious elements that such parents can introduce, through agency policy on such issues as unscheduled visits or phone calls, as well as carefully worked-out treatment plans in collaboration with the placing agency. Such a plan might include gathering evidence to resolve in court the possibility of returning home. A second task is to work with the child who has such fantasies about reunification and such feelings of intense loyalty to fuel them. These feelings might be so strong that little or no confrontation on this issue can happen for some time. The main effort would focus on helping the child develop important relationships with peers and adults, as well as define in what way he can have a relationship with his parents. Finally, the agency can develop the next placement, hopefully a long-term foster care setting leading to guardianship or adoption. Stoeffler (1960) described an enriched pilot program that ended after three years. He also described the regression and panic that developed among children who did not know where they would be going. His description is a poignant but powerful reminder of how important it is to include a child's future placement in treatment planning. It obviously is advantageous for an agency to have its own foster care program. In that kind of setting, the slow, painful work of building new relationships and giving up older ones can continue with some consistency.

Ambivalent Parent

In this kind of family situation, the child may have spent significant time outside the home. Reunification efforts have failed at least once. The problem that characterizes this family and confounds treatment is ambivalence. Jackson and Dunne (1981) outline a powerful way of working with the ambivalent parent. The approach is time-consuming and structured by written contracts, and rests on the worker's ability to develop an effective and nonjudgmental working relationship. If a private agency does not possess the resources to replicate their program, a second choice may be to divide up the work with other agencies, including the placement worker from the public sector. It also may be that PL 96-272, with its emphasis on procedures, will tolerate only a certain period of ambivalence, by placing limits on the length of stay in placement for those children about to be returned home.

Morawetz and Walker (1984) describe a vignette using family therapy techniques in which several levels of ambivalence are resolved. The case involves the struggle between birth and foster mothers, with agencies taking sides and the child caught in the middle (pp. 337–345).

Impoverished Parent

In this situation, the parents are overwhelmed by an array of external problems, and the basic issue for the family is survival. With so many difficulties facing the family, the most difficult problem is to know where to start. Minuchin et al. (1967) seemed to give priority to the family's own organization. Only later would they help them work with the community-based resources they needed. Montalvo (Minuchin, 1974) follows this approach by reorganizing a family to stop a child's fire-setting behavior in the first session. However, he worked with the family over the next eighteen months and helped other family members obtain what they needed from the community. A different emphasis is to concentrate on the community resources needed to support the family and to prepare for the child's return home. Specific problem areas are addressed, and plans for obtaining help are outlined. Weissman (1978) describes a placement prevention program that emphasized contracts, signed not only by the client but also by representatives from community resources that were offering help.

Several common factors can be seen in both approaches. Much of the work is done in the parents' community and even in their home. Someone must regulate and oversee all of the treatment, lest the interventions become just another burden for the family. The goals of the work are very specific and expressed in concrete terms.

Addicted Parent

The use of drugs or alcohol is increasingly seen as a problem that can be approached from a family perspective (Stanton and Todd, 1982; Wegscheider, 1981). Although the one abusing drugs or alcohol may be dependent, the other family members are codependent or play reactive roles in the family. Increasingly, mental health professionals are concluding that little can be done unless the dependent person stops using or abusing drugs and alcohol. However, that is only the beginning of treatment. As Janzen and Harris (1986) point out, the most effective methods of treatment are those that involve family members. Still other services such as Alcoholics Anonymous are necessary to support the lifestyle changes that must occur if family members are to continue in a recovery process.

The dilemma for the therapist is to gain some level of certainty in a time-limited period about whether the child in residence should return home. Rzepnicki (1985) presents a task-centered approach that works within certain time limits. One case example contains a contract that addresses the father's reported abuse of alcohol.

Abusive Parent

Increasingly, parents who are reported for child abuse are offered place-ment prevention services. If the child is removed, he may be returned home within a short period of time, provided he no longer is in danger. Residential care would seem to be a choice of treatment if extenuating circumstances were present, or if reunification efforts had failed. Nevertheless, family-based approaches toward this population are worth considering. Janzen and Harris (1986) take an interactional view of child abuse and support approaches that might foster more appropriate interaction within the family, such as teaching parenting or communication skills. Also, there are self-help support groups for parents who have abused their children. Finally, specialized interventions have been developed for adult children of abusing parents (Gil, 1983). This latter approach may be helpful because so many abusing parents may have themselves been victims.

In this sketchy outline of family types, no mention has been made of other approaches such as those outlined by Whittaker (1979) in his chapter called "Parents as Partners in Helping." One major reason for this selective view is the author's bias about the changing nature of residential care caused by PL 96-272: children referred will be from families that have already experienced family-based interventions, namely, placement prevention and reunification efforts. With this kind of scenario, residential programs should be emphasizing a collaborative and comprehensive effort at determining under what conditions a child should return home, as well as the development of permanent substitute care for those children who cannot return home. Each residential program might well be advised to develop its own rule of thumb regarding what it can do for a particular type of family. To inadvertently foster a false hope of reunification or to focus on a child's misbehavior and ignore a serious addiction problem would be tragic. Likewise, to offer counseling in an office when the need is for intensive home-based services might result in another failure experience and make reunification even less likely. The task is to determine what can be done with what family at what time, realizing that for many the pieces cannot be put back together. Although that realization is a heavy burden, it can be shared with others involved with a family and within the context of the permanency planning continuum.

REFERENCES

Fanshel, D. (1975). Parental visiting of children in foster care. *Social Service Review, 49*, 493-514. Reprinted in Sinanoglu, P. A. and Maluccio, A. N., eds. (1981). *Parents of Children in Placement.* New York: Child Welfare League of America.

Fisch, R., Weakland, J. H., and Segal, L. (1982). *The Tactics of Change.* San Francisco: Jossey-Bass.

Gil, E. M. (1983). *Outgrowing the Pain.* San Francisco: Launch Press.

Jackson, A. D. and Dunne, M. J. (1981). Permanency planning in foster care with the ambivalent parent. In A. N. Maluccio and P. A. Sinanoglu, eds., *The Challenge of Partnership.* New York: Child Welfare League of America.

Janzen, C. and Harris, O. (1986). *Family Treatment in Social Work Practice,* 2nd edition. Itasca, Ill.: Peacock.

Knitzer, J. (1982). *Unclaimed Children.* Washington, D.C.: Children's Defense Fund.

Lawder, E. A., Poulin, J. E., and Andrews, R. G. (1984). *Helping the Multi-problem Family.* Philadelphia: Children's Aid Society of Pennsylvania.

Maluccio, A. N. and Sinanoglu, P. A., eds. (1981). *The Challenge of Partnership.* New York: Child Welfare League of America.

Minuchin, S. (1974). *Families and Family Therapy.* Cambridge, Mass.: Harvard University Press.

Minuchin, S. et al. (1967). *Families of the Slums.* New York: Basic Books.

Morawetz, A. and Walker, G. (1984). *Brief Therapy with Single-Parent Families.* New York: Brunner-Mazel.

Rzepnicki, T. L. (1985). Task-centered intervention in foster care services. In A. E. Fortune, *Task-Centered Practice with Families and Children.* New York: Springer.

Schultz, S. J. (1984). *Family Systems Therapy.* New York: Jason Aronson.

Sinanoglu, P. A. and Maluccio, A. N., eds. (1981). *Parents of Children in Placement.* New York: Child Welfare League of America.

Stanton, M. D. and Todd, T. C. (1982). *The Family Therapy of Drug Abuse and Addiction.* New York: Guilford Press.

Stoeffler, V. R. (1960). The separation phenomenon in residential treatment. *Social Casework, 41,* 523–530. Reprinted in Whittaker, J. K. and Trieschman, A. E., eds. (1972). *Children Away from Home.* Chicago: Aldine.

Van Hagen, J. (1982). Aftercare as a distinct and necessary treatment phase. *Residential Group Care and Treatment, 1,* 19–29.

Van Hagen, J. (1983). One residential center's model for working with families. *Child Welfare, 62,* 233–241.

Wegscheider, S. (1981). *Another Chance: Hope and Health for the Alcoholic Family.* Palo Alto: Science and Behavior Books.

Weissman, H. M. (1978). *Integrating Services for Troubled Families.* San Francisco: Jossey-Bass.

Whittaker, J. K. (1979). *Caring for Troubled Children.* San Francisco: Jossey-Bass.

Part II

MANAGEMENT ISSUES

The importance of an effective administrative team in a residential treatment center cannot be overemphasized. The administration is responsible for delineating the mission and goals of the center, procuring adequate funding, attracting and keeping competent staff, negotiating salaries and personnel practices, developing a sense of community within the agency, and advocating for children's services in the legislature and community.

The following chapters discuss what we consider to be a number of key but complex administrative issues in residential treatment, including the need for strong leadership, staff development, permanency planning, quality assurance, program evaluation, and the prevention of staff burnout and child abuse.

9

The Establishment and Maintenance of the Director's Influence on a Residential Treatment Program

Andrew Diamond

It is safe to speculate that when Ralph Waldo Emerson wrote that an "institution is the lengthened shadow of the man," he was not contemplating the enormous complexity of administering a residential treatment center. However, a secure executive with a knowledge of principles of residential treatment, an understanding of operating requirements, and a sensitivity to board, client, and staff needs, can still cast an imposing silhouette.

A colleague recounted the following analogue from a talk with an executive who had recently resigned from a large agency:

> I was thrilled to assume the position of executive director of a prestigious agency. My office had the most modern equipment available. I had a large console on my desk with dozens of push buttons, and I assumed that I could reach anywhere in the agency by pushing the correct button. As the weeks passed, I was hard at work sending out instructions, reordering agency priorities, and making crucial management decisions. One day in the middle of preparing a very significant policy change, I accidentally dropped my pen on the floor and it rolled under the desk. I crawled under the desk to look for my pen, and saw a mass of wires on the floor coming from the back of the console. As I searched for my pen, I learned an important lesson in administration. I observed that none of the wires coming from the console were connected to anything. It was no wonder that I was unable to make any substantive changes in the agency's program.

Although this parable is overdrawn, its message is apparent. The appointment of an executive director by a board of directors will not automatically put the executive's philosophy into operation.

The establishment of a director's impact on a residential treatment center develops during an evolutionary process. The final result (i.e., a milieu in which the director has maximum influence on the treatment program) can be referred to as "the director's milieu." In a director's milieu, the presence of the director will be reflected in agency practices such as the nature of specific therapies provided and the prescribed roles and functions of treatment team members. In addition, the quality and nature of interpersonal relationships among children and staff will reflect the director's standards and values. Other important areas of impact include behavioral expectations, discipline, recreational activities, home visiting, dress code, and activities of daily living (e.g., meal and bedtime procedures).

There are three phases in the process of establishing and maintaining a director's milieu. The first phase consists of a thorough assessment of the current institutional power structure as it pertains to the delivery of services. In the second phase, the director begins to translate his own philosophy into agency practice. The final phase, which is ongoing, consists of maintaining and reinforcing the director's influence on a day-to-day basis.

The executive's direct impact on the residential treatment program is inversely proportional to the size of the agency. The director of an agency in which the residential treatment program is a division of a larger agency, cannot have the same influence as the director whose agency consists of a treatment center as the sole or primary service provided. In large multiservice agencies, an administrator is usually appointed with direct responsibility for the residential program. However, the executive director and the residential administrator may share some board and program functions, and will let practicalities determine who has the primary impact on the establishment of the director's milieu. This chapter is most directly applicable to the role of an executive of an agency in which residential treatment is the primary service provided.

PHASE ONE: ASSESSING THE CURRENT POWER STRUCTURE

This phase is critical for new executives, particularly those appointed from outside the agency, who are not generally privy to board expectations and to the actual practices and procedures within the agency. A director must gain an understanding of the existing power structure. The milieu is not a tabula rasa. The functioning of a treatment program depends upon current board policies, procedures established by the previous administrator(s), and actual staff adherence to board and executive expectations. An executive's ability to operate efficiently and effectively requires an appreciation of these variables.

Board and Executive Interaction

The administrative latitude of the executive is determined in part by the degree to which the board and the executive function within traditional organizational standards. Boards establish and modify agency policy, maintain the agency's fiscal integrity, and have a legal and moral obligation to the community for the agency's functioning. The executive and the administrative staff ensure that the goals established by the board are put into practice.

The roles of the executive and the board do not always remain distinct. The extent of board participation in policy execution, and the degree of the executive's involvement in policy formation, are a function of fiscal considerations, agency traditions, and the values and priorities of the executive and board members. In addition, program transitions and crises within the milieu that affect the community's perception of the agency may dissipate traditional boundaries between board and executive functioning. Examples follow of role overlap based upon the preceding variables.

Fiscal considerations: The executive of a medium-sized residential center believed that a change was necessary in the educational program of the children. All children attended a special education school on the grounds of the agency. The executive believed that as many as twenty of the children could benefit from mainstreaming into the neighborhood public school. The program committee of the board of directors validated this approach despite concerns over losing rental income for the classroom space on grounds that would be vacated by this move. The executive then arranged a meeting with the principal of the local junior high school. The principal was unhappy with the prospect of twenty children "from the institution" entering the school. As the discussion between the executive and the principal continued, it became evident that for the children to have the best chance of succeeding, one new agency staff member would need to be hired. That employee would be present at the school to provide support to the children and backup to the teachers. In addition to losing rental income, the board was faced with the expense of adding a new worker to the budget. As a result of the total expenditure necessary to implement the program, the board reluctantly did not approve the funding. Therefore, the program could not be initiated.

The executive in the above example was unable to proceed with this project simply because the agency could not afford the program. The most frequent and frustrating situations of role overlap for the board and the executive occur when the board must make a program decision dictated by fiscal realities.

Agency tradition: For twenty years, the board of one residential treatment center did the actual hiring of the top three administrators of the agency.

Besides the director, the board hired the assistant director and the clinical director. At the time of the director's appointment, the other two positions had already been filled. A short time after the director's arrival, the assistant director resigned. The director wanted and needed an assistant with whom he felt he could work comfortably in bringing about program changes. The board was adamant in its resolve to make the final decision on the candidate to be hired. The person employed was not the director's first choice, and as a result the director felt hindered in the accomplishment of his goals.

In this example the director did not understand a tradition that existed before he was hired, that impinged upon his functioning as the executive. A director's time is well spent learning about agency traditions that support board involvement or control over areas traditionally delegated to the executive.

Values and priorities of the executive and board members: A residential treatment center contracted with a local gardening company to tend the grounds. The foliage was healthy and attractively arranged around the living units. Visitors were always impressed with the appearance of the grounds, which looked more like a college campus than a residential treatment center. The professional staff decided that the children would benefit from taking responsibility for the gardening. Such an undertaking would teach new skills and provide jobs for the more responsible children. In addition, the residents would have a sense of pride in their involvement in maintaining the grounds. Some members of the board objected strenuously, believing that the boys could not maintain the level of care provided by the gardeners. They felt that the appearance of the grounds would deteriorate, that the center would look less attractive to visitors, and that needed financial contributions would be affected. After a lengthy and at times heated discussion, a compromise was reached. The children and the gardeners would share landscaping responsibility.

Was the issue of who does the gardening a board or an executive issue? Obviously each side believed that its position was best for the agency. In establishing a director's milieu, an executive must be cognizant of individual and collective values of board members, and must consider the potential effect of those values on program determination.

Program transition and crises within the milieu: A new executive of a small child-care facility was determined to develop a more sophisticated treatment program. The agency was well known as a custodial institution, but did not provide intensive individual treatment or family treatment for its residents. The board of directors seemed enthusiastic about the plan. The social workers, many of whom had worked within the program for years, were not trained in working with families. As the executive began meeting with the social work

staff to outline his plan, including biweekly family meetings, parental participation in treatment planning, and home visiting, the staff became angry and
resentful. They felt that their years of service were not appreciated, and that
the executive was implying that the social workers had not performed their job
adequately prior to his arrival. The social work staff drafted a petition and wrote
letters to the board of directors complaining that they received autocratic and
insensitive treatment from the executive. As a result of the petition, and staff
unrest, the board asked for the executive's resignation.

In this case, the executive did not correctly assess the board's ability to
withstand the upheaval created by his attempt to make a major change in
agency practice. Despite initial enthusiasm for the executive's plan, the
board reacted strongly when the agency's stability appeared to be threatened.

The Executive's Assessment of the Existing Program

Prior to the implementation of any program changes, the executive must
consider current written policies, the organizational hierarchy, existing
treatment approaches, and the influence of veteran staff members. A
thorough understanding of these factors can facilitate program acceptance and increase chances of success.

Current Policies. The executive should review all agency manuals,
program statements, and written policies to clarify existing expectations
regarding program content and procedures. Following such a review, an
assessment should be made of whether these guidelines are representative of the actual functioning of the program. The paucity of such
documents can indicate either a lack of direction for line staff or an
administrative or staff autocracy.

Some larger children's residential centers are divided into smaller administrative departments or units. The primary purpose of such a division is to provide
more individualized attention to the needs of each child. In one agency with
four units, one unit administrator was responsible for the treatment of forty
children. The executive director of the agency had very little direct impact on
the milieu. He was an easygoing administrator who enforced basic guidelines
which coincided with licensing requirements (no physical or corporal punishment,
no withholding of food or sleep, no interference with parent–child visiting,
etc.). The written policies sent to staff consisted of these regulations.

The unit administrators were given broad latitude in supervising their units.
One unit administrator sent many memos to staff outlining policies and
procedures governing all aspects of cottage life. He spent a great amount of
time meeting with children and staff to ensure adherence to the guidelines. He
also exerted strong pressure on the staff and children to meet high expectations

and to take responsibility for their actions. The group living atmosphere fostered positive peer and child–staff interactions.

The second unit administrator had the same approach as the executive. He passed the written licensing regulations to the staff, and left the day-to-day running of the unit entirely to the child care staff, irrespective of their capabilities or experience. As a result, daily routines were followed haphazardly, and consequences for deviant behavior were not consistent among the child care staff. The tenor of the cottage depended entirely upon which line staff were on duty. Individual acting-out and negative group interaction became the norm rather than the exception.

Both units were part of the same treatment center. The actual functioning of each unit, however, was determined by the action or inaction of the unit administrator. The lack of specific written policies made it more difficult to assess current practices. In other situations an executive may send out voluminous material, but the content may not be reflected in the functioning of the agency.

The Organizational Hierarchy. Understanding the organizational hierarchy is an essential task for an administrator, and is critical to an appreciation of the institutional power structure. An organizational chart, however, can tell us as much or as little about the agency as the existing written policies. In the preceding example, both unit administrators were on the same administrative level, but in reality their impact on the milieu differed greatly. An organizational chart can be of assistance to an executive who is aware of each worker's job description and actual level of performance.

Existing Treatment Practices. An executive intending to make a program change should anticipate how the change would affect the existing program. If contemplated changes seem to conflict with entrenched practices, the implementation needs to be planned carefully.

The director of a large residential center believed that the children should have the experience of shopping for their clothes in the community, instead of receiving them from a storeroom located on the grounds of the center. The current system for the acquisition of clothes was simple. The child care worker took the resident who needed clothes to the storeroom. The child would look through the clothes and choose what he needed from the limited selection on hand. After the clothing was selected, the storeroom supervisor would make a notation in the child's clothing book. The system had worked extremely well. The children had an ample supply of attractive clothing. The director's plan included the closing of the storeroom and reassignment of the storeroom supervisor to another position in the agency. Before the director could make any changes, he had to understand the ramifications of the proposed change.

1. *Possible staff resistance:* The existing system of obtaining clothes for the children was simple and efficient for the child care workers. The extra time

consumed in taking the children shopping in the community and the increased possibility of acting up during the trip might create resistance to the plan by the staff.

2. *Effects on the children:* Some children might experience anxiety in choosing and purchasing clothing outside the institution.
3. *Possible staff morale problems:* The storeroom supervisor had worked at the center for many years and would be upset by the closing of the storeroom and by the new job assignment. She had many friends on the staff, who would be quite sympathetic to her reactions to the changes. A staff morale problem could result.
4. *Large budgetary increase:* Clothing could no longer be purchased in bulk at wholesale prices. A large budgetary increase requiring board approval would be necessary.
5. *Increased bookkeeping requirements:* A new bookkeeping system would be needed to track purchase orders and billing. Individual clothing accounts would have to be set up for the children.

The director had to consider all these ramifications before implementing the program change. He anticipated resistance because the plan required new, complex procedures that would have to be implemented by a staff invested in the existing system.

Influence of Veteran Staff. The feelings and reactions of long-term employees to proposed program changes should be considered before their implementation. In the previous case, the reactions of the storeroom supervisor and her coworkers were of legitimate concern to the director. Veteran staff members serving in supervisory and nonsupervisory positions can provide reassurance to the executive. Over the years a mutually dependent relationship can develop. Staff rely on the encouragement and support of a director in the performance of their jobs, and the executive appreciates the stability that veteran staff provide. Often, these employees are the backbone of the treatment program. During periods of change in an agency, veteran staff may feel vulnerable, may become angry, and may even resign. Staff discontent and/or the loss of experienced workers can undermine an existing program and inhibit implementation of the most worthwhile plan.

After considering all the ramifications of proposed changes, an executive may begin to put the new ideas or concepts into practice.

PHASE TWO: IMPLEMENTING THE DIRECTOR'S MILIEU: TRANSLATING THE DIRECTOR'S PHILOSOPHY INTO AGENCY PRACTICE

Executives attempting to impact on the treatment program should be aware that their success is dependent upon the director's presence in the milieu and the skill with which the director proceeds to implement any changes in the agency's philosophy and practice.

The Executive's "Presence" in the Milieu

The executive's "presence" in the milieu is determined by the authority inherent in the role of director, in combination with the director's personality and the responses of staff and residents to the director as an object of transference.

Children and adolescents struggle with issues relating to authority and autonomy. In most situations in which residential treatment is indicated, a breakdown in the functioning of the family unit has occurred, and the child's symptomatology is manifested by a deterioration in self-control and social adaptation. By temporarily extricating the child from intense conflicts within the home, professionals may treat these issues in a thoughtful, unemotional manner, unencumbered by familial strife.

At the time of admission to a residential treatment program, children enter a social system in which predictability, consistency, and order are the norm. It is anticipated that their experience with the authority figures at the treatment center will not coincide with their preconceptions. The director personifies the limits and demands placed upon the residents. The newly admitted child sees that the other children in the program are conforming to adult expectations. In addition, the child knows that the executive is also the authority for the staff. The director, possessing such power and authority, becomes an intense object of transference by both children and staff (Mayer, 1960).

The director's legitimate authority combines with transference factors to create an important tool in the establishment of the director's milieu. The children and staff look to the director for modeling and as a frame of reference for their own social interaction. The director's personality traits (e.g., values, ethics, and quality of interpersonal relationships) exert a strong influence on the therapeutic program.

It is important to distinguish between personality traits and charisma. A charismatic director may impress and influence staff and children by his appearance and style of communicating. However, a charismatic administrator, lacking training or skill, cannot have a sustained influence on the milieu.

In the 1960s a young administrator was appointed to direct a small treatment center of forty adolescent boys. The previous director was ten or more years his senior, so his appointment came as a surprise to the predominately young staff.

The new administrator was bright and engaging and elicited positive feelings from everyone with whom he came in contact. In the early 1960s less attention was paid to men's fashions, and facial hair was not yet in vogue, however, the director had a neatly trimmed moustache and wore oxford button down shirts, paisley ties, and khaki pants. Within a few weeks almost all of the male child care staff had sprouted moustaches and sported the oxford, paisley, khaki look. Even some of the delinquent boys began wearing similar clothes. It was amusing to watch the children and staff walking as a group to the main dining hall for dinner. Nevertheless, the director's charisma could not compensate for his lack of experience. After a short period of time, as problems in the program and with individual children remained unsolved, the initial impressions changed, and his influence waned.

Charisma is a valuable but not crucial quality in an effective administrator. Skill, knowledge, personal integrity, and commitment to a treatment philosophy are the critical traits of the director seeking to establish and maintain an impact on the milieu.

Board Support of Executive Action

The board of directors should be kept informed of all program changes that affect the budget, the stated goals and policies of the agency, or the agency's standing in the community. The board, committees of the board, and key board members should be advised, in advance, of any possible ramifications of changes that might temporarily affect program stability or staff morale. This is crucial even if the authority for the changes lies exclusively in the executive's domain. An executive who maintains open communication with the board is more likely to receive board support for any program or policy change than one who is less communicative.

Staff Support of Executive Action

When staff understand and accept a change in philosophy or policy, they are likely to align with the executive to facilitate implementation of that change. There are several steps an executive may take to precipitate staff acceptance. These tasks include an articulation of the executive's philosophy, solicitation of staff input, and the development of relevant staff training. If indicated, staff roles or functions may have to be modified. These steps are taken with the knowledge gained by the executive's previous appraisal of the current system in operation.

An executive of a residential treatment center planned to make some major changes in the existing therapy program. The system that existed is illustrated by the following organizational chart:

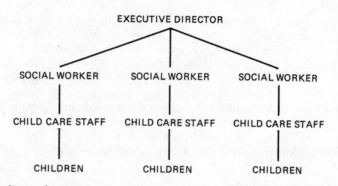

The lines of supervision are evident; the executive director supervised the social workers, who in turn supervised the child care staff. The role of the social workers was twofold: they provided therapy for the children and families, and they supervised the group living unit. The executive thought that the social workers' role should be more distinct and should not overlap with the role of the child care staff.

Under the existing system, a child who acted up received a consequence from the child care worker and the social worker, and was then expected to go into therapy with the social worker to discuss his reaction to authority and his feelings about the behavior.

The executive wanted to remove the social worker from the position of authority, with the expectation that in the therapy sessions children then would be freer to discuss their ambivalence around issues related to their behavior, group living, and their families. The executive decided to hire a staff member who would supervise the child care staff directly. The program change is reflected in the following organizational chart:

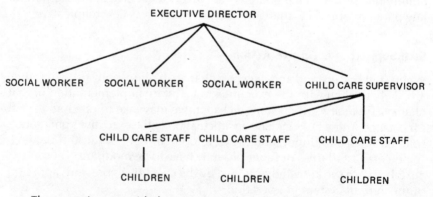

The executive met with the appropriate board members to discuss personnel and program ramifications of the plan. The board was enthusiastic. The executive began a series of meetings with the child care staff and the social work staff to receive their imput and to explain the rationale for the change. After a few

meetings, the child care staff had positive feelings about the change. The
. social workers remained skeptical, indicating that they were comfortable with
their dual roles. The executive then met with the individual social workers in
order to understand their reactions more thoroughly. The executive decided to
implement the plan and to hire the new child care supervisor even though one
of the social workers was still very resistant. The executive rewrote the social
workers' job description and hired a consultant to train the social workers on
techniques that would put the executive's plan into practice.

In this example the director showed great skill and sensitivity in handling the anxiety and anger that the new treatment approach triggered in
the staff. A less thorough approach might have created grave problems
that could have prevented adoption of the plan or doomed it to failure.

PHASE THREE: MAINTAINING THE
DIRECTOR'S MILIEU

The director's milieu is nourished by the institutional system designed
and administered by the director. Adherence to a treatment philosophy
and adoption of certain administrative practices will ensure the maintenance of the director's impact on the milieu.

   Adherence to a Treatment Philosophy. The director's treatment philosophy is the product of board directives, agency traditions, current staff
capabilities, and the personal beliefs and professional knowledge and
experience of the director. In order for this philosophy to be maintained, it
must be reinforced and supported by current procedures and practices.
Any proposed change in policies will impact upon the existing philosophy
and need careful consideration. The director's milieu is not static and
needs to be flexible enough to allow for modifications in specific practices as well as in the overall philosophy.

   Other important factors in maintaining the director's milieu include the
in-service training program, and personnel selection and promotion.
In-service training should be designed to reinforce and improve current
practices and enhance staff's understanding of the overall treatment
philosophy. Personnel selection and promotions should be based upon
the applicant's capabilities and compatibility with the existing philosophy.

   Accountability. One of the most important decisions an executive
makes is the determination of responsibilities that can or should be
delegated. The degree of delegation varies with the size of the agency and
with other demands placed upon the executive. Delegation is not abdication,
and the executive still has to assess whether the overall philosophy and
treatment approaches are being followed by middle management and

line staff. This is accomplished through formal supervision and informal monitoring.

Supervision of middle managers and line workers should be scheduled on a regular basis, irrespective of the tenure or expertise of the employee. Supervisory conferences provide an opportunity to focus on areas where improvements or changes are sought, and to discuss and modify existing practices that may not be consonant with the director's milieu. Follow-up is indicated until the practice is consistent with existing policies and philosophy. Issues that were problematic in the past need periodic reexamination to assure a satisfactory resolution.

Direct observation of institutional practices can provide a valuable supplement to supervisory conferences. Visits to the living units and recreation activities, review of case records, and informal discussion with direct treatment staff and children can provide a comprehensive view of the milieu.

Maintaining Staff Effectiveness. Staff members in a residential treatment center may face the angry, defiant, aggressive, and self-destructive behavior of children on a daily basis. This continuous barrage can cause disillusionment, stress, and burnout.

The morale of the staff is conveyed to the children either consciously or unconsciously, and can impact on the treatment milieu. The director needs to create and perpetuate a positive atmosphere for the staff. Support of staff decisions, staff input in program planning, acknowledgment of exemplary service, relevant and creative in-service training, and remuneration consistent with their value to the program are necessary ingredients to keep staff motivated and committed to the program.

Certain staff members may have unique skills and talents, but they may not understand or entirely agree with the prevailing philosophy. Others may have been trained at other facilities with a different treatment approach. These employees, although quite gifted, may become too threatened by the expectation for change and decide to leave the treatment center. The executive, aware of the value of such staff, should make every effort to retain them as members of the treatment team while still anticipating compliance with the existing philosophy.

Communication. Accessibility to the director, and methods of communication between staff and director and among staff, are critical processes in the functioning of a residential center.

An aloof administrator may not be aware of valid concerns or complaints. Problems that remain unaddressed may undermine the integrity of the treatment program. Scheduled meetings and informal conversations with staff create a forum for open communication, and the skillful director is able to relate to and interact with line staff without compromising the authority and influence of the supervisory staff. An established system of communication results in greater visibility of staff performance, and thus increased administrative awareness of the staff's adherence to the agency's treatment philosophy and practice.

SUMMARY

The establishment and maintenance of the director's milieu can be viewed as an evolutionary process consisting of three phases. In the first phase, the director assesses the existing power structure as it affects decision making. In the second phase, the director uses his presence, with an awareness of the existing system of decision making, to influence the treatment milieu. In the third phase, the director uses supervisory techniques, ongoing in-service training, methods of support of staff, and the established system of communication to ensure adherence to the prevailing treatment philosophy.

REFERENCE

Mayer, M. F. (1960). The parental figures in residential treatment. *Social Service Review, 34,* 281.

10

Professional Development for a Therapeutic Environment

Richard M. Kagan

A comprehensive professional training program can help to achieve two vital goals for residential treatment programs: (1) to enhance and promote the knowledge, skills, and attitudes necessary for effective programs; and (2) to foster a consistent environment based on common therapeutic philosophies and teamwork between disciplines and programs (Kagan, 1983). To accomplish these goals, most staff development programs must surmount several major challenges, including: a lack of resources (staff time, funding, instructors); staff apathy; competition between staff groups; internal conflict; criticism; and low priority in comparison with pressing demands from clients, emergencies, or mandates from funding or accrediting agencies. This chapter examines premises for effective professional development programs and outlines practical tips for avoiding typical snag points (Pittman, 1984) that can defeat training programs.

PREMISES

Effective professional development programs are based on the following premises:

1. Children from troubled families repeat behavioral patterns experienced in their homes and previous placements. Children in group care, in effect, reenact family dilemmas with staff. Accordingly, the child who has experienced abuse, abandonment, and neglect will often provoke the same interactions with staff members. The child in stress will create in staff his or her feelings—and, *without staff training,* his or her behaviors (Long, 1986). Professional development programs that foster an understanding of clients' dilemmas, the meaning of interactions, and practitioners' self-awareness are

thus essential for creating an environment that can facilitate change and growth in children and families.

2. Professional development programs reflect the agency's development, efficacy, and dilemmas. The agency that has many scattered programs without a central set of priorities will typically have training programs that are specific to different units. Similarly, an agency that lacks a strong mission statement with clearly outlined priorities and commitments will typically have a professional development program that has little focus or depth. The professional development program of an agency will reflect the agency's: organization/disorganization, unity/division, openness/repression, creativity/rigidity, and progress/regression.

3. The focus for a professional development program must be on the organization as a whole rather than on specific problems or individuals. Professional development programs can be a means of fostering organizational development. The challenge for professional development programs is to assess agency needs, to set realistic objectives based on the agency's primary goals, and to maintain a clear sense of direction and movement toward accomplishment of the agency's priorities.

4. A therapeutic environment requires a common philosophical base and consistent approaches carried out by many staff from different backgrounds and disciplines. Accordingly, the scope of professional development programs must include programs for program directors, members of the board of directors, clinicians, educators, child care workers, and support staff (maintenance, kitchen, secretarial, accounting, etc.). Training programs can facilitate the common language and understanding necessary for effective teamwork.

5. Programs must address the self-awareness necessary for staff to provide needed services to families and children/adolescents. Lectures alone are insufficient, as staff, like all other human beings, will typically fall back on old values and behaviors when stress mounts. And, children in group care seem to have an uncanny sense of what can provoke an otherwise competent staff member into feeling the frustration, terror, or rage that the children themselves have so frequently experienced.

Professional development programs can offer staff resources for their own lives and for their work with clients. In order to help families, staff must be aware of their own family issues, cultural values, and their own vulnerabilities. As staff develop their own potential, they become more capable of helping troubled families.

SNAG POINTS

Apathy

The best curricula will have little impact if participation is low and staff members do not apply to their day-to-day practice the information and skills developed in training sessions. Staff apathy, resentment, or frustration can defeat the finest programs.

To mobilize staff participation, the following steps have been useful in developing programs (Kagan, 1983):

1. Soliciting staff needs and requests for programs through surveys, discussions in program meetings, discussions in committees, and personal consultation with all program directors and supervisors.
2. Involving key staff from the major disciplines in a training committee.
3. Developing a tentative outline of programs from the list of staff needs.
4. Sharing the tentative outline with program directors and supervisors, for input and suggestions.
5. Adjusting topics, formats, and scheduling to meet the needs of staff members from different programs.
6. Including an evaluation component in every program to obtain participants' feedback on the value of the program for their work and their suggestions for improvement.

Within this framework, staff recommendations and criticisms provide the foundations for training programs, and they serve as an ongoing measure of program value. Staff needs and agency priorities serve as guidelines for adjusting programs to be most productive.

"No Time"

Participation of staff members in training programs is directly related to the priority and encouragement their supervisors provide for attendance. Supervisors must go to a great deal of effort and expense to arrange coverage for absent staff, as staff time is the most valuable resource that an agency has. Training is a very expensive proposition for an agency, regardless of the dollar amount listed for it in the agency's budget. Supervisors thus can be expected to say they have "no time" for their staff and themselves to attend training sessions. To facilitate the support of supervisors from staff to participate in seminars or workshops, all training programs need to be developed conjointly with supervisors and senior staff members.

Staff participation can also be stimulated by using program directors and supervisors from all disciplines as instructors in large workshops. For example, "Creating a Context for Change," a key part of the orientation program at Parsons Child and Family Center, was developed and led by the supervisor of group care, the assistant director of education, a child care supervisor, and a clinical psychologist. Use of program supervisors as trainers can also facilitate implementation of training material in day-to-day practice, and can promote interdisciplinary cooperation. If supervisors are actively involved, they are likely to encourage staff members to implement training materials. Giving supervisors an investment in the training curriculum can lead to increased support from them, as well as the commitment of staff members' time to both participation in sessions and actual implementation of techniques presented through staff development (Kagan, 1983).

The pressure on staff time must be recognized and respected by training directors. At the same time, the need for training must be emphasized to avoid the countless crises and difficulties that result when staff work without a clear understanding of the complex factors affecting the behaviors of clients and themselves. Training programs need a commitment of adequate staff time from supervisors and agency directors. Moreover, supervisors need to follow up with checks on staff attendance and the value of programs for their staff. The best way to facilitate this is to involve supervisors in both the development and the evaluation of training programs.

Staff Criticism

Staff criticism can be very disconcerting to seminar/workshop leaders. Staff members often use training programs to point out discrepancies between agency policies and what actually takes place. In-house instructors may find themselves put on the defensive as representatives of the agency's administration, and challenged to either change a given situation immediately or admit the impossibility of the approach or technique that is advocated. An instructor or training director who responds directly to such complaints, criticisms, or apathy often becomes embroiled in a prolonged discussion (or, more likely, argument) with the participant; and such a win/lose struggle will disrupt the best of programs (Kagan, 1983).

Instead of responding in that way, the instructor can acknowledge a staff member's challenge, accept issues as real problems, and admit mistakes when wrong. The instructor can work to mobilize staff members (participants in the workshop) to work on the situation in question (Kagan, 1983). The training program can have the additional value of stimulating needed change by the staff members directly involved in a problem, and tying staff concerns to the agency's administrative and quality assurance process. Criticism of training programs themselves can be sought routinely in every workshop or seminar and then used to improve future programs. This approach serves as a model for improving other programs and services in the agency.

Conflict

Professional development programs can easily become the focal point for staff members to express frustrations and animosities. Debates about the value of a particular treatment program or particular approach can snarl a training program in a deadly morass. Philosophical differences in an agency can lead to stagnation in the training program, as different sides compete over which approach (e.g., the X model of family therapy or the Y model) is preferable. In such situations, the training director may easily be perceived as advocating a particular side in the ongoing battle for control of the agency. One part of the agency may have an aversion to the training program, while another part thinks it is wonderful. In this way, the training program itself comes to reflect organizational dynamics and gets locked into a specific position or role that permits little creativity or change.

Conflict is present in all organizations and can be a healthy part of a growing and progressive facility. Several strategies may be useful in preventing a training program from becoming locked into a dysfunctional role:

1. Incorporate a training program as part of a research–training center, and tie training programs to ongoing research on the effectiveness of treatment approaches.
2. Encourage innovative work and assessment of the effectiveness of services for client groups.
3. Avoid advocating a specific approach to treatment; instead work on developing strengths within the agency and improving upon specific models of service to meet the needs of agency clients.

Kahlil Gibran, in *The Prophet,* wrote that: "The teacher who walks in the shadow of the temple, among his followers, gives not of his wisdom but rather of his faith and his lovingness. If he is indeed wise, he does not bid you enter the house of his wisdom, but rather leads you to the threshold of your own mind." An effective training program promotes self-development rather than advocating a certain specific approach as a panacea and mandating its use with all clients.

"It's Boring"

When staff say a program is boring, it is important to find out if the subject matter is irrelevant or too basic. Was the instructor unable to engage the group? Were expectations clear? Did staff feel pressured to attend?

Training programs need to be geared to the developmental level of staff in terms of knowledge, skill, and experience. Programs can be too basic, redundant, or too sophisticated. Beginning staff need a lot of basic survival skills and intensive supervision, followed by more theory and regular supervision of the implementation of program concepts and strategies into their work with clients. Advanced staff need stimulation and opportunities for self-development and learning, on their own and with colleagues. Sending advanced staff out to major conferences can help to prevent stagnation and boost creativity. For beginning staff, on the other hand, it will usually be more important to provide opportunities to learn the basics and to receive much-needed supervision.

"Local Saints Perform No Miracles"

Every training program must address the question of whether to bring in outside resources, usually at great cost, or utilize in-house staff to lead seminars and workshops. Workshop leaders from outside the agency often can gain immediate command of staff attention, and they typically are thought to know more than in-house authorities—in almost direct proportion to the distance they have traveled to get to the host agency! Outside workshop leaders can be very successful in bringing in new perspectives, stimulating staff to explore new areas, and providing excitement in the week-to-week routine of an agency. On the other hand, brief visits by distinguished guests often have a very limited impact over time because the instructors are not available for ongoing supervision and consultation with actual cases. Stimulating ideas and provocative videotapes are often forgotten when a practitioner is alone with an acting-out adolescent or a violent family.

In-house instructors often feel undervalued by their colleagues and are very sensitive to intra-agency conflicts over philosophies, approaches, workloads, and so on. It is valuable to encourage in-house instructors to publish and present elsewhere, as this can add to their esteem within the agency. Similarly, including participants from other agencies in training programs may cause staff members of the sponsoring agency to see in-house instructors from a different perspective (i.e., as leaders in the field). It also is essential to gain administrative support for training programs and in-house trainers. Trainers need time for preparation and deserve special compensation for carrying out training programs. This not only increases the incentive for in-house leaders to teach, but also demonstrates the agency's commitment to the training programs offered.

The best training programs provide ongoing sessions that cover an approach (e.g., family systems) over a period of years. From this perspective, it is very important to think of three- to five-year curriculum for staff development rather than one-shot workshops. The work involved in group care is much more difficult than anything that can be encompassed in a simple focused workshop. A combination of consistent ongoing training with local instructors, and opportunities for a few intensive but time-limited workshops with distinguished guests, can be very productive.

"No Money"

Training programs typically are beset by financial constraints and lack of funding. Moreover, when funding becomes tight, the training budget is often one of the first to be trimmed, slashed, or eliminated. Direct services to clients must be provided first.

It is helpful to view expenditures for training from the perspective of the agency's overall fiscal management of resources. From this perspective, staff time is the overriding expense for the agency, compared to relatively low expenses for actual payments to trainers, and so forth. With a clear understanding of staff time as a resource, it becomes imperative to utilize staff time in the most efficacious manner possible, in order to best serve clients and meet the agency's primary commitments. Small expenses for equipment or trainers may be acceptable, given the vital need for specialized training programs to provide quality services and the much larger cost of staff time already committed to training programs. A small investment in improving the quality of training programs can result in a big improvement in the productivity of training time for staff.

An agency that has time but lacks funding can still provide quality programs. Grants can be sought for specific training. Moreover, the agency may offer regional training programs for professionals in other human services agencies. Fees from outside participants can help to offset the direct expenses of bringing in instructors for programs.

"Prove It"

In an era of fiscal cutbacks and restraints on funding for children's services, training programs will be pressed to prove their effectiveness.

Evaluation of training programs is essential in order to maintain ongoing input of staff into programs and as a means of developing the next set of programs based upon staff needs. Simple evaluations can be utilized to assess the value of each program. Moreover, it is very helpful to conduct an annual evaluation of programs offered by each discipline. Please see Attachment A for a sample evaluation instrument.

Attachment A
PROFESSIONAL DEVELOPMENT SERIES

PARTICIPANT EVALUATION*

PROGRAM TITLE _____ DATE _____

1. On a 1-5 basis (5 being excellent), what number reflects your rating for the following (please circle):

    a. overall value of this program for your work   1   2   3   4   5
    b. content   1   2   3   4   5
    c. presenters: overall   1   2   3   4   5
             comments on individuals _____

    _____

    d. teaching materials   1   2   3   4   5
    e. methodology   1   2   3   4   5
    f. achievement of objectives   1   2   3   4   5
    g. facility   1   2   3   4   5

2. The level of the subject matter for the workshop you attended was (please circle #):

    1 much too basic
    2 somewhat too basic
    3 about right
    4 somewhat advanced
    5 much too advanced

3. Suggestions for improving the workshop you attended _____

    _____

    _____

4. Which of the following areas would you like to see covered in future seminars or workshops? Please rate on a 1-5 basis (5 being highest priority):

    a. human services management   1   2   3   4   5
    b. family systems therapy   1   2   3   4   5
    c. developmental disabilities   1   2   3   4   5

---

*Developed with the assistance of Pat O'Connor.

d. special education	1	2	3	4	5
e. child care	1	2	3	4	5
f. diagnostic assessments	1	2	3	4	5
g. organizational development	1	2	3	4	5
h. application of computers for human services agencies	1	2	3	4	5
i. certificate program in family therapy with multi-problem families	1	2	3	4	5
j. permanency work	1	2	3	4	5

5. Please list specific topics you would like to see addressed _____

_____

_____

6. Please use the space below and the reverse side for additional comments:

Objective measures also can be developed to assess the impact of training programs. For instance, an increase in the use of family therapy or a decrease in dropouts could be measured (Silverman, 1985). Objective indicators of change can be developed from the actual needs of the agency (e.g., to increase client referrals, to increase applicants for clinical staff positions, to reduce incidences of physical restraints or injuries, etc.).

Problem-Maintaining Solutions

Agencies, like families, seek help when under stress. However, most families (and agencies) are not seeking change but instead want relief from pain (Pittman, 1984). In fact, help is often sought primarily to reduce discomfort and get the family (or agency) back to a previous stage of development with as little conflict as possible.

Training programs often are introduced to handle disturbing problems (e.g., a high rate of dropouts, increasing turnover, or violence). Too often, however, these programs become problem-maintaining solutions by ignoring the underlying dilemmas of staff and clients. Instructors may be brought in to lecture to staff on policies and procedures. Training programs may have too little depth to be effective, or may fail to address the real needs of staff. The programs can come to be seen as penalties for poor performance or a waste of time because they stress training in areas (e.g., documentation) that appear only tangential to the pressures and strains of actual day-to-day work with high-risk clients.

As frustrations grow, training programs may come to resemble exercises in ventilation therapy, with expression of concerns that wind up in the wastebasket. This in turn leads to increasing frustration as hopes are raised but little or no substantial change results. In some agencies training programs may come to be regarded as perks for a privileged few who are allowed to go to conferences (Silverman, 1985). Or training programs can lead to frustration if trainees have no authority to implement changes in their agencies (Silverman 1981a, b).

In contrast, professional development programs can be the focal point of an agency committed to the ongoing development of improved services. An agency dedicated to enriching staff and providing the highest quality of services can become a center for research and training. In such agencies, training serves to broaden perspectives, to enrich staff, and to provide an ongoing stimulus for improved services. Staff development programs can be tied to the agency's quality assurance programs in a productive fashion (Kagan, 1984), building on staff strengths to improve services and manage problem areas. Such training is geared for adults and based on their needs, with an emphasis on use of self and a clear focus on the priorities of the agency for serving clients. Training can become a resource for staff and a shared endeavor in expanding knowledge and skills. Training programs can symbolize the agency's efforts to learn, to improve, and to take a leadership role in the community, region, or nation.

A PROFESSIONAL DEVELOPMENT CURRICULUM

The following curriculum provided a framework at Parsons Child and Family Center (PCFC) for continually evolving training programs in three areas: (1) an orientation program for all staff, (2) required training by discipline, and (3) advanced training for experienced staff members (across disciplines).[1] All programs were developed to meet current needs of staff and combined didactic and experiential training that stressed use of self. Programs were conducted by practitioners and designed to help staff adopt theoretical approaches to the specific client situations encountered in the agency. This curriculum illustrates how a training program can address agency needs for a common theoretical base and promote skill development for all staff (new and advanced), stress the importance of teamwork, provide opportunities for self-development, and identify the agency's primary commitments.

Curriculum Goals

Professional development programs were designed to promote the knowledge, skills, and self-awareness necessary for staff to provide a contiuum of child welfare, educational, clinical, and child care services to families and children/adolescents with special needs. Programs for new and advanced staff address the need for a consistent therapeutic milieu, based upon the agency's commitment to:

1. Strengthening families and fostering ongoing relationships that can provide children and adolescents with consistent nurturing parenting.
2. Responding to community needs.
3. Provision of the highest quality services in the least restrictive environment.
4. Teamwork across disciplines and programs.

Basic Curriculum

A developmental and family systems perspective is emphasized by agency supervisors and trainers to promote a common foundation for interdisciplinary teamwork. The basic plan is shown here in outline form.

I. *Orientation for New Staff*
    A. A first-day training program is provided to new staff by their supervisors, which focuses on the immediate skills needed by professionals in direct contact with children and families. The following information is offered in a full-day training session:
        Part I—First-Day Orientation[2]
        1. Fire safety
        2. Emergency procedures
        3. Tour
        4. Accident and injury reports
        5. Introduction to behavioral management
            a. Observation of two instructional videotapes, focusing on discipline and prevention of physical involvements.
            b. Reading packets of information.
            c. Participation in a one-hour "hands on" training session with supervisor/trainers. Training is provided in handling emergencies and the safe use of physical restraints as a last resort.
            d. Supervised practice in driving an agency vehicle (as appropriate).
            The First-Day Checklist is distributed upon completion of the orientation to assure both the professional and the supervisor that all the immediate training needs have been satisfied.
    B. The second component of orientation (Part II) is designed to familiarize the new employee with the philosophies, policies, and programs of the agency. Part II is offered by interdisciplinary instructors in three half-day sessions. Session I is provided within the first sixty days of employment, and Sessions II and III are given in the first four months of employment.

Session 1—Agency Overview
1. Agency history, mission, and philosophies
2. Program overviews
3. Agency slide show

Session 2—Permanence[3]
1. The meaning of permanence
2. Dynamics of attachment and loss
   a. Grief, loss, and separation
   b. Impact of placements
3. Practical implications for work with families and children

Session 3—Creating a Context for Change[4]
1. Systems perspectives
   a. Agency's mission
   b. Family–community system
   c. Whose child is it? (relationship with referral sources)
   d. Agency interventions within a systems perspective
   e. The child's and the family's experience in placement
2. Developmental stages of children and families
   a. Individual and family assessment from a developmental perspective
   b. How to use an understanding of cognitive, physical, emotional, social, and sexual development to "speak a child's language" and work from a child's strengths
3. Starting with ourselves
   a. Values, goals
   b. "Helping" adults
   c. Working at PCFC
4. Application of a systems model
   a. Assessment: separation and loss issues
   b. Engaging families
   c. Permanence
   d. Teamwork and a therapeutic milieu
   e. Review conference
   f. Conflict management
   g. Evaluation and follow-up
5. Creating a context for change
   a. Using a child's system: family, community, team
   b. Behavioral management programs for classroom and group living situations
   c. Constructive methods of crisis and conflict management
   d. Alternatives to physical involvements with acting-out youth
   e. Use of messages

II. *Safety Issues*
Through in-house workshops, direct-line staff will receive the following safety training within one year of employment (and repeated annually thereafter):
A. Multi-media first aid (Red Cross–approved)
B. CPR (Red Cross–approved)

    C. Suicide prevention
    D. Substance abuse
III. *Specialized Curricula*[5]
    A. Education staff curriculum
    B. Developmental disabilities program staff curriculum
    C. Clinical staff curriculum: certificate program in family systems
      1. Multi-generational family systems training
      2. Strategic family systems training
    E. Management curriculum
IV. *Advanced Training Curricula*
    1. Consultant in residence: An expert in child welfare provides ongoing seminars for one to five days each year with an emphasis on practical issues for child care, clinical, and educational staff.
    2. Study groups: Staff are encouraged to participate in study groups that research relevant topics related to serving clients of the agency (e.g., violent families, long-distance families with children in placement).
    3. Parsons/Sage professional development programs[6] and other outside conferences: Training and professional development opportunities are offered for professionals at the agency and other human service agencies in the upstate New York region through the following presentations:
      a. The Parsons/Sage Fall Institute, a conference that speaks to the vital concerns of professionals working with children and families.
      b. Parsons/Sage Winter/Spring Series of workshops and seminars designed to meet the needs of practitioners serving special need children and their families.

Critical Issues in Making Professional Development Programs Work

Professional development programs play an essential role in determining whether a child's placement will be productive or just another episode in failure for the child and his or her family. The best interventions by one staff member can be undone by contradictory messages from another staff member operating with a different approach. Development of a comprehensive training program can pull together staff members and promote a consistent environment in which families and children can change (Kagan, 1983).

Frustration, apathy, conflicts, and complaints of "no money," "no time," and "prove it first" can be surmounted with professional development programs that focus on building from strengths and working with staff as professionals. Training programs begin with a careful assessment of agency strengths, needs, and dilemmas. In-house training programs can become an integral part of the agency's ongoing efforts to carry out its basic mission (i.e., whom it will serve as clients and how it will serve them). Programs based on actual needs usually will be welcomed and can provide staff with the opportunity to develop skills and increase their self-awareness and resources as individuals and practitioners. An ongoing evaluation component can help training programs to evolve along with the agency, with a focus on current needs and agency objectives.

"Local saints may perform no miracles," the expression goes; however, in-house training programs can have a great impact on services provided. The crucial element in effective programs is to engage staff in common efforts to improve services, as we push back the frontiers of our knowledge about helping families and children. Staff motivation and investment in training programs are correlated with their involvement in program development. The Chinese philosopher Lao-Tse is quoted as saying, "Of the best leaders, when their task is accomplished, the people all remark 'We have done it ourselves'" (Hudson, 1983). Of the best training programs, staff may say, "It was our program."

NOTES

1. The author wishes to thank Brian Aylward, Mary Lou Baum, Marylynne Brady-Johnson, Wander deC. Braga, Dave Bryan, Jeanne Burk, Nadia Finkelstein, Pat Geary, Ruth Hartman, Jim Hudson, Larry Krohmal, Adele Pickar, Steve Roberts, Ray Schimmer, Shirley Schlosberg, Debbie Singer, Steve Sola, Lenore Sportsman, Linda Smith, Micki Sumpter, Tom Walsh, and Kathy Raymond for their help in the development and implementation of these programs.
2. Developed with Jim Hudson, Joanne Matias, and supervisory staff.
3. Developed by Shirley Schlosberg.
4. Developed with Adele Pickar, Brian Aylward, Tom Walsh, Bill Martone, and Mike O'Conner.
5. Detailed descriptions of the specialized curricula are available from the R. M. Kagan.
6. Developed by Parsons Child and Family Center and Russell Sage College.

REFERENCES

Hudson, J. L. (1983). Measuring the costs and benefits of QA. *Quality Review Bulletin, 9*(6), 164–166.

Kagan, R. M. (1983). Staff development for a therapeutic environment. *Child Welfare, 62*(3), 203–211.

Kagan, R. M. (1984). Organizational change and quality assurance in a psychiatric setting. *Quality Review Bulletin, 10*(9), 269–277.

Long, N. (1986). Understanding and managing the behavioral disorders in the classroom. Workshop presented at Parsons Child and Family Center, Albany, N.Y., Mar. 19, 1986.

Pittman, F. S. (1984). Wet cocker spaniel therapy: an essay on technique in family therapy. *Family Process, 23,* 5.

Silverman, W. H. (1981a). Self-designed training for mental health advisory/governing boards. *American Journal of Community Psychology, 9,* 67–82.

Silverman, W. H. (1981b). Self-designed continuing education for supervisors in community mental health. *Journal of Community Psychology, 9,* 347–354.

Silverman, W. (1985). Agency based staff development. *Administration in Mental Health, 12*(4), 284–292.

11

Promoting Permanency Planning

Anthony N. Maluccio

The philosophy of permanency planning emphasizes that every child or youth has a right to grow up in a family setting. This philosophy is most pertinent to youngsters in residential care, who are especially vulnerable to impermanency in their living arrangements. Following a brief overview of the definition and context of permanency planning, this chapter will consider the role of residential care in permanency planning and delineate guidelines for overcoming barriers and promoting permanency planning.

DEFINITION AND CONTEXT

Permanency planning has been defined as "the systematic process of carrying out, within a brief time-limited period, a set of goal-directed activities designed to help children live in families that offer continuity of relationships with nurturing parents or caretakers and the opportunity to establish lifetime relationships" (Maluccio et al., 1986: 5). Its essence is that practitioners have a responsibility to take prompt, decisive action to maintain children in their own homes or place them permanently with other families. Permanency planning thus encompasses both prevention and rehabilitation, with attention not only to children and youth in care but also to those who are at risk of out-of-home placement.

Emergence

Permanency planning emerged nearly two decades ago as a response to the abuses of the child welfare system, especially the inappropriate removal of children from their homes and the recurring problem of drift of children from one home or institution to another. It was soon viewed as a vital means of dealing with the needs of children and youth living away from their own families with little sense of stability or continuity in their living arrangements. In the 1970s, it was widely promoted by the "Oregon

Project," a landmark, federally funded program that demonstrated that children who had been adrift in long-term care could be returned to their biological families or placed in adoption through intensive agency services emphasizing aggressive planning and casework techniques (Pike, 1976).

Permanency planning was subsequently hailed as a popular movement, representing a revolution in child care comparable to the earlier closing down of mass congregate institutions (Fanshel and Shinn, 1978). Whether or not a revolution is in the making, there is no question that the philosophy and methodology of permanency planning have influenced policy and practice. The federal government has enacted the "Adoption Assistance and Child Welfare Act" of 1980 (Public Law 96-272), which mandates that states promote permanency planning for children and youth coming to their attention, through such means as subsidized adoption; requirement of case plans, case reviews, and other procedural reforms; and preventive supportive services to families. Each state in turn has passed legislation or established policies to guide implementation of the federal law; and public as well as private child welfare agencies have been reshaping their programs in accordance with the philosophy of permanency planning and related laws and policies.*

Key Features

As it has evolved in recent years, permanency planning has come to embody the following key features (Maluccio et al., 1986):

- A *philosophy* highlighting the primacy of the biological family and the value of rearing children in a family setting.
- A *theoretical* perspective stressing that stability and continuity of relationships promote a child's growth and functioning.
- A *program* focusing on systematic planning within specified time frames for children who are placed out of their home or at risk of such placement.
- A *case management method* emphasizing practice strategies such as case reviews, contracting, and decision making, along with participation of parents in the helping process.
- Active *collaboration* among various community agencies, child care

---

*For discussion of Public Law 96-272 and corresponding state laws as well as their impact on child welfare and child care agencies, see Hardin (1983); Maluccio et al. (1986); McGowan and Meezan (1983); and Pine (1986).

personnel, lawyers, judges, and others working with children and their parents.

Hierarchy of Options

Implicit in permanency planning philosophy and practice is the following hierarchy of options, in descending order of desirability: (1) maintaining a child with his or her own family; (2) reuniting a child with his or her own family (or relatives) when a temporary placement out of the home cannot be prevented; (3) adoption; and (4) permanent foster family care.

While in theory there is agreement regarding such a hierarchy, in practice it is often difficult to choose the most appropriate plan for a particular child. It should be stressed in this regard that alternatives such as adoption, permanent foster care, or reunification of children with their families are not inherently good or bad for every youngster. In each case there should be careful assessment to determine the best permanent plan for the child. It is particularly in this area that residential care can play a prominent role in permanency planning.

ROLE OF RESIDENTIAL CARE

The permanency planning movement began out of concern primarily for children placed in foster family care; but it has grown to encompass also the needs of children and youth in residential care. The challenge of permanency planning with these youngsters is a demanding one, as they constitute a highly vulnerable group. They tend to be older, have emotional or behavioral problems or other handicaps, have a history of multiple placements, come from disorganized families, or have no home available to them at all.

A key question is whether placement in residential care can be regarded as a permanent plan, and this option is generally seen as a last resort. It is argued that most youngsters can be helped to tolerate and profit from living in some type of family setting, and that a suitable family or family-like setting can be found or created for nearly every child (Maluccio et al., 1986).

Functions of Residential Care

Although its use as a long-term or permanent plan for children and youth is controversial, there is no question that residential child care can be used to promote the goals and values of permanency planning. As seen increasingly in residential centers throughout the country, there are many opportunities for residential care to play a vital role within a permanency planning framework, through functions such as the following:

- Evaluating children and their situations to determine the best permanent plan (Weitzel, 1984).
- Facilitating reunification of children with biological families by means of rehabilitation of children and/or families (Carlo, 1985).
- Providing support services (e.g., respite care; day treatment) to prevent out-of-home placement or help maintain children with their own families or in another family setting.
- Preparing children for placement in adoption or in permanent foster family care and providing postplacement services to foster parents or adoptive parents (Powers and Powell, 1983; Weitzel, 1984).
- Serving as a time-limited option and treatment of choice in certain situations, such as those of teenagers who are moving toward emancipation, or children who are involved in intensely conflictual relationships with their parents.

Barriers to Permanency Planning

Carrying out the above functions in residential care is complicated by a variety of barriers to permanency planning—barriers that may be system-related, worker-related, or case-related (Fein et al., 1983; Miller et al., 1984; Regional Research Institute for Human Services, 1976).

Barriers related to such systems as child welfare agencies, the courts, and schools are complex and multiple. Typical examples include a lack of resources for helping families, legal constraints or delays in obtaining termination of parental rights, and a lack of adoptive homes. Worker-related barriers include biases against biological parents, reluctance or inability to make decisions in complex cases, and lack of experience or training. Examples of case-related barriers are the complexity of a parent's problems, the special needs of a child, and the financial needs of a prospective adoptive family.

Specific barriers to permanency planning in residential treatment include:

- The traditional child focus or orientation of most residential centers, which does not encourage attention to the needs of families in general, and parents in particular.
- Unclear or insufficient commitment to a permanency planning philosophy.

- Budgetary constraints, which result in such consequences as inadequate outreach services to parents or pressure to keep beds full.
- The relationship between the residential center and the referral agency or other community agencies, with inadequate coordination, role conflict and confusion, and disagreement regarding the time or choice of a permanent plan for a child.
- Lack or inadequacy of resources such as adoptive homes or social supports for children and parents in the community, which complicates efforts to reunify the child with the biological family or place the child in adoption, and at times leads to the undoing of gains made by the child during residential treatment.
- The complexity of moving children through the legal system, including difficulty in obtaining termination of parental rights.
- Differences in perspectives, expectations, and values among staff members, which can create confusion or delays in selection and implementation of permanent plans.
- Bureaucratic requirements for paperwork and accountability, which at times place excessive or inappropriate demands on staff members' time and energies.
- Bias of practitioners against certain features of permanency planning methods and programs, such as, reluctance to maintain the kinds of records that are required for documentation in court, concern about the confrontation with a parent that a service agreement may necessitate, and discomfort with case reviews or other monitoring procedures.

As this selective listing of typical barriers suggests, implementing permanency planning in a residential center, as in many other settings, presents staff, administration, and boards with numerous challenges. Various guidelines are available, however, for overcoming barriers such as those noted above, promoting permanency planning, and thus enhancing the contribution of residential care to children and families.

GUIDELINES FOR PROMOTING PERMANENCY PLANNING

Adoption of a Permanency Planning Philosophy

The most crucial early step is for members of the board, administration, and staff of residential centers "to adopt wholeheartedly a permanency planning philosophy" (Maluccio et al., 1982: 105). In settings where permanency planning is a new approach, this is a painful but essential process (Maluccio et al., 1982):

> Exchanging a "going" philosophy for a new one is inherently difficult. There is always resistence to the new and unknown, the process of introducing procedures to implement changes may be unsettling, and the cost of staff re-training may be substantial. In addition, coping with staff anxieties is a formidable task; these anxieties may be not only about dealing with a new philosophy but may also have to do with the impact of separation and loss when the plan is to move children out as quickly as possible. While these difficulties are real, it is essential to introduce changes that can enhance the effectiveness of services provided for children and their families, (p. 105).

Among the changes that can promote permanency planning are: creation of a manual spelling out policies and procedures to be followed from intake to aftercare; formulation of a policy statement that unequivocally reflects the center's mission in relation to permanency planning; introduction of an ongoing staff development program focused on the philosophy, theory, and methodology of permanency planning; and clarification of the roles of administration, board, and staff at all levels.

The point about role clarification should be elaborated. The success of a comprehensive approach to permanency planning depends on the commitment of all involved with the center and their mutual support of each other's efforts. Board members, for instance, can offer leadership in such areas as child advocacy, changes in public policy, linkages with other community systems, and mobilization of community resources on behalf of children and families.

It should also be stressed that attitudinal changes on the part of staff, board, and administration are often required to implement a permanency planning philosophy. Above all, there may be a need to examine biases against biological parents, which are common in child welfare programs, policies, and practice (Knitzer and Allen, 1978). It is important to regard parents as resources in their own behalf, as partners in the helping process rather than simply carriers of pathology. As we shift away from a pathological view of parents, we are better able to identify strengths in parents themselves and to involve them in growth-producing activities. As they are given adequate opportunities, parents and other family members can mobilize their own potentialities and adaptive strivings, and contribute to permanency planning for their children.

Finally, changes in attitude must be accompanied by strong support of staff by administrators and board members. Permanency planning work can be satisfying, but it also involves frustrations and dissatisfactions that often lead to burnout. Administrators need to "deal with the loss of energy, purpose, and enthusiasm that can be experienced by staff over a period of time as a result of a variety of causes: client overload, insufficient training, too many things to do in too little time, low pay, unchanging clients, and bureaucratic constraints" (Maluccio et al., 1986: 286). Administrative and other supports are essential and can be provided through such means as "training, adequate time for job performance, manageable caseloads, peer support groups, and opportunity to deal with personal feelings" (Maluccio et al., 1986: 286).

Adoption of a Family-Centered Orientation

A key feature of the permanency planning philosophy is a family-centered orientation to service delivery. In response to contemporary needs, children's centers are increasingly shifting from their historical child focus to a family focus. For example, residential programs are being reshaped to turn the center into a "living laboratory for family members" (Carlo, 1985).

Whittaker (1979, 1981), Finkelstein (1981), and others have written extensively about the shift toward a family orientation. In particular, they have described programs designed to change the residential treatment center into a comprehensive resource for parents. In these programs, the staff recognizes the importance of parents to the child as well as the parents' own needs, and mobilizes agency and community resources on behalf of parents and the family as a whole.

There has been progress in the direction envisioned by these authors. As noted by LeCroy (1984: 89), "perhaps the most significant recent change in residential treatment services is an increased commitment toward parent involvement." Group child care centers and other foster care agencies are increasingly involving parents in the therapeutic process as well as the child care program in general, through a variety of innovative approaches (Blumenthal and Weinberg, 1984; Bryce and Lloyd, 1981; LeCroy, 1984; Maluccio and Sinanoglu, 1981). As discussed below, an explicit shift to a family-centered orientation can help in various ways to enrich the contribution of residential centers to permanency planning.

Maximizing Parental Involvement. By regarding the family as the central unit of service or focus of attention, staff members are likely to maximize the involvement of parents in the helping process and the overall treatment program. This is very important for permanency planning because the family has the potential for providing resources throughout the life cycle, especially as its members are sustained and supported by community services.

As various projects have demonstrated, many parents can be rehabilitated and helped to plan responsibly for their children, through provision of comprehensive help involving both counseling and support services; emphasis on skill training and systematic case management based on principles of decision making; goal setting and contracting (see Bryce and Lloyd, 1981; Kaplan, 1986; Maluccio and Sinanoglu, 1981; Stein et al., 1978).

It has been shown that, even in situations in which children cannot be returned home, parents can be helped to participate in the planning process in a way that reflects their caring, helps maintain their dignity, and frees the child to move into another family (Jackson and Dunne, 1981). A common denominator in these programs is that parents are regarded as human beings with feelings and needs of their own, instead of being approached primarily in relation to what they may offer or mean to the child.

Preserving Family Ties. The family-centered orientation underscores the challenge of preserving family ties as much as possible. The natural bonds between children in care and their parents continue to be prominent, for parents as well as children, long after they are physically separated, reflecting the significance of the biological family in human connectedness and identity (Jenkins, 1981; Laird, 1979). Staff members of residential centers should regard the goal of preserving family ties as a major imperative of residential treatment.

A key means of accomplishing preservation of family ties is parental visiting of children in placement. The findings of various studies have highlighted the crucial role played by parent–child contact or parental visitation in the outcome of the placement as well as the child's functioning and development. For instance, research has demonstrated the importance of parental visiting of children in foster care as the best single predictor of the outcome of placement; in their longitudinal study of foster care, Fanshel and Shinn (1978) found that children who were visited frequently by their parents during the first year of placement "were almost twice as likely to be discharged eventually as those not visited at all or only minimally" (p. 96).

Of course, these findings only show correlations, and it may be that those children whose families seem most promising are the ones whose parents are encouraged most by professionals to be involved with the child. Further research is needed to demonstrate convincingly that visitation plays a causal role in the outcome of the placement; but, in the meantime, we should assume that it plays at least some role and promote such visitation.

In line with these findings, researchers have stressed the importance of encouraging and monitoring visiting: "agencies should be held accountable for efforts made to involve the parents in more responsible visitation" (Fanshel and Shinn, 1978: 111). Practice guidelines have also been formulated for encouraging staff members to arrange visits; using parent–child visiting as a means of achieving permanency planning; and coping with the negative aspects of parental visiting, such as children getting more upset before or after a visit (White, 1981).

As noted by Aldgate (1980), parent–child contact can have various beneficial results, such as, assuring the child that he or she has not been rejected; helping the child to understand why he or she cannot live at home; preventing the child's idealization of the parent; and helping parents maintain their relationship with their children. Others have called attention to a neglected dimension: the significance of sibling relationships and the importance of maintaining sibling ties while children are in placement (Ward, 1984).

Involving Parents in Decision Making. This family focus leads to emphasis on the participation of parents in decision making about issues involving their children. These issues range from everyday matters to complex decisions, including choosing and implementing a permanent plan for the child. Methods for working directly with parents are beyond the scope of this chapter, and are covered elsewhere in this book. In addition, specific principles and techniques for promoting parents' involvement in decision making and goal planning for their children are discussed by Blumenthal and Weinberg (1984), Hoejsi et al., (1981), Kaplan (1986), Maluccio et al., (1986), and Stein and Rzepnicki (1983).

One strategy that should be stressed here is use of the service agreement or contract with parents (Stein and Rzepnicki, 1983). The service agreement can be an effective means of involving parents, increasing their sense of control over their lives, and monitoring their progress as well as the efficacy of professional intervention. It can help staff and parents to determine when sufficient efforts have been made, or when the parents have gone as far as they can. Through active, therapeutic use of the service agreement, practitioners and parents can not only establish treatment goals but also consider concretely when goals have been accomplished, when there is reason to renegotiate new or additional goals, and when it is time to stop because the parents have demonstrated that they are unable to effect change or make use of the service.

Following a Decision-Making Framework

The preceding discussion of parental involvement indicates the importance of deliberately following a decision-making framework in permanency planning. Decision making "consists of the process of actively and deliberately making choices among alternative options by following specific steps and procedures, so as to lead to a permanent plan for a child" (Maluccio et al., 1986: 11).

Decision making about crucial issues, particularly the timing and choice of a permanent plan, is complex and demanding. In most case situations, choices are not clear-cut, and alternatives are not readily available. Guidelines for choosing a permanent plan have been delineated elsewhere (Janchill, 1981; Maluccio et al., 1986; Pike et al., 1977; and Stein and Rzepnicki, 1983). The following factors, in particular, should be considered: the child's age and developmental needs, parental resources and potentialities, previous placement experiences, and legal status. In addition, particularly with older children and youth in residential care, the youngster's perceptions and preferences regarding a permanent plan should be carefully considered.

The above factors also influence the time frame for making permanency planning decisions after a child enters residential care. Although idiosyncratic factors such as the child's age should be taken into account, a permanent plan for each youngster should be made within a maximum period of eighteen months in residential care or other placement. This assertion is based on research indicating that unless a child is discharged from out-of-home care within eighteen months, he or she is likely to remain in placement indefinitely (Fanshel and Shinn, 1978). For this reason Public Law 96–272 mandates a double review system for every child in out-of-home care: (1) a *case review every six months*, to monitor the need and appropriateness of the placement, examine the progress being made, and establish a likely date for the child's return home or another permanent plan; and (2) a *dispositional hearing* by a court or its sanctioned agent within eighteen months of placement, to determine the most appropriate permanent plan and the services required to accomplish it.

As with the choice and timing of a permanent plan, it is often difficult to reach decisions regarding the extent, nature, and duration of parental involvement. In some situations, continuing parental involvement is inappropriate. Many parents can be sufficiently rehabilitated to be able to maintain, sustain, or resume care of their children, or they can be helped to accept their inability to do so and participate in making an alternate permanent plan; but there are also parents who are not able to respond or who cannot be helped toward rehabilitation.

In many of these cases, practitioners must ask: How can we manage to help the family overcome its difficulties within a time scale that does not damage the child? How far do we go in trying to help the parents? When should we move decisively to make another plan for the child? When is it time to give up, and seek termination of parental rights? Although there are no precise prescriptions, workers should consider certain factors in resolving these questions (Maluccio et al., 1986):

- *Age of child*: In general, the younger the child, the more quickly a decision about a permanent plan needs to be made, to facilitate the child's bonding with parental figures.
- *Time*: A parent's potential for rehabilitation "over time" is not enough. There must be an ability to rehabilitate within a "reasonable length of time," as determined on the basis of careful assessment of the child's needs, sense of time, and interests.
- *Previous efforts at rehabilitation*: When comprehensive and good quality services have been provided for a sustained period with no indication of progress, the value of additional efforts should be questioned.
- *Chronicity of problems*: When the family's history reflects no stable time, and dysfunction has been a "way of life," we can have little optimism about its potential for positive change. This is especially so when there is an established pattern of child abuse or neglect, or an extensive history of incapacitating drug addiction.
- *Parents' investment*: When parents are unwilling to participate in rehabilitative efforts despite energetic, repeated, varied, creative attempts to enlist their participation, reunification of the child with his or her family is questionable.

In view of the complexities and pressures affecting decision making in permanency planning, the process must involve a team approach. Permanency planning is not a solitary or individual undertaking. As the following sections on case management and interagency collaboration show, it involves many persons, agencies, and systems. The team approach is a cornerstone of permanency planning work.

Case Management Strategies

Permanency planning requires consistent and systematic attention to the needs of the child and his or her family, prompt and deliberate decision making, careful monitoring and follow-through on decisions and plans, and avoiding the risk of having the child fall between the cracks of the service delivery system. Certain case management strategies have proved valuable in this context.

Team Approach. Because of the complexities and pressures inherent in these cases, it is important to have staff members of the residential center and service providers from other agencies adopt a team approach. Permanency planning is facilitated as staff and others function as a team, pooling their resources and expertise to help children and their families.

Although team participation may increase the cost of service provision, the ultimate cost-effectiveness of this approach makes it worthwhile. In addition, given the complex decisions to be made and the range of services often required, collaboration among professionals with different training, perspectives, knowledge, and skills is essential in most case situations. In residential treatment settings, child care workers, in particular, play a role in permanency planning that deserves to be recognized; for instance, child care workers can help the team to appreciate a child's needs, determine the child's readiness for alternatives being considered, and prepare him or her for the chosen plan.

The functions of the team include: clarifying goals, plans, and tasks in a particular case; providing consultation to key staff working with children and parents on such matters as formulation of a service contract; evaluating the case's progress and outcome; and dealing with conflict among collaborators.

Case Manager. The appointment of a case manager, who plays a leadership role in each case, contributes to the success of permanency planning activities. The case manager may be a staff member of the residential center or, more typically, someone from a collaborating agency, such as the public child welfare agency legally responsible for the child's care. When someone from the outside serves as the official case manager, it is also useful to appoint a member of the center's staff to coordinate the center's activities in a given case.

The case manager has overall responsibility for coordinating and monitoring permanency planning efforts and ensuring that everyone is working on one focused plan. His or her specific tasks may include (Maluccio et al., 1986):

- Ensuring that a decision is made regarding a permanent plan, and that the child and family are involved in the decision-making process.
- Clarifying and negotiating respective roles and tasks of different service providers.
- Monitoring the implementation of roles and tasks by service providers.
- Planning case reviews, including those that are mandated by federal and state regulations.
- Identifying gaps or breakdowns in service delivery.
- Mediating between the clients and service providers and advocating on behalf of clients.

Goal-Oriented Recording and Checklists. Other case management strategies include the use of goal-oriented records and checklists. Goal-oriented records are useful in documenting client and staff activities, monitoring progress, and enforcing decision making. Checklists can help ensure timely completion of agreed-upon tasks. Checklists and goal-oriented recording forms and procedures have been extensively described and illustrated (Maluccio et al., 1986; Stein and Rzepnicki, 1983).

Permanency Planning Consultant. Some agencies have found it useful to designate as the permanency planning consultant a staff member who is especially interested in this area of practice. The selected staff member has, or acquires, expertise on permanency planning, and offers consultation, training, and support to center staff.

Interagency Collaboration

Interagency collaboration is an essential ingredient in permanency planning. For most children and youth in residential care, the process of formulating and implementing a permanent plan involves a range of social agencies, formal and informal helping systems, and other community organizations. Much effort is needed to create a climate that facilitates coordination and collaboration among child welfare personnel, mental health personnel, lawyers, judges, educators, and others working with the children and their parents.

To promote collaboration and help overcome barriers to permanency planning, residential centers can consider strategies such as forming a consortium with other agencies to facilitate continuity of care, provision of services, and creation of needed resources; establishment of linkages with family service agencies, child guidance clinics, child welfare agencies, adoption programs, and other systems, to help maximize the use of residential care facilities by families; forming a partnership with public child welfare agencies, which are responsible for the care and treatment of the overwhelming majority of children in out-of-home care or at risk of such placement; and participation with other community systems and organizations in child advocacy activities.

Aftercare Services

Finally, to promote permanency planning, residential centers must provide services to help maintain the permanent plan made for a child or youth. In conjunction with other resources in the community, staff members of residential centers can contribute immeasurably to maintenance of a permanent plan by continuing to work with the child and his or her biological parents or other caretakers.

For such reasons as limited resources, aftercare services have long been neglected in child welfare practice, even though various studies have shown that continued professional and community supports are necessary to sustain the gains made by children and youth during residential treatment (Taylor and Alpert, 1973). Moreover, many biological families need basic services in the aftercare period—services such as housing, employment, financial assistance, recreation, and counseling. A prominent role for residential centers, then, is to connect parents and children with needed community agencies and resources, and to monitor the provision of services once the child returns to the family or is placed in adoption or with another permanent family. In short, aftercare services constitute an indispensable link in the continuum of child, youth, and family services that promote permanency planning.

CONCLUSION

Permanency planning means a deliberate commitment to keep or reunite children and youth with their families, or to place them with alternate permanent families if necessary. In line with this commitment, residential care can play a significant role by providing varied services and supports to an especially vulnerable group of youngsters and their families. Staff, administration, and board members of residential centers will experience an enduring sense of accomplishment as they help make permanency planning a reality for the children and youth in their care.

REFERENCES

Aldgate, J. (1980). Identification of factors influencing children's length of stay in care. In J. Triseliotis, ed., *New Developments in Foster Care and Adoption.* London and Boston: Routledge and Kegan Paul, pp. 22–40.

Blumenthal, K. and Weinberg, A., eds. (1984). *Establishing Parental Involvement in Foster Care Agencies.* New York: Child Welfare League of America.

Bryce, M. and Lloyd, C., eds. (1981). *Treating Families in the Home—An Alternative to Placement.* Springfield, Ill.: Charles C. Thomas.

Carlo, P. (1985). The children's residential treatment center as living laboratory for family members: a Review of the literature and its implications for practice. *Child Care Quarterly, 14,* 156–170.

Fanshel, D. and Shinn, E. B. (1978). *Children in Foster Care—A Longitudinal Investigation.* New York: Columbia University Press.

Fein, E., Maluccio, A. N., Hamilton, V. J., and Ward, D. (1983). After foster care: outcomes of permanency planning for children. *Child Welfare, 62,* 485–558

Finkelstein, N. E. (1981). Family-centered group care—the children's institution, from a living center to a center for change. In A. N. Maluccio and P. A. Sinanoglu, eds., *The Challenge of Partnership: Working with Parents of Children in Foster Care*. New York: Child Welfare League of America, pp. 89–105.

Hardin, M., ed., (1983). *Foster Children in the Courts*. Boston: Butterworth Legal Publishers.

Horejsi, C. R., Bertsche, A. V., and Clark, F. W. (1981). *Social Work Practice with Parents of Children in Foster Care: A Handbook*. Springfield, Ill.: Charles C. Thomas.

Jackson, A. D. and Dunne, M. J. (1981). Permanency planning in foster care with the ambivalent parent. In A. N. Maluccio and P. A. Sinanoglu, eds., *The Challenge of Partnership: Working with Parents of Children in Foster Care*. New York: Child Welfare League of America, pp. 151–164.

Janchill, M. P. (1981). *Guidelines to Decision Making in Child Welfare*. New York: Human Services Workshops.

Jenkins, S. (1981). The tie that binds. In A. N. Maluccio and P. A. Sinanoglu, eds., *The Challenge of Partnership: Working with Parents of Children in Foster Care*. New York: Child Welfare League of America, pp. 39–51.

Kaplan, L. (1986). *Working with Multiproblem Families*. Lexington, Mass.: D. C. Heath.

Knitzer, L. and Allen, M. L. (1978). *Children without Homes*. Washington, D.C.: Children's Defense Fund.

Laird, J. (1979). An ecological approach to child welfare: issues of family identity and continuity. In C. B. Germain, ed., *Social Work Practice: People and Environments*. New York: Columbia University Press, pp. 174–209.

LeCroy, C. W. (1984). Residential treatment services: a review of some current trends. *Child Care Quarterly, 13*, 83–97.

Maluccio, A. N., and Sinanoglu, P. A., eds. (1981). *The Challenge of Partnership: Working with Parents of Children in Foster Care*. New York: Child Welfare League of America.

Maluccio, A. N., Fein, E., Hamilton, J., Sutton, M., and Ward, D. (1982). Permanency planning and residential child care. *Child Care Quarterly, 11*, 92–107.

Maluccio, A. N., Fein, E., and Olmstead, K. A. (1986). *Permanency Planning for Children—Concepts and Methods*. New York and London: Tavistock Publications.

McGowan, B. G. and Meezan, W., eds. (1983). *Child Welfare: Current Dilemmas—Future Directions*. Itasca, Ill.: F. E. Peacock Publishers.

Miller, K., Fein, E., Bishop, G., Stilwell, N., and Murray, C. (1984). Overcoming barriers to permanency planning. *Child Welfare, 63*, 45–55.

Pike, V. (1976). Permanent planning for foster children: the Oregon Project. *Children Today, 5*, 22–25, 41.

Pike, V., Downs, S., Emlen, A., Downs, G., and Case, D. (1977). *Permanent Planning for Children in Foster Care: A Handbook for Social Workers*. Washington, D.C.: U.S. Department of Health, Education and Welfare, Publication No. (OHDS) 78-30124.

Pine, B. A. (1986). Child welfare reform and the political process. *Social Service Review, 60*, 339–359.

Powers, D. and Powell, J. (1983). A role for residential treatment in preparation of adoption. *Residential Group Care and Treatment, 2,* 31–44.

Regional Research Institute for Human Services (1976). *Barriers to Planning for Children in Foster Care.* Portland, Oreg.: Regional Research Institute for Human Services, Portland State University.

Stein, J., Gambrill, E. D., and Wiltse, K. T. (1978). *Children in Foster Homes— Achieving Continuity of Care.* New York: Praeger Publishers.

Stein, T. J. and Rzepnicki, T. (1983). *Decision Making at Child Welfare Intake.* New York: Child Welfare League of America.

Taylor, D. A. and Alpert, S. (1973). *Continuity and Support Following Residential Treatment.* New York: Child Welfare League of America.

Ward, M. (1984). Sibling ties in foster care. *Child Welfare, 63,* 321–332.

Weitzel, W. J. (1984). From residential treatment to adoption: a permanency planning service. *Child Welfare, 63,* 361–365.

White M. (1981). Promoting Parent-child visiting in foster care: continuing involvement within a permanency planning framework. In P. A. Sinanoglu and A. N. Maluccio, eds., *Parents of Children in Placement: Perspectives and Programs.* New York: Child Welfare League of America, pp. 461–75.

Whittaker, J. K. (1979). *Caring for Troubled Children: Residential Treatment in a Community Context.* San Francisco: Jossey-Bass.

Whittaker, J. K. (1981). Family involvement in residential treatment: a support system for parents. In A. N. Maluccio and P. A. Sinanoglu, eds., *The Challenge of Partnership: Working with Parents of Children in Foster Care.* New York: Child Welfare League of America, pp. 67–88.

12

Quality Assurance

Peter H. Cormack

Providers of human services are being held increasingly accountable for their actions. This accountability is to patients and their families, to the communities where service delivery facilities are located, to organizations that finance health care and related services, and to the larger society. A variety of psychological, sociocultural, and economic factors have converged to produce this situation in the current service delivery milieu. Among these influences are the increasing political conservatism of the post-Watergate era, increasing concerns about the fate of fundamental human rights in the face of the needs of large bureaucracies, the increasing emphasis on tort law within the judicial system, and needs to control costs that escalate faster than inflation rates.

In the field of mental health care, there has been accountability to professional organizations, governmental bodies, and other standard-setting groups for many years, although standards have been minimal, at times conflicting, and based on a set of assumptions that many find unacceptable in light of current realities. Initial attempts at standard setting focused on physical plant safety and staff qualifications, the assumption being that if the setting is safe and the staff qualified, then good-quality care will ensue. This type of thinking emanated from governmental agencies and from the early efforts of the Joint Commission on Accreditation of Hospitals, and was aimed at upgrading the care given in large mental hospitals. Indeed, the setting of standards in these areas was a necessary first step in an evolving process of upgrading the quality of care, and it contributed to a trend of increasing professionalization of service delivery.

The establishment of training standards for mental health professionals was the next step, with the American Association of Psychiatric Clinics for Children providing leadership in the area of children's mental health services through accreditation of agencies as service delivery units and as training sites. This remains an active area, with recent trends being for professional associations to set standards for service providers, to establish credentialing processes and procedures, and to upgrade the effectiveness of their efforts at ensuring that members of their discipline practice within established professional guidelines. Professional psychologists have been particularly active in this arena. Specialty boards have been established, definitions of service providers have been developed, and directories of practitioners who meet published standards have been produced. The duties and responsibilities of licensing bodies and ethics committees have also been more clearly defined and, in many cases, expanded. Similar trends are occurring in the social work profession and, to a more limited extent, in the child care field. These developments parallel those in organized medicine, particularly in psychiatry and child psychiatry in the 1940s and 1950s.

The early 1970s saw a reevaluation of concepts of accountability in mental health services, particularly child services, as became evident when the Joint Commission on Accreditation of Hospitals published the first edition of the *Consolidated Standards for Child, Adolescent, and Adult Psychiatric, Alcoholism and Drug Abuse Facilities* in 1979. Implicit in this document was the concept that having a qualified staff working in a safe environment was no longer enough. It now became necessary also to define the processes and procedures through which service was delivered, the policies governing service delivery, and the roles that various practitioners play in the treatment process. The standards also required that everything be in writing to ensure a common understanding. Apparently it was again assumed that the process of making policies and procedures explicit would contribute to an increase in the quality of service delivered. A trust in the capacity of service providers to consistently adhere to written policies was also implicit. Subsequent editions of the consolidated standards have paralleled developments in the thinking of other standard-setting bodies, and have moved in the direction of assuming less and less about what will happen if certain conditions are present, instead requiring ongoing analysis and evaluation of what is occurring, how it is occurring, who is providing service, and the impact of services on recipients. A "penetration model" is also implicit in child mental health service standards, with agencies and/or programs being held accountable for a patient's overall welfare in direct proportion to the amount of control they exert over the patient's life. Day treatment programs are more accountable than outpatient services, but less so than a residential treatment program. In recent years, efforts at accountability have been called quality assurance, with an entire subspecialty evolving within the mental health system. Standard-setting bodies require that quality assurance activities occur, and bodies that fund programs specify that a specific staff member be designated to look after and report on quality assurance activities. The Residential Treatment Facilities Program of the New York State Office of Mental Health is an example of this emerging trend.

It is likely that these trends will continue, and that demands for more thoroughly ensuring and documenting the quality of services delivered to emotionally disturbed patients will continue. The American Association of Psychiatric Services for Children, formerly the American Association of Psychiatric Clinics for Children, is again providing leadership in this area. The association recently (1985) published standards that attempt to increase the breadth and depth of quality assurance activities through requiring that treatment programs increase their conceptual clarity and sophistication.

Quality assurance activities, as presently conceptualized by the Joint Commission on Accreditation of Hospitals and other standard-setting bodies, have abandoned the assumptions that were characteristic of earlier approaches. In their place are requirements for extensive documentation in a variety of areas, including requirements for ongoing monitoring and evaluation of current program processes, staff functioning, and the state of the service delivery milieu. Services must be matched to patients, with quality and appropriateness of service being the unifying concepts.

The establishment of a quality assurance program within the context of a residential treatment center presents unique challenges. Some of these are common to establishing a quality assurance program in any mental health treatment facility, and some are peculiar to residential treatment. The initial issue involves achieving an understanding of the nature of quality and developing some operational definitions of the concept. The next steps are solution of the measurement problems involved in assessing quality and development of procedures and processes for gleaning data from these measurements that reflect on quality issues. The final steps include the development of methodologies for monitoring the overall effectiveness of the quality assurance program.

The question of what constitutes quality is a thorny one that can lead program planners into a thicket of problems. Equating quality with a favorable outcome makes the definitional process unnecessarily complex. It also misses the essential nature of program quality, namely, that a quality program is one that is targeted at a particular patient group, has a clearly delineated method of operation, and operates consistently within its defined parameters. The definition of quality for a residential treatment program thus lies in the policies and procedures manual of the program. The remainder of this discussion will extend the discussion of the elements of a quality program and present an approach to how they can be woven together into an integrated quality assurance program for a residential treatment center.

A quality assurance program must have at least four discrete elements along with some kind of administrative structure to tie them together. These elements include: quality and appropriateness standards aimed at what is being done and how it is being accomplished; utilization review procedures to assure that service is targeted at a defined population with a defined need; staff credentialing, privileging, and reprivileging procedures to assure that staff providing service are adequately prepared for their work, and that they maintain their competancies at an acceptable level; and p.)cedures aimed at ensuring the integrity of the treatment milieu in the areas of safety, infection control, housekeeping, maintenance, sanitation, and the like. The procedures in each of these areas must address what is actually occurring, have the capability of identifying potential problems, and have the capacity for following problems through from identification to resolution.

QUALITY AND APPROPRIATENESS STANDARDS

These standards define what should occur if service is being delivered as intended in the residential treatment program. They cover each program area and are stated in terms of expected performance. Some examples include: "Children will attend at least 90% of scheduled psychotherapy appointments," "Patients will demonstrate at least one year of academic growth for each calendar year in the school program," "Patients will participate in 90% of planned milieu activities," and "Parents will keep at least 90% of scheduled visits with patients." Using this format, we can develop any number of explicit statements detailing what should happen so that the areas where standards are established, time frames, and/or frequencies adopted reflect the clinical judgment of the treatment staff. In a residential treatment program, standards should pertain to cottage life, the school experience, specific treatment experiences such as psychotherapy, work with parents and/or collaterals, and the administrative processes and procedures that tie the program together and integrate it into a meaningful whole. These standards then serve as markers or red flags for potential problems. Records are maintained tabulating which cases are in compliance with the various standards and which are not. The cases that do not comply can be further reviewed to determine why the pattern of service delivery in individual cases is at variance with expectations, whether the variance is justified by clinical realities, and whether any significant service delivery system problems exist. This same mechanism allows evaluation of the total service delivery system or subsets of it through examination of program performance in relation to specific standards.

UTILIZATION REVIEW PROCEDURES

Residential treatment programs should continually review patients, using specific criteria for the appropriateness of admission to the program and the appropriateness of continuation in it. These criteria should weigh both evidence of significant emotional disturbance and evidence of the capacity to benefit from the therapeutic experiences offered. The reviews should be completed by individuals not directly involved in delivering service to the patients, and organized in such a way as to distinguish patients whose status requires intense, in-depth evaluation from those whose issues are clear-cut. Inevitably, there will be times when the clinical needs of the patient do not dovetail with the ability of either more or less intensive treatment facilities in the patient's community to receive the patients; the utilization review system must account for these times so that continuity of the therapeutic experience is assured. Patient need, rather than institutional or other needs, should drive not only the utilization review program but all quality assurance activities.

PROGRAM STAFF AND QUALITY ASSURANCE

The quality of any residential treatment program hinges on the quality of the staff who deliver service to patients. This group includes the traditional mental health professionals (child psychiatry, clinical child psychology, and clinical social work) as well as various types of special educators, psychiatric nurses, child care workers, and other support staff. Particularly crucial are the knowledge base that staff members bring, their skills in developing and utilizing therapeutic relationships with disturbed patients, their ability to continue to grow and develop as caregivers, and the clarity with which roles and functions of each person serving a child are defined.

The quality assurance issues here are several, and each needs to be addressed individually. They include: development of an understanding of the kinds of people necessary to carry out the mission of the residential treatment program; defining roles, functions, and degree of supervision and/or autonomy for each staff member; defining procedures and processes of staff orientation to their jobs; selecting and defining methods for monitoring and evaluating each staff member's ongoing performance; and defining ways that allow staff to function with increasing degrees of independence as their skills and training permit.

Each of the staff-related issues noted above must be dealt with directly through organizational processes that seek to unite people with diverse backgrounds and training into a common effort. The administrative processes of any residential treatment program or, for that matter, any child mental health facility may be seen as efforts to translate concepts of quality care into a method of doing business. Quality assurance is the monitoring process that provides ongoing information about whether what is supposed to happen actually does occur on a continuing basis. When what has been mandated occurs, programmatic definitions of quality have been realized. When what was mandated does not occur, the lack of success may reflect diminished quality, previously unrecognized needs, processes and procedures in need of revision, or other problems. Failure to meet a standard means that it is time for program planners to rethink and reevaluate procedures, and does not necessarily indicate a deficit.

In terms of credentialing, there must be processes for determining what kinds of "treatments" individual staff members may administer, and what sort of evaluations they may conduct. For persons who are professionals in disciplines other than mental health (e.g., special education), who work in areas lacking national standards and full professionalization (e.g., child care work or sociotherapy), or who are program support personnel (e.g., housekeeping, dietary, maintenance, etc.), what they can and cannot do vis-à-vis patients, and under what circumstances they can act (e.g., only with ongoing supervision), must be clearly delineated in job descriptions, definitions of career ladders, and so forth.

The process of peer review of staff performance, and the subsequent granting or withholding of practice privileges, is a complex one. It is further complicated by the realization that peer reviewers may carry a legal responsibility and liability for their decisions, particularly if what is decided has an adverse impact on the professional or economic well-being of the individual whose performance is evaluated. A jury in the State of Oregon awarded triple damages of $2.4 million to a surgeon whose clinical privileges at a local hospital were revoked by peer reviewers. This case, known as *Patrick* v. *Burgitt,* is currently in the appeal process, with one major issue in the appeal being whether or not peer reviewers enjoy immunity from prosecution in legal matters arising from their decisions. Although other cases (e.g., *Marrese* v. *Interqual, Inc.* and *Doe* v. *St. Joseph's Hospital*) have affirmed peer reviewer immunity, it appears to remain a live issue, and one that any residential treatment program that develops a peer review system should be aware of when establishing policies and procedures.

Processes of supervision and staff development also relate to program quality and require monitoring and periodic review. Residential treatment requires meticulous attention to detail to ensure that the residential treatment center becomes and remains a psychologically safe arena where patients can confront the sources of their distress and develop adaptive ways of meeting life's challenges. Staff supervision is often a major vehicle for keeping divergent threads tied together in a coherent, consistent treatment effort. Supervision systems should be created for each professional and paraprofessional discipline. These systems should have the capacity to deal with both clinical and administrative issues, tying the two together when the occasion demands. These systems should also complement a program of ongoing educational experiences that help ensure that staff remain well-grounded in the basic conceptual framework of the treatment program, as well as keep abreast of current developments in the field. A quality program cannot exist without these elements, as they stimulate and nurture staff needs for growth and development while bringing in new ideas and different ways of thinking about problems. The quality assurance program should keep track of whether or not these events occur as anticipated, and monitor their contribution to the overall program.

THE TREATMENT MILIEU

In a residential treatment center, environmental messages are twenty-four-hour-a-day ones. They communicate a wealth of information to patients about their physical and emotional safety, their perceived worth and value, and the program's sense of its own worth and value. The quality assurance issues here are numerous, and relate to the monitoring of a program's efforts to use the physical plant as a treatment tool.

Residential treatment centers are required by statute, regulation, and accreditation standards to maintain their physical plants in specified ways and to monitor whether this maintenance is occurring on a regular basis. The current (1985) edition of the Joint Commission on Accreditation of Hospitals *Consolidated Standards* manual has standards for these areas listed under the titles "Therapeutic Environment," "Infection Control," "Housekeeping Services," "Functional Safety," and "Sanitation & Building and Grounds Safety." The quality assurance program should monitor compliance with the relevant standards in each of these areas and make the results of these activities available for review, along with other types of quality of care-related information. The Joint Commission on Accreditation of Hospitals standards were employed to illustrate the specific areas that must be addressed, largely because these standards have become prototypical and are quite similar to those of other standard-setting bodies.

AN ADMINISTRATIVE STRUCTURE FOR
COORDINATING QUALITY ASSURANCE ACTIVITIES

A quality assurance program in a mental health facility, whether it is a freestanding residential treatment program or a series of interrelated programs with differing levels of service intensity, is a set of mechanisms and procedures for monitoring the ongoing clinical and administrative process of the program(s). The role of the quality assurance program is not one of decision making or establishing program direction, but is to help ensure that these events occur in an orderly way, and that necessary details receive attention. The quality assurance program brings to the attention of decision makers things that do not happen as expected. When a service delivery system identifies a problem within itself and deals with the issue, it is noted in a quality assurance report. If the problem is identified and not dealt with, the role of the quality assurance program is to bring this information to decision makers. Quality assurance activities are thus part of a system of checks and balances that helps a system operate at maximum efficiency.

Quality assurance data must flow to a single point to be reviewed, digested, and integrated, so that recommendations can be generated for consideration by decision makers and those who establish policy. The precise mechanisms for accomplishing this vary from program to program, with either a quality assurance committee or a quality assurance office employed in the majority of programs. The manner in which this is accomplished should receive critical attention, as it is important to maintain the concept that quality is the concern of each practitioner even though certain staff have been designated to coordinate responsibility for the quality of care issues.

The remainder of this chapter consists of a quality assurance document, produced by the author and a number of his colleagues, that defines a plan currently in operation in a multi-service child and adolescent mental health facility. This plan was developed to address the issues noted above and contains narrative material, statements of specific standards, and forms for summarizing and reporting data.

CONVALESCENT HOSPITAL FOR CHILDREN
QUALITY ASSURANCE PLAN

INTRODUCTION
The Quality Assurance plan is a set of mechanisms and processes designed to permit ongoing monitoring and periodic, systematic evaluation of the overall operation of Convalescent Hospital for Children and each service delivery unit within the hospital (i.e., Residential Treatment, Day Treatment, Preschool Program, Outpatient Services, and Summer Programs). There are four major areas which are focused upon in this plan. These areas include the following:

SERVICE DELIVERY SYSTEMS
CLINICAL STAFF COMPETENCE
ADEQUACY OF THE PHYSICAL ENVIRONMENT AND TREATMENT MILIEU
PATIENT UTILIZATION REVIEW PROCEDURES

I. *QUALITY ASSURANCE COMMITTEE:*
The primary working group which focuses upon quality assurance issues is the QUALITY ASSURANCE COMMITTEE. This committee meets at least quarterly and is composed of representatives of each service delivery unit and discipline. The data base for the Quality Assurance Committee consists of reports from each specific service delivery unit within the Convalescent Hospital for Children as well as reports detailing various total agency administrative activities. The manner in which quality assurance data are generated is the responsibility of the administrative head of the reporting unit; however, each reporting unit will generate data in predetermined areas. The data are meant to reflect the overall functioning of each service and the activities of the several disciplines and departments. Reports concerning ongoing quality assurance activities are submitted on a monthly basis to the President of the Convalescent Hospital for Children and the Director of Quality Assurance. These reports contain discussions of current performance, trends, quality issues, and steps that have been taken toward resolution. The results of monitoring of steps taken to resolve previously identified problems are also reported.

The overall responsibility of the Quality Assurance Committee is to ensure that ongoing monitoring activities are occurring in a manner consistent with this plan, that the results of these monitoring activities are reviewed on a regularly scheduled basis and to periodically review whether or not the Quality Assurance Plan is realizing its stated objectives.

Specific responsibilities of the individual service delivery units within the context of this plan include the following:

A. Designing methods for carrying out prescribed monitoring activities.
B. Reviewing data collected.
C. Formulating results.
D. Developing recommendations for dealing with identified problems.
E. Consulting with the Chief Executive Officer for the purpose of finalizing methods for dealing with each identified problem.
F. Assessing the impact of implemented recommendations.
G. Reporting of results to the Chief Executive Officer and to the Quality Assurance Committee.
H. Assigning a representative to the Quality Assurance Committee.
I. Each service will develop a written plan describing methods for data generation and methods for monitoring its own activities. This plan must be approved by the President of the Convalescent Hospital for Children prior to its implementation.

Memberships on the Quality Assurance Committee will be based on the following criteria:

A. Each member will have a minimum of two years experience within his or her field.
B. Each member will have been employed at Convalescent Hospital for at least one year.

The QUALITY ASSURANCE COMMITTEE is chaired by the Director of Quality Assurance and is the agency-wide quality assurance body. This committee is composed of representatives from each of the several service delivery units of the hospital. This committee must include a minimum of one representative of each professional discipline included on the hospital staff. The actual work of the Quality Assurance Committee may be accomplished by subcommittees that report to the total committee. The role of these subcommittees is to examine specific issues and make recommendations to the Quality Assurance Committee for consideration. Every twelve months the composition and function of the committee will be reviewed.

Responsibilities of the Quality Assurance Committee include the following:

A. Reviewing monitoring activities, data, results and recommendations of the services.
B. Developing recommendations around issues pertaining to the overall functioning of the hospital and/or specific service delivery units.
C. Reporting recommendations to the Chief Executive Officer of the hospital for action.
D. Developing support systems to assist service delivery units with their responsibilities.
E. Reviewing the Quality Assurance Plan in terms of its effectiveness.

Responsibilities of the Chief Executive Officer/Administrative Council shall include:

A. Review of each recommendation of the QUALITY ASSURANCE COMMITTEE.
B. Advising the QUALITY ASSURANCE COMMITTEE on:
    1. the action taken on each recommendation,
    2. the subsequent impact of that action
C. Reporting on Quality Assurance activities to the governing body or Board of Directors.

II. *MAJOR QUALITY ASSURANCE AREAS:*
There are four major areas upon which this plan focuses:

- SERVICE DELIVERY SYSTEMS
- CLINICAL STAFF COMPETENCE
- ADEQUACY OF THE PHYSICAL ENVIRONMENT AND TREATMENT MILIEU
- PATIENT UTILIZATION REVIEW PROCEDURES

This section of the plan will discuss each of these areas individually:

A. *Service Delivery Systems:*

Each service delivery unit exists to provide patients with the type of services they need in a timely and efficient manner. Each service delivery unit is required to insure that this occurs within its programs by establishing checkpoints in its procedures that enable them to collect the needed data to document that patients are receiving the services they need.

Seven areas have been identified where each service delivery system shall generate data and report on its findings. These include:

1. Case assignments.
2. Review of impact of delivered services.
3. Completeness and thoroughness of documentation.
4. Review of impact of other related service delivery systems on patient care.
5. Review of unusual events including untoward incidents, accidents/injuries, restraint and premature termination (child discharged by the program although discharge goals are not met) and/or unplanned termination (child withdrawn by the parent or another source).
6. Review of appropriateness of patient placement and continuation.
7. Review of unmet needs for service.

Each service delivery unit maintains statistics, and guidelines have been developed that define relevant data centers and interpretive standards concerning those centers. On a monthly basis each service delivery unit reports on these seven areas to both the President of the Convalescent Hospital for Children and the Director of Quality Assurance. These reports detail current performance trends and quality issues. They contain statistical data that documents the conclusions offered and provide documentation concerning actions taken around identified problems and the impact of those actions. These reports are presented on the "Quality and Appropriateness of Services Data Summary Form."

B. *Clinical Staff Competence:*

A carefully selected, thoroughly trained and effectively supervised staff are crucial to each service delivery unit. Processes for selection, hiring, credentialing and evaluating staff have been developed and are described elsewhere. It is the role of the Quality Assurance Committee to monitor ongoing compliance with these policies and procedures.

1. Selection Hiring and Evaluation:

    Each month, a report will be filed with the Quality Assurance Committee by the secretary to the President of the Convalescent Hospital for Children detailing administrative activities concerning staff. This report will contain the following information:

    a. Number of candidates hired for the clinical staff on a probationary status,
    b. Was each item in Part I, "Pre-employment Screening Phase" of the clinical staff appointment checklist completed for each hired candidate; if not, how many are incomplete and anticipated completion dates.
    c. Number of staff transferred from "Probationary Status" to "Permanent Staff Status."

    d. Was each item in Part II, "Probationary Phase" of the "Clinical Staff Appointment Procedures Checklist" completed for each transferred employee. If not, how many are incomplete and anticipated completion dates.

    e. Number of evaluations of permanent staff requested.

    f. The number of evaluations of permanent staff completed.

    g. Actions taken concerning delinquent evaluations.

2. Clinical Credentialing:

One hallmark of quality mental health care is that the service provided is delivered by individuals with adequate training and experience, with all practitioners functioning within the scope of their defined competence. There is a Credentialing and Clinical Privilege process that functions to define the scope of practice for each member of the clinical staff. It is the role of the Quality Assurance Committee to monitor the activities of the Credentialing and Clinical Privilege Committee to assure that clinical privilege decisions have been made concerning all clinical staff and that ongoing reviews of staff competence are conducted. This monitoring is based on reviews of minutes of the Credentialing and Clinical Privilege Committee meetings and review of the monthly reports submitted to the Quality Assurance Committee by the secretary to the President of the Hospital.

C. *Adequacy of the Physical Environment and Treatment Milieu:*

If a treatment program is to be effective, the physical surroundings, environment and treatment milieu where services are delivered must be conducive to the provision of high quality therapeutic services. Attention in this arena is focused upon the areas of functional safety and sanitation, therapeutic environment, housekeeping, infection control and building and grounds safety where specific standards have been developed and are described in the Policy and Procedures Manual of the Convalescent Hospital for Children.

Compliance with these standards is monitored by the Safety Committee which is chaired by the Safety Officer. The results of these activities are reported to the Quality Assurance Committee through a monthly report submitted to the Quality Assurance Committee by the Safety Officer.

D. *Utilization Review:*

This program addresses issues of whether or not the hospital is making appropriate use of its resources to provide maximum benefit to the largest group of patients while assuring that adequate services are provided to assure a consistently high quality of service. Utilization Review is a process through which appropriateness of admission and continuing treatment for patients in each treatment division is examined on a regular basis. This function is accomplished within each service by persons not directly involved with a case. The Utilization Review Committee reviews children who require treatment within a given service that extends beyond established length of stay norms as well as cases that do not satisfactorily pass through the review process in the individual services. The agency-wide Utilization Review Committee has four members, two of whom must be physicians.

The review of the appropriateness of admission and continuing treatment for patients is accomplished in the following manner:

1. Appropriateness for admission is determined through the procedures of the Diagnostic Service for all patients entering intensive services for the first time and by the outpatient service assignment committees for the outpatient service. Patients transferring from one intensive service to a second intensive service are evaluated by a committee consisting of the heads of each involved intensive service and the Chief Executive Officer of the Hospital. The outcome of these conferences is documented in each patient's clinical record. This documentation is contained in the written summary of the Diagnostic Service Diagnostic Conference, or it is written on the "Record of Agency Contacts" form by the chairperson of either the Outpatient Service Assignment Committee or the Intensive Service Transfer Committee, indicating the results of the evaluation. The documentation includes a statement of which criteria were met at the time of the review as justification of the decision.

2. All reviews for admissions are in terms of pre-established criteria for admission to the service in question.

3. Appropriateness for continuation of services is determined within each service. Each service establishes its own frequency of case review standards in accordance with the most stringent requirements of its licensing and regulatory bodies. The results of these case reviews are documented in the clinical record according to established procedures for this activity. One of several decisions may be made in these clinical care reviews (continued treatment at the present level of intensity, an increase or decrease in the level of intensity, or discharge from treatment). The treatment plan shall document these decisions in the established manner and shall contain a plan for implementation of the decision. These evaluations may be conducted as part of any larger treatment conference on a case or independently.

4. Each treatment case is also reviewed according to length of stay norms. Each service establishes length of stay norms through an analysis of the length of stay of the last fifty cases discharged from the service. Percentiles will be established for duration of treatment in this group, and the 75th and 95th percentiles will serve as marker points for evaluation. These norms are revised annually.

The process for review of clinical decisions for admission and continuation of care occurs at three levels. All cases are reviewed at Level I. Cases failing a Level I review are reviewed at Level II. Cases failing at the Level II review, cases requiring independent review because of length of stay, and cases requiring independent review due to other special circumstances are reviewed at Level II.

1. Level I Review Procedure:

Each case record is reviewed according to the Acceptance Criteria/ Continuation Criteria Checklist within ten (10) working days of a decision-making meeting concerning a case. Reviews are also conducted as frequently as mandated by regulatory body requirements of each service. A case satisfactorily passes this review if all relevant items on the checklist are satisfied. Satisfactory completion of this review is noted in the clinical record on the "Utilization Review Form." Cases failing Level I review are automatically referred for Level II review. This referral consists of notification of the Head of the Service and the Utilization Review Committee.

2. Level II Review Procedure:

Level II Reviews occur within each Service, with the Service Head having responsibility for ensuring that the review occurs. Senior clinical staff shall be designated by the service head to perform this review. They shall not have direct involvement in the case under review. The purpose of this review will be to address the reasons for the failure at Level I. This review shall be done and a report sent to the Utilization Review Committee and the service head within ten (10) working days of the date that the service head was notified of the Level I review failure. Failure at a Level II review or failure to notify the committee within ten (10) working days generates a Level III review. The Utilization Review Committee will consider each report of Level II evaluations and may either accept the report and terminate the review process or decide that a Level Three review is necessary.

3. Level III Review Procedure:

These Reviews are the responsibility of the agency Utilization Review Committee. The purpose of these reviews is to address reasons for failure at Level II reviews, to review cases exceeding length of stay norms, or other cases requiring exceptions to continuation criteria. These reviews are conducted by a senior member of the clinical staff who is credentialed as an independent reviewer, who is not a member of the service delivery team, who is not a member of the service managing the case and who is appointed by the Utilization Review Committee. The independent reviewer examines the patient's records and makes a recommendation for consideration by the Utilization Review Committee. If the recommendation is for continuation at the present level of intensity and the Utilization Review Committee concurs, this will be so noted in the clinical record of the patient, and the review process will terminate. If either of the following occurs:

1. The level of treatment intensity being offered is judged inappropriate by the independent reviewer and the utilization review committee concurs; or,
2. The committee does not accept the reviewer's recommendation;

then, a final review will be conducted by the Chief of Clinical Staff which will also involve the independent reviewer, the head of the affected service and the chairperson of the Utilization Review Committee. A disposition will be made based on the consideration of clinical need and other issues that are relevant to the case.

The results of this final review will be noted in the patient's clinical record. When the period of time that a patient has been in treatment in a given service reaches the 75th percentile, or treatment duration for that service, an independent review of that case is conducted by a senior member of the clinical staff using the procedures outlined above. Cases will be reviewed again when they reach the 95th percentile marker point and on a bi-monthly basis thereafter. All reviews will be done according to established criteria for continuation in a particular level of service.

APPENDIX 1
ACCEPTANCE/CONTINUATION CRITERIA CHECKLISTS: ALL SERVICES

CONVALESCENT HOSPITAL FOR CHILDREN
UTILIZATION REVIEW COMMITTEE
ACCEPTANCE CRITERIA/CONTINUATION CRITERIA CHECKLIST

OUTPATIENT SERVICE

Acceptance Criteria	Continuation Criteria
Age 5.5–18. . . . . _____	Age under 21. . . . . _____
Diagnosis other than V71.09 (No Diagnosis) on either Axis I or II. . . . . _____	Minimum of one treatment goal partly met. . . . . _____
Signed Financial Form. . . . . _____	Minimum of 65% parent appointments kept. . . . . . _____
	Minimum of 65% of child appointments kept. . . . . . _____
	Diagnosis other than V71.09 (No Diagnosis) on either Axis I or II within one year. . . . . _____
	Case seen minimum of once monthly. . . . . _____

CONVALESCENT HOSPITAL FOR CHILDREN
UTILIZATION REVIEW COMMITTEE
ACCEPTANCE CRITERIA/CONTINUATION CRITERIA CHECKLIST

PRESCHOOL PROGRAM

Acceptance Criteria	Continuation Criteria
Age: Day Program 3-6 . . . . . _____	Age: Day Program 3-7 . . . . . _____
Outpatient 3-5.5 . . . . . _____	Outpatient 3-6 . . . . . . _____
*P.D.D. Prog. 3-12 . . . . _____	*P.D.D. Prog. 3-12 . . . . _____
Infant Stim. Under 3 . . _____	Infant Stim. under 4 . . . _____
Average intellectual	Diagnosis other than V71.09
potential . . . . _____	(No Diagnosis) on either
Diagnosis other than V71.09	Axis I or II within one
(No Diagnosis) on Axis	year . . . . _____
I or II . . . . _____	Treatment plan requires
Signed Admission Form . . . . _____	input from three or more
Diagnostic conference	modalities (Day & Autistic
recommendation for	Programs only) . . . . _____
specialized day treatment	Treatment plan specifies
program (Day and P.D.D.	need for day program
Programs) . . . . _____	(day/P.D.D. only) . . . . . . _____
	Minimum of 65% parent
	appointments kept . . . . . . _____
	At least one treatment goal
	partly met . . . . _____
	Case seen minimum of once
	monthly (outpatient
	only) . . . . _____
	Child attends at least 90%
	of program days in Day and
	P.D.D. programs . . . . _____

*P.D.D. means Pervasive Development Disorders

CONVALESCENT HOSPITAL FOR CHILDREN
UTILIZATION REVIEW COMMITTEE
ACCEPTANCE CRITERIA/CONTINUATION CRITERIA CHECKLIST

DAY TREATMENT

Acceptance Criteria	Continuation Criteria
Age: 6–17 . . . . ____	Age: 6–21 . . . . ____
Average or better intellectual potential . . . . ____	One treatment goal partly met . . . . ____
Diagnosis other than V71.09 (no diagnosis) on either Axis I or II . . . . ____	Diagnosis other than V71.09 (No Diagnosis) on Axis I or II within one year . . . . ____
Signed Admission Form . . . . ____	Treatment plan requires input from three or more modalities . . . . ____
Diagnostic or transfer conference recommendation for specialized Day Treatment Program . . . . ____	Minimum 65% parent appointments kept . . . . . . ____
	Treatment plan specifies need for Day Treatment Program . . . . ____
	Patient attends minimum of 90% of treatment days . . . ____

CONVALESCENT HOSPITAL FOR CHILDREN
UTILIZATION REVIEW COMMITTEE
ACCEPTANCE CRITERIA/CONTINUATION CRITERIA CHECKLIST

RESIDENTIAL PROGRAMS

Acceptance Criteria

Age: Residential 5–11.6.... _____
    Mills 10–16......... _____
Average intellectual
   potential............. _____
Sex: Male (Mills only)...... _____
Signed Admission Form.... _____
Diagnostic or transfer con-
  ference recommendation
  for Residential
  Treatment............. _____
Diagnosis of severe mental
disorder:
RTF Program:
  Schizophrenia (295.xx)... _____
  Conduct Disorder
   (312.xx)............. _____
  Pervasive Developmental
   Disorder (299.xx)...... _____
  Personality Disorder
   Axis II (301.xx)....... _____
  Major Affective Disorder
   (206.xx)............. _____
Residential Treatment
Program:
  Diagnosed Mental Disorder
  other than V71.09 (No
  Diagnosis) on Axis
  I or II............. _____
  Approval by PACC (RTF).. _____

Continuation Criteria

Age: Residential 6–13..... _____
    Mills 10–18......... _____
Diagnosis of severe mental
  disorder within 1 year
  (RTF Program)........ _____
Minimum of one treatment
  goal partly achieved..... _____
Treatment plan requires input
  from three or more
  modalities............ _____
Minimum of 65% parent
  appointments kept...... _____
Treatment plan specifies need
  for 24 hour care........ _____
Diagnosis other than V71.09
  (No Diagnosis) on Axis I
  or II within one year
  (Residential Treatment
  only)............... _____
Meets level Disability
  determination (RTF)..... _____

APPENDIX 2
UTILIZATION REVIEW SUMMARY FORM

CONVALESCENT HOSPITAL FOR CHILDREN
UTILIZATION REVIEW COMMITTEE

UTILIZATION REVIEW SUMMARY FORM

Case Name: _____   Case Number: _____

DATE	TYPE OF REVIEW	LEVEL OF REVIEW	OUTCOME	SIGNATURE

APPENDIX 3
QUALITY AND APPROPRIATENESS OF SERVICES: DATA SUMMARY FORM

I. Current performance, tends and identified quality issues:

A. Case assignments: _____
_____
_____

B. Review of the impact of delivered services: _____
_____
_____

C. Completeness and thoroughness of documentation: _____
_____
_____

D. Review of the impact of other related service delivery systems on patient
care: _____
_____
_____

E. Review of unusual events including, untoward incidents, accidents/
injuries, restraint and premature and/or unplanned terminations: _____
_____
_____

F. Review of appropriateness of patient placements and continuation: ___
_____
_____

G. Review of unmet needs for service: _____
_____
_____

II. Actions initiated regarding identified Quality of Care issues:

ISSUE	ACTION
_____	_____
_____	_____
_____	_____

III. Current status of previously identified Quality of Care Issues:

ISSUES	DATE IDENTIFIED	CURRENT STATUS
_____	_____	_____
_____	_____	_____
_____	_____	_____

APPENDIX 4
SERVICE DELIVERY SYSTEM QUALITY ASSURANCE GUIDELINES

The guidelines listed below represent the thinking of the members of the senior clinical staff regarding the hallmarks of quality patient care. They are grouped into seven areas in order to make the organization and reporting of quality assurance data more efficient. Individual service delivery units shall use these guidelines when preparing the "Quality and Appropriateness of Services Data Summary Form" for submission with their monthly reports. Service delivery units are expected to maintain statistics in each of the data centers enumerated below although reporting out shall be in terms of trends and statistics that indicated a need for some type of clinical or administrative intervention.

Seven reporting areas have been defined. These include:
1. Case Assignments.
2. Review of the impact of delivered service.
3. Completeness and thoroughness of documentation.
4. Review of the impact of other service delivery systems on patient care.
5. Review of unusual events including untoward incidents, accidents/injuries, restraints, premature and unplanned terminations, and patients discharged as unimproved.
6. Review of appropriateness of patient placement and continuation.
7. Review of unmet needs for service.

The specific guidelines in each of these areas are as follows:
1. *Case Assignments;*
   a. A worker(s), as defined by the service and including at least someone to work with the parent and someone to work with the child, shall be assigned to each case assigned to a service delivery unit within ten (10) working days of parental acceptance of the recommendation for treatment in the unit.
   b. Assigned worker(s) shall contact each new case assigned within five (5) working days of receiving the assignment for the purpose of scheduling an initial appointment.
   c. Intake appointments shall be offered within five (5) working days of a call requesting such an appointment.
2. *Review of the impact of delivered services:*
   a. Treatment plans shall be reviewed according to the following schedule:

SERVICE DELIVERY UNIT	FREQUENCY OF TREATMENT PLAN REVIEW
Residential Treatment	1/60 Treatment Days; months 1-12. 1/84 Treatment Days thereafter.
Day Treatment	1/60 Treatment Days
Preschool	1/60 Treatment Days
Outpatient	1/12 weeks
Seasonal Programs	1/20 Treatment Days

b. It is expected that intensive service patients and family members of patients will keep at least 80% of their scheduled appointments. In the Outpatient Service it is expected that patients and family members will keep at least 65% of their scheduled appointments, and that no more than two consecutive appointments will be missed.

c. Each service shall review its rate of success in achieving stated treatment plan objectives through comparing the number of objectives achieved against the number of objectives established.

d. It is expected that parents of children in residential treatment shall visit their children in accordance with their individually established visiting plan. The service will maintain a record of visits scheduled and visits held in order to evaluate compliance with this expectation and highlight cases where more than 20% of scheduled visits are missed.

3. *Completeness and thoroughness of documentation:*
   a. All conference reports and treatment plans will be filed with the record room within five (5) working days of the conference.
   b. Records shall be reviewed on a regular basis to ensure that they contain all necessary entries, signatures, etc. Each service shall review 8.334% of its records each month to ensure that each record is reviewed annually.

4. *Review of the impact of other related services on patient care:*
   a. Each service shall monitor the time needed to obtain data concerning and/or services for patients from "out of house" providers and determine whether the needed data or service was obtained within a time frame consistent with good patient care.
   b. Each service shall monitor the time needed to obtain data concerning and/or services for patients from "in house" providers and determine whether the needed data or service was obtained within a time frame consistent with good patient care. "In-house" providers consist of any department, service or discipline which contributes to a treatment program.
   c. Each service providing meals for patients shall conduct periodic food acceptance studies.

5. *Review of unusual events including untoward incidents, accidents/injuries, restraint, premature and/or unplanned terminations, and patients discharged as unimproved.*
   a. Each service shall maintain statistics regarding the number of events that occur in each of these categories.
   b. Each event shall be individually reviewed.
   c. Programs utilizing mental health station or administrative appointments as treatment tools shall maintain records of each use of these tools. Use of these tools shall be reviewed on a monthly basis.

6. *Review of appropriateness of patient placement and continuation:*
   a. Each service shall maintain the following data:
      i.   The number of cases scheduled for utilization review.
      ii. The number of cases reviewed.
      iii. The number of cases out of compliance with continuation criteria.
      iv. The number of cases referred for further review.

7. *Review of unmet needs for services:*
   a. Each service shall maintain a record of:
      i. The size of its waiting list.
      ii. Staff availability to provide services, including caseload size, number of appointments scheduled/held.
      iii. Size of waiting list for specialized treatment services. (e.g., art and dance therapy).

APPENDIX 5
SERVICE DELIVERY SYSTEM—STATISTICAL SUMMARY FORM

1. *Case Assignments*
   A. 1. Number of cases this month where parent or guardian has accepted the recommendation for treatment in the service _____
      2. Number of cases assigned to worker(s) within ten working days of their receipt _____
   B. 1. Number of new case assignments transmitted to worker(s) this month _____
      2. Number of cases where contact for initial appointment was made within five working days of the workers' receipt of the case _____
   C. 1. Number of requests for intake appointments _____
      2. Number of cases where appointment was offered within five days of the call _____

2. *Review of the Impact of Delivered Services*
   A. 1. Number of treatment plans reviewed this month _____
      2. Number of treatment plans reviewed within the established time frame for review _____
   B. 1. Intensive Services
         a. Number of patients failing twenty or more percent of scheduled appointments _____
         b. Number of parents and/or families failing twenty or more percent of scheduled appointments _____
      2. Outpatient Services
         a. Number of patients failing thirty-five or more percent or missing two consecutive scheduled appointments _____
         b. Number of parents and/or families failing thirty-five or more percent or missing two consecutive scheduled appointments _____
   C. 1. Number of treatment plan objectives planned for achievement this month _____
      2. Number of treatment plan objectives realized _____
      3. Number of cases reviewed _____
      4. Percent objectives realized per case _____
   D. Number of cases where twenty percent or more of parent and/or family visits to a Residential Treatment child or adolescent were failed _____

3. *Completeness and Thoroughness of Documentation*
      a. Number of Clinical Conferences held _____
      b. Number of "treatment plans" received in the Record Room six or more days after the conference _____
      c. Number of "Conference Summary and Report Packets" received in the Record Room six or more days after the conference _____
   B. 1. Number of active cases in the service _____
      2. Number of cases reviewed for completeness (this number should be at least 1/12th of the total) _____

4. *Review of the Impact of Other Related Services on Patient Care* ____
   A. 1. Number of requests for data or services from "out-of-house" providers ____
     2. Number of requests that were not responded to in a time frame considered reasonable for good patient care ____
   B. 1. Number of requests for data or services from "in-house" providers ____
     2. Number of requests not responded to in a time frame considered reasonable for good patient care ____
   C. 1. Number of meals for which food acceptance studies were conducted ____
     2. Number of food acceptance studies reviewed with the dietician ____

5. *Review of Unusual Events including untoward incidents, accidents/ injuries, restraint, premature (child discharged by the program although discharge goals not realized) terminations, unplanned (child removed from the program by parent, guardian or other source) terminations* ____
   A. 1. Number of untoward incidents this month ____
     2. Number of untoward incidents presented to the special review committee ____
   B. 1. Number of accidents/injuries this month ____
     2. Number of accidents/injuries reviewed by Service Head and the Chief of Clinical Staff ____
   C. 1. Number of restraints this month ____
     2. Number of restraints reviewed by Service Head and the Chief of Clinical Staff ____
   D. 1. Number of premature terminations this month ____
     2. Number of premature terminations reviewed with the Chief of Clinical Staff ____
   E. 1. Number of unplanned terminations this month ____
     2. Number of unplanned terminations reviewed with the Chief of Clinical Staff ____

6. *Review of the Appropriateness of Patient Placement and Continuation*
   A. Number of cases scheduled for utilization review ____
   B. Number of cases reviewed ____
   C. Number of cases found to be out of compliance ____
   D. Number of cases referred for further review ____

7. *Review of Unmet Needs for Service*
   A. Number of patients waiting for service ____
   B. Number of staff in service seeking less than their established patient quota ____
   C. Size of waiting list for specialized therapeutic services:
        Art Therapy. . . . . ____
        Dance Therapy . . . . ____
        Video Therapy . . . . ____
        Total ____

CLINICAL STAFF APPOINTMENT PROCEDURE CHECKLIST

1. *Pre-employment Screening Phase*
   A. Completed application submitted　　　　　　　　　　_____
   B. At least two references received　　　　　　　　　　_____
   C. Credentials verified　　　　　　　　　　　　　　　_____
   D. Resume received　　　　　　　　　　　　　　　　_____
   E. Items A, B, C, D reviewed by relevant discipline head and decision to interview applicant or to cease considering applicant made　_____
   F. Applicant informed of his/her status (copy of letter to be attached)　_____
   G. Interviews held with discipline head, service head, chief executive officer and other staff as necessary, with interviewers' comments documented on the application form in the appropriate place.　_____
   H. Decision to hire/not hire made
       Decision: _____　_____
   I. Decision communicated to the Candidate by the discipline head　_____
   J. Candidate hired on a probationary status, formal letter of appointment sent and signed copy of the letter returned indicating acceptance of the appointment (copy of letter attached)　_____
2. *Probationary Phase*
   A. Starting date established　　　　　　　　　　　　_____
   B. Immediate administrative supervisor appointed　　　_____
   C. Clinical Privileges and level of supervision determined by credentialing committee　_____
   D. Clinical Privilege and level of supervision decisions communicated to staff member by administrative supervisor.　_____
   E. Personnel paperwork processed　　　　　　　　　_____
   F. Necessary supervisor assigned　　　　　　　　　_____
   G. Orientation to agency, services, and facility completed　_____
   H. Probationary evaluations completed, discussed with individual and filed in personnel record　_____
   I. Decision made to grant or not grant permanent staff status to the employee.
       Decision: _____　_____
   J. Decision communicated to employee　　　　　　　_____
   K. Formal letter of appointment sent to employee (copy attached) notifying employee of permanent staff status　_____

NEW STAFF ORIENTATION PROCEDURE
CHECKLIST

This checklist contains items that are to be covered in orientation process for each clinical staff member while in the probationary period. Enter the date completed and sign after each item after it has been completed.

ITEMS	DATE	SIGNATURE
A. Organizational Structure of the Hospital		
B. Individual Service Plans		
C. Infection Control Policies and Procedures		
D. Quality Assurance Plan		
E. Review of Job Description and Responsibilities		
F. Review of Patient's Rights Policies		
G. Disaster and Evacuation Plans		
H. Intake/triage/admission Policies and Procedures		
I. Policies and Procedures Governing the Use of Restraint		
J. Child Abuse Reporting Procedures		
K. Policies and Procedures for Suicidal Patients		
L. Accidents and Untoward Incident Procedures		
M. Tour of Facilities		
N. Review of Hospital Service Programs		
O. Review of Personnel Practices and Policies		
P. Review of Clinical Records Policy & Procedures		
Q. Review of Organization of Clinical Records		
R. Observation of the Ongoing Activity of the Services		

REFERENCES

Accreditation Standards for Psychiatric Services for Children and Youth (1985). Washington, D.C.: American Association of Psychiatric Services for Children.

Consolidated Standards Manual for Child, Adolescent and Adult Psychiatric, Alcoholism and Drug Abuse Facilities (1985). Chicago: Joint Commission on Accreditation of Hospitals.

Everstine, L. and Everstine, D. S., eds. (1986). *Psychotherapy and the Law.* Orlando: Grune and Stratton.

13

Evaluating Treatment Effectiveness

John B. Mordock

Over two decades ago, Adessa and Laatsch (1965) cautioned those professionals who were disenchanted with residential care and imbued with the
concept of community psychiatry, that effective treatment of some children takes many years. In addition, they warned that even workers involved
in residential programs were prone to make constant errors in judgment
that affected their ability to formulate appropriate treatment plans. These
errors included: (1) failure to recognize how "ill" most children are who
are placed in residential centers, there being a widespread, anxious
disinclination of many workers to acknowledge the seriousness of a
disorder; (2) the difficulty of fully grasping the nature and complexity of
psychic growth, with workers proceeding on the assumption that deep
personality changes and growth can be accomplished with minimal effort
in a relatively short time period; (3) a notion that the child is being held
for short-term repair in residential centers to escape intolerable home
situations, situations that will quickly improve after the child's departure—an
idea that ignores that placement itself results in reactive disturbances
(i.e., emotional traumas, object loss, guilt, fear, decrease in self-esteem)
that require reworking over long periods of time; and (4) the infusion of
economic issues, standards, and concerns into professional decisions—if
money is available for only a certain period, then the child will be "cured"
in that period.

In addition, new "errors" are emerging. For example, the American
Academy of Child Psychiatry published a handbook of professional standards for child psychiatrists (Silver, 1976), in which the average length of
stay is given for children in certain diagnostic categories in three inpatient
psychiatric units—the suggestion being that programs will be evaluated
by how closely the child's stay approximates these time periods. Yet effectiveness of these programs themselves has never been evaluated, and we
know how unreliable psychiatric diagnoses are! Menninger (1977) states:

No one would seriously assert that such a formula-based approach to patient care is likely to result in quality, and yet the pressure to develop measurable definitions of quality for the benefit of third-party payment schemes is pushing sophisticated thinking about a complex reality aside in favor of the convenience and simplicity of standards that a clerk can apply. (p. 185)

Adessa and Laatsch (1965) state that most children placed in residential centers have severe ego defects and seriously impaired object relationships. Consequently, placed children need a program designed to (1) promote a stronger ego with more adaptive capabilities, (2) modify and sublimate drives, (3) develop more mature ego defenses, and (4) make more use of identifications. The children need to repeat their basic difficulties with a variety of people. Years are needed in which patterns of relationships to adults can be tested, threatened, and tried again. Consequently, improvement must be measured in terms of improved ego development and more mature object-relations, rather than in symptom change or in symptom disappearance. Such a notion is supported by earlier work as summarized by Mordock (1978, 1979a, 1986). Adessa and Laatsch caution professionals not to be satisfied with the substitution of acceptable for unacceptable symptoms. Impoverishment of affect, reduction of learning capacity, or psychosomatic complaints are as "unhealthy" as hostile or hyperactive behavior.

Yet many scoffed at these warnings, believing strongly that children should not be separated from families. Community psychiatry, family therapy, extended casework, day treatment centers, and other community approaches would help the family cope effectively with their child. Yet at the same time community agencies were offering brief therapies to avoid waiting lists, and viewed changes as resulting from crisis resolutions rather than personality reconstruction. As Martion et al. (1976) state:

It has become popular recently to seek a "community solution" to certain problems rather than face the "inevitable horror" of institutional care. A client's community and his family are viewed in the same way as mother, apple pie and country; eternally with us, they're definitely better than available alternatives. The reality is that some families and communities are dangerous and destructive places to educate and socialize children. Other communities and families are inadequately prepared to deal with severe disturbances in children. (p. 269).

Mordock's (1978) study indicated that in most instances, referral for residential treatment was not taken lightly; the majority of children referred had been exposed to serious attempts by numerous community agencies to reverse the pattern of behavior that was causing concern. Consequently, most children placed met the following critieria: (1) there was a history of deterioration in behavior in both home and school; (2) clinical evaluation indicated the need for intensive therapeutic contacts across several modalities; (3) intensive restructuring of the child, his family, and his environment was indicated; (4) the child needed a great deal of external support and structure that could not be obtained in his current environment; (5) significant others in the home environment reported that if the child was not removed, harm (psychological or physical) to either himself or others would result; (6) significant responsible others in the environment were not able to control the child and would not be able to establish control as long as the child was present.

Such children include those whose parents depersonalize them, where separation and individuation are not taking place, and where the child is so enmeshed in family pathology that overall emotional development is halted (Rinsley, 1974). Such children are those with firmly structured intrapsychic conflicts that cause repetitive life patterns transcending the specifics of the current family situation. Promotion of growth outside the family is required. The children often control and manipulate their parents and display persistent acting-out. The parents of such children usually display massive pathology, require individuation themselves, and are highly resistant and distrustful, if not deceitful. Most parents are inappropriate for family therapy and need considerable individual long-term, ego-supportive work (Weitzman, 1985).

Follow-up data (Mordock, 1978; Prentice-Dunn et al., 1981) reveal that most children referred for residential treatment do need the type of extended care suggested by Adessa. Changing the personality or behavioral patterns of the child and his parents is no simple matter. Bloom (1964), in his classic work on stability and change in human characteristics, states:

> A major thesis of this work is that change in many human characteristics becomes more and more difficult as the characteristics become more fully developed. Although there may be some change in a particular characteristic at almost any point in the individual's history, the amount of change possible is a declining function as the characteristics become increasingly stabilized.
>
> Furthermore, to produce a given amount of change (an elusive concept) requires more and more powerful environments and increased amount of effort and attention as a characteristic becomes stabilized. In addition, the individual not only becomes more resistant to change as the characteristic becomes stabilized, but change, if it can be produced, must be made at greater emotional cost to the individual. (pp. 229–230)

For effective evaluation of the outcome of residential treatment and of the various therapeutic modalities offered to children admitted and families served, three requirements to be met: (1) the characteristics of the children served must be carefully described; (2) treatment goals for children with differing characteristics must be clearly delineated, and the milieu plan to achieve these goals described; and (3) the social networks available to assist the child must be identified.

CHARACTERISTICS OF CHILDREN SERVED

One would think it obvious for evaluation efforts to include careful descriptions of children served. Yet Project Re-Ed, which was lauded by the Joint Commission on Mental Health of Children (David, 1972) for its inexpensive yet effective treatment of children, failed to present either a conceptual or a statistical description of the children it served. Yet traditional residential treatment centers were compared unfavorably with Re-Ed centers on the basis of one follow-up study of the Re-Ed children, performed six months after children were withdrawn (Weinstein, 1974). This study is still being cited today, yet it is the only outcome study performed by Re-Ed staff. The Astor Home for Children (Mordock, 1978) has completed three follow-up studies, after ten, fifteen, and twenty years of operation, and the results are clear: while disturbed children do make progress, the effectiveness of programs is significantly enhanced by the provision of long-term group or foster care.

Although admitted children will have differing developmental needs, children in residential centers display serious developmental imbalances, with many revealing character disorders such as the borderline syndrome, narcissistic personality disorder, and primitive hysteria, all syndromes where symptoms wax and wane and where developmental arrest predominates in the clinical picture. For this reason, I disagree with the notion that "more objective measures of behavioral functioning such as observational ratings and standardized assessment inventories" (Baenen et al., 1986, p. 267) should be utilized in outcome studies. Instead, I recommend returning to the traditional approach of assessing the client's level of emotional development and adaptive ego functioning.

Developmental Diagnosis

Experienced clinicians such as Anna Freud (1965) and developmental psychologists such as Peter Kohlberg (Kohlberg et al., 1972) have repeatedly emphasized that diagnosticians should ask themselves whether the child being evaluated has reached developmental levels that are adequate for his age, to what degree the child has remained behind these levels, and whether regression or arrest is responsible for developmental imbalances. Psychoanalytic research and child observation at the Hempstead Clinic and elsewhere demonstrated that pinpointing and describing developmental imbalances of emotionally disturbed children lead to greater understanding of their difficulties than do characterizations of these children according to symptomatology. Consequently, a scheme for understanding the normal phases of development was essential. Such a scheme, developed by Anna Freud and Hempstead Clinic staff, is called the Developmental Profile (Nagera, 1963). Unfortunately, because many clinicians in residential settings are not analytically or developmentally trained, the Profile is not widely used. Others, however, have developed some procedures that allow for developmental assessment by less sophisticated staff (Goldfarb, 1970; Klein and Mordock, 1975; Wood, 1975). Although it is beyond the scope of this chapter to discuss developmental assessment, professionals in residential treatment should become well versed in this topic if they want to develop meaningful base-line data with which to assess client change. Family systems theorists have also developed ways to classify families developmentally.

The reader is referred to the classic work of David Beres (1952, 1956, 1965), whose experience with ego-impaired children at the Pleasantville Cottage School led him to delineate conceptually the various functions of the ego that an evaluator should examine in order to evaluate a child's functioning adequately. Twenty years later, Klein and Mordock (1975) presented a somewhat similar classification scheme. Some investigators believe certain ego functions to be more important than others. Bowlby (1977), for example, would emphasize affectional bonds, as would Masterson (1972). Goldfarb's (1970) developmental classification scheme for psychotic children is an excellent example of the developmental approach applied to this group. Beardslee and his colleagues (Beardslee et al., 1985) have developed an approach to assessing adaptive processes that can assist those working with adolescents.

Mordock is not biased against other approaches, as he has described the use of behavioral techniques in school settings (Grieger et al., 1970; Mordock and Phillips, 1971). Behavioral approaches can be of use in residential programs with children at certain developmental levels, but at the same time, Mordock (1970) has argued against their wholesale application. To understand a child's developmental needs is not a bias—it is a must. Although some problems of children are not developmental (see, for example, Tanguay, 1984), their disabilities create developmental difficulties. The developmental approach is useful for understanding the difficulties of handicapped children (Mordock, 1979b) and in planning for retarded–disturbed adults (Mordock, 1987).

Behavioral Data

Arriving at a developmental diagnosis does not preclude the clinician's gathering "hard" data on a child. Risley and his colleagues (Risley et al., 1975) have been examining the "impersonal" aspects of group care. They examined the percentage of time a child is involved in each type of activity offered in the group care setting. Change in time spent by a child in a particular activity could be used as a measure of change.

Other investigators also recommend behavioral observations of children as the measure of change. An operational definition of target behaviors is made with systematic sampling of the behavior over specified time periods (Konstantareas and Humatidis, 1984). Most treatment settings document "incidents" displayed by a child, and a decrease in number of reported incidents could be a sign of change. Unfortunately, however, the reliability of behavioral counts typically is poor (Mordock, 1986). The investigator considering the use of behavioral observations would do well to review the earlier work of Rausch (1959), which appeared in part of a series of papers on observational research with emotionally disturbed children published in the *American Journal of Orthopsychiatry*.

To decide what type of "hard" data to gather, one needs to know the attributes or skills a child possesses that can be changed and are related to outcome (unlike IQ, which correlates highly with outcome but is relatively unchangeable). Stiffman et al. (1986), for example, found that two competence measures have predictive power for mental health status— school competence and activity competence. School competence is predictive of a child's level of behavior problems, whereas activity competence (successful participation in different hobbies, clubs, and sports) interacts with the proportion of mentally ill family members—the more ill family members there are present, the less activity-competence the child is. Interpersonal competence was not predictive. Similarly, academic adequacy facilitates the maintenance of behavioral adjustment following discharge (Baenen et al., 1986). The reader is referred to Mordock (1978, 1979a, 1986) and to Fineberg et al. (1980) for a review of client variables that relate to outcome of milieu treatment.

TREATMENT GOAL DELINEATION

The effectiveness of treatment cannot be determined without clarity of treatment goals. Mordock (1979a) states:

> The struggle to define success exists in all residential treatment centers and in many child-caring institutions, and highlights the difficulties involved in evaluation. Psychiatrically oriented accrediting bodies, such as the Joint Commission on Accreditation of Hospitals, want

evaluation in terms of psychiatric diagnosis, psychiatric symptomatology, symptom-oriented indices. Social service agencies want evaluation in terms of family change and the results of such change upon individual client adaptability. They also want evaluation of different types of aftercare. For example, schools want outcome measured in terms of academic achievement, and courts in terms of decreased delinquent activity. Not all agencies can evaluate change in all these areas. Each will have to make a choice. (pp. 300–301)

Because symptom reduction is not an adequate criterion of therapeutic growth, I have chosen to look at developmental advancement as the measure of client progress. What type of advancement do we expect from placed children? Of course, we could simply say that each child's progress can be assessed by comparing him against a relative standard of developmental mastery for his age group.

This is the procedure employed by Matsushima (1979). He describes a goal attainment procedure that he thinks answers the accountability needs of the agency as well as providing data consonant with principles of a developmental approach to classifying children. Behaviors reflective of normal growth and development were used as benchmarks of improvement. Because children enrolled were latency age children, they were expected to master the principal developmental tasks facing children of this age. Target behaviors hypothesized as reflective of progress along designated dimensions were placed within time intervals from admission to discharge. Children were expected to master the tasks of latency in approximately three years.

Unfortunately, except for stating that the program is based on psychoanalytic ego psychology (although later descriptions of disciplinary techniques, such as limits on privileges, fines for damages, and individual cottage grading sheets, would suggest a more behavioral orientation), Matsushima included no discussion of how the milieu was designed to help each child achieve mastery of developmental tasks. This procedure holds promise, but simply comparing each child against his equal-age peers results in our ignoring what we already know about the developmental imbalances of children in residential treatment and their therapeutic needs.

Developmental Arrest in Residential Populations

Children in residential treatment typically fall into two major categories: those with *no internal controls* and those with *variable controls.*

A youngster with no control shows the following characteristics:

- Fears injury and punishment without the ability to anticipate the expected consequences of aggressive acts.
- Shows a prominence of magical thinking where rage is projected onto others, and consequently the child feels that he is in a continually threatening environment. As a result, he shows a prominence of paranoid ideation, and his use of displacement abounds.
- Shows no signs of remorse, concern, or empathy for the "victim" whom he may attack. Concurrently, he does not expect a response when he is hurt; in other words, he does not seek the protective comfort of others when attacked.
- Shows little or no engagement in overt fantasy expression; and when he does show any, the content of such fantasy is limited.
- Has a background devoid of nurturance, protection, and prideful experiences of pleasing and being pleased. Consequently, the child maintains the rage characteristics of earlier phases of development and needs his aggressive powers to cope with his own sense of unsafety, pseudoautonomy, and aloneness. Such behavior blocks the development of internalization of moral injunctions and ideas.

The second major category is the child with variable internal controls. Such a child may show these characteristics:

- Has a degree of identification with the aggressor.
- Shows marked changes in his attachment to caretakers. Such a child both "loves" and "hates" the same person, depending upon whether the person satisfies or frustrates his needs.
- Engages in global self-condemnation (the forms of such condemnation are indicators of internalization of conflict, and are prognosticators of superego constancy or variability).
- Has experienced an abrupt, sustained loss of closeness to and ability to please adults around the ages of twenty-four to thirty-six months, and shows: (a) ambivalence about the need for close contact; (b) better control when in the presence of the cared-for adult; (c) violent alienations from the "baby-self" and a mimicry of adult talk; (d) lightning-swift unpredictable changes in behavior; (e) isolated play often following bad behavior; (f) a struggle to be good that is often a fear of the consequences if bad, but with some desire to please adults.

Consequently, assessment of development should include an examination of the child's ability at self-control, an area of development classified primarily under the heading of socialization in Klein and Mordock's (1975) approach to developmental diagnosis.

Over thirty years ago, Beres (1952) delineated the therapeutic needs of most children in residential treatment, and these needs remain unchanged. Their aggression must be treated (1) by efforts toward promotion of ego development, particularly defenses against anxiety; (2) by therapy of sadomasochistic disturbances; and (3) by minimization of external factors that promote frustration. Crenshaw (see Chapter 4) has described the treatment needs of abused and abandoned adolescents, incorporating what has been learned about the effects of sexual abuse.

The aggression of placed children is predominantly the manifestation of disturbed ego development, and the principles of its treatment have been discussed by many authors. They have not changed much (compare, for example, Rank and MacNaughton, 1956 with Crenshaw et al., 1986). The treatment includes developing opportunities for satisfactory relationships with adult persons, with whom identifications may be established to make up for gaps in earlier life experiences. In this phase of treatment the direct activity of the person or persons with whom the child is living is more important than direct therapy by a psychiatrist or psychologist.

Clinician's Role

The mental health worker's function is to interpret the child's behaviors to others concerned with his care. Part of the plan includes searching out some person to whom the child becomes attached, such as a cottage parent, child care worker, or maintenance man, and then strengthening this attachment with whatever practical means are available. Albert (1959) calls such treatment an effort at a "corrective emotional experience." Similarly, Geleerd (1946) showed that such children often progressed when they could develop a dependency relationship with an adult figure.

A further role for the therapist in a residential treatment center is to design a milieu that fosters the development of maturational processes and removes conditions that may hinder them. The child's ego must be strengthened through provision of masterly experiences and experiences that enhance self-esteem.

If the child is functioning at the level of a sadomasochistic relationship, individual psychotherapy is needed to help promote fusion of the aggressive and libidinal impulses so that splitting does not occur. In such cases object-relations may be developed to a considerable degree, and the treatment aims are to resolve ambivalent relationships and alleviate neurotic symptomatology. Similarly, Weil (1956) believes that we should simultaneously deal with deviational development and neurotic symptomatology.

Gould (1972) describes the response of caretakers to the child who is not developing internal controls. First, they should protect and rescue the child from situations in which he is frightened. Second, they should avoid exposing the child to experiences of loss of face or should mitigate such experiences. Third, they should make restraints and prohibitions predictable and limit punishment as much as possible, verbalizing the reasons for a disciplinary action ("I want to help you stop hurting yourself and others"). Fourth, they should make frustrations objective issues. Fifth, they should broaden the horizons of the child's "dos," and sixth, they should expand the child's concrete skills.

If such efforts are successful, the child will display any one or all of the following behaviors. First, he will begin to check with adults before he does things ("Is this right?"; "Can I do this?"). The ability to delay long enough to ask an adult marks the first step in the development of self-control; it reflects a desire to please an adult rather than the fear of punishment. The child will then begin to verbalize his desires and complaints with tattletale-like statements ("Billy hit me"). Such behavior is to be encouraged rather than discouraged. Second, when the child does throw a tantrum, his reactions will be less violent, and he should be praised for this change. Third, the child will become more focused on others, making statements such as, "My teacher went to the ball game," "My therapist did such and so," or "My friend went here." Fourth, the child will show jealous and possessive behavior, becoming dependent upon a particular adult and demanding that the adult "stay with him." Such behavior sometimes is misunderstood by adults, and the child is rejected for what the adult considers infantile, clinging behavior. In other words, the child goes from pseudoindependence to real dependence, a progression the caretaker fails to appreciate. Sixth, the child learns to concentrate longer and to take pleasure in school and recreational activities.

In general, the child is now developing the beginnings of a trust-dependency relationship. Correspondingly, there will be development of impulse control because with such control comes pleasurable involvement in activities and investment in learning. The first sign is a *wish to please*. He begins to experience parental demands and prohibitions as "joining forces with his own ambitions" ("I do things for you because you do things for me"). Guilt in a child can occur only when the child feels attached to an adult toward whom he is angry. He must have conflict. In other words, he must have a desire to please and must feel bad when he has let the adult down.

The child with variable internal controls needs continued growth based on opportunities the environment offers him to feel good and to be admired for his ego achievements. He must have the chance to be admired for behaviors other than compliance with an adult; in that way he can begin to feel that he should want to do what the caring adult wishes. He must develop trust in his basically good impulses and his ability to mitigate and control his bad and aggressive impulses. Prohibitions upon his behavior have to be seen as protective rather than as punitive or humiliating (Gould, 1972).

Knowing the stages a child must go through to arrive at a level of improved development allows one to develop procedures to assess the presence of more advanced behaviors. Staff can ask themselves questions such as, "Does he show a desire to please anyone?"; "Does he talk about others in a positive manner?"; "Does he show jealous behavior?"; "Does he concentrate longer?" The same set of questions first used to assess the child can be used to reassess his functioning and, thereby, assess his progress. In addition, we know from Ekstein (1967) that the fantasies displayed by a child can help staff to assess his progress. The further from reality the child's fantasy, the more his disturbance. For example, fantasizing that he is a Planet X creature is a more distant fantasy than being "Action Jackson" and therefore more disturbing.

Problems Encountered

Under pressure to resolve each crisis that the child and family experience during placement, staff at treatment planning meetings often neglect asking the questions needed to assess the child's current developmental level. Pressures for symptom reduction and immediate resolution of problems (Ekstein, 1962; King, 1976) take precedence over reassessing development. Hence, the clinician serving as case manager needs considerable help and support from peers to keep the child's treatment team focused on this task. Use of a simple behavior checklist, devised to assess developmental level, does not serve this purpose, as it will be routinely completed, with staff forgetting its original purpose.

Clinical staff as well as program staff meetings should include time for reemphasizing that developmental advancement is the goal of all treatment planning. Maintenance of such a therapeutic environment requires a kind of evaluation that is perhaps more important than evaluation of client progress and yet is rarely undertaken: the effort to evaluate the status of the milieu environment. I know of very few studies where the "milieu" is varied and the outcome examined (see, for example, Schopler et al., 1971) Fineberg et al. (1980, p. 928) conclude from their review of milieu treatment research that the "weakest area has been the delineation of active treatment ingredients," as they found no studies of the effect of modalities offered in residential centers or of the milieu itself.

Assessing the Milieu Environment

Ample evidence exists that milieu therapy (however defined) can assist seriously ego-impaired children to make developmental advancement. Yet can staff of residential centers continue to produce and maintain the type of environment necessary to foster such development? My own twenty-year experience indicates that continued effort is needed to "reinvent the wheel"; that residential centers go through cycles in which they are sometimes therapeutic, whereas at other times they simply provide child care and education. Treatment planning in these latter times is superficial and often ritualistic. At their worst, residential centers, because they group together children with serious psychopathology, become a collection of disturbed children who negatively influence others as well as staff.

Rabkin et al. (1966) define milieu therapy as follows:

> Milieu therapy, as we conceptualize it, means the planned creation of a very special and unique life space for each child, an environment delicately and constantly tuned to adapt to the child's ever-shifting needs. Our treatment philosophy assumes that the essence of the therapeutic experience for the child is residence in an environment which emphasizes growth, change, and adaptation—dynamic, constructive processes diametrically opposed to the static, destructive ones which characterizes his previous world. We therefore attempt to create, through regular reassessment of the child's current emotional needs, a wide variety of new learning contexts. The creation and maintenance of these positively reinforcing situations require constant communication between the various staff members and the vigilant awareness of a coordinator, most frequently the child's psychotherapist. (p. 273)

The authors give an example of the type of constant communication needed to maintain a therapeutic milieu. They go on to state:

> There is no magic in the words "therapeutic milieu," but there can be much seductive magical thinking following its initial creation. Such thinking assumes that the therapeutic milieu is self-perpetuating; that it can maintain a constant strength without continual surveillance; and that it can automatically mend a gap created by the loss of significant people. (p. 282)

What kind of surveillance is necessary to maintain the therapeutic milieu? Earlier in this chapter we presented the response required of caretakers to foster the development of children with no controls and those with variable controls. The milieu designed for the child with no controls considers the following principles:

1. The child is protected and rescued from situations in which he is frightened.
2. The program is designed to avoid or mitigate experiences of loss of face.
3. Restraints and prohibitions are made predictable.
4. Punishment is limited, and when a child is disciplined, statements such as "I want to help you control yourself" are employed as part of the control techniques.
5. Frustrations are made objective issues by clarification of the ambiguous and uncertain atmosphere the child experiences.
6. Staff members broaden the horizons of "dos" because the child has experienced many "don'ts."
7. A strong effort is made to expand the child's concrete skills so that he participates in many skill-building activities.
8. The child's defenses are supported, and more mature defenses are reinforced.

The milieu designed for the child with variable controls focuses on:

1. Efforts that will enable the child to please a cared-for adult.
2. Expanding the notion of good behavior to include notions broader than that of simple obedience.
3. Helping the child to feel good and to be admired to his ego achievements.
4. Opportunities for the child to be admired for behaviors other than compliance so that he begins to feel that he should want to do what the caring adult wishes.
5. Developing trust in his basically good impulses and his ability to control or mitigate his bad or aggressive impulses.
6. Providing prohibitions that are protective rather than punitive or humiliating.
7. Reinforcing the child's sustaining fictions (beliefs that the child holds about himself or his past that are not necessarily true but maintain his sense of well-being), and reaffirming past positive relationships.

In addition, staff following a developmental model (Klein and Mordock, 1975) attempt to develop milieu environments on the basis of developmental notions. Table 1 serves as an example of such thinking.

Table 1. Developmental levels and treatment environments.

STAGE OF EMOTIONAL DEVELOPMENT	OPTIMAL LEARNING CONDITIONS	TEACHING TECHNIQUES
Age 0–1½ years The child feels and behaves like an impulsive, demanding infant.	Give maximum gratification and loving acceptance with minimal demands to create a desire for the teacher's approval and a feeling of success.	Concrete rewards. Ample supplies. Visual objects. Teacher demonstrations. Rote learning. Avoidance of general discussions.
Age 1½–3 years The child both defies and clings to adults. He is often unreasonable and shows poor self-control.	A highly structured environment is needed for external support so that rules can be learned. Inconsistency is to be avoided.	Order and routine. Few distractions. Simple directions. Short, definite tasks. Labeling and sorting. Emphasis on standing in relation to norms.
Age 3–6 years The child seeks pleasure rather than achievement. He will control his behavior to please a liked teacher.	Maximum opportunity for independent self-assertion. Autonomy rather than enforced compliance.	The discovery method. Individual activities. Free discussion. Exploration to provide sensual gratifications for eyes, ears, hands. Experience in all modalities—music, games, storytelling. Use child's relationship with teacher for approval and disapproval.
Age 6–10 years The child is interested in mastering skills and making friends.	Opportunity to achieve in accordance with internalized aims, interests, and values.	Groups projects. Learning of information about the environment. Mastery of skills with practical applications. Use of peer competition and peer approval.

MILIEU TREATMENT IMPLICATIONS	MILIEU TECHNIQUES
Meet needs unreservedly, lovingly, consistently. Don't demand self-denial, sharing, etc. Provide a permanent one-to-one relationship. No volunteer visits with unfamiliar people; use staff instead.	Material gifts in abundance. Use food as a highly personal and pleasurable experience; special dishes, feeding, etc. Much cuddling and touching. Extra persons so that the maximum of individual attention can be given. Counselors should not specialize according to their talents, but stick closely to the same children.
Approval and disapproval by the loved person only can be accepted and used to gain internal controls. Reassurance without overprotection, and external support of controls, without letting the child control the environment is most helpful. Avoid punishment, impatience, and criticism.	When the loved person is absent, use group and institution rules as firm guidelines. Tolerate food fads, and provide sweets freely. Provide a great deal of individual, free, recreational activity leading to physical mastery, such as bike riding, roller skating. Neat collections and well-controlled paint and clay activity are helpful.
Explanation and reassurance. Acceptance of masturbation within limits. Nonacceptance of peer sex play. Freedom and encouragement for initiative. Approval of sexual characteristics and role. Continued use of approval and disapproval by loved person with further demands for self-control. Start using shame for destructive or unethical behavior and logic to aid control.	The child has relatively little need for mothering, but needs close contact with adults of both sexes. Overemotional attitudes toward these adults are to be tolerated. Offer encouragement toward fantasy play and storytelling; also toward many individual creative projects. Trips and exposures to new experiences are meaningful and enriching from now on.
Have realistic expectations. Provide compensatory experiences and skills. Give opportunities for practical achievement. Moral attitudes should be consciously taught. Acceptance of delay, frustration, and self-sacrifice should be demanded.	Create high status for educational progress by admiration, interest, modeling. Similarly, foster other ego skills and talents, particularly in the poorest school achievers. Deemphasize athletic prowess unless it is the child's sole asset. Real jobs should be available. Contributions to group living should also be rewarded. Discussion groups, using rationality and empathy, are profitable now in forming character and resolving conflicts.

The developmentalist assumes that a child must have his needs met at any one level before he will move up to the next stage of development. Meeting the child's needs leads to developmental progression. An important, but as yet untested, assumption of this approach is that general developmental progression can be best achieved by concentrating on the areas where the child is developmentally weakest. The plan is to treat the child, by and large, in accordance with his weaknesses instead of trying to develop his relative strengths to even higher stages. Pulling the child up from the lowest levels would produce a greater balance in development, and it is balanced development that is associated with emotional maturity.

Maintaining the type of milieu environment necessary to foster development in each child requires continuing examination, to determine whether staff are constantly aware of and focused on developing and implementing appropriate activities for children grouped according to developmental needs. In general, staff have difficulty responding to older children as if they were younger. Staff need much support and encouragement to allow regressions such as sucking on baby bottles, wrapping up in blankets, preferring to play rather than learn, or making messes. Training programs utilizing Maslow's concepts of need hierarchies, in addition to developmental information, help staff to accept the fact that children with unmet infantile needs must have these needs met before they can advance developmentally.

Evaluation Methods

Moos (see Moos and Fuhr, 1982) developed a ward atmosphere scale that permits assessment of the type of atmosphere that exists in a psychiatric ward. Earlier Moos had determined empirically that patients treated in a ward characterized as having a more democratic atmosphere have the fewest readmission rates. In addition, Moos's work has contributed to the growing body of knowledge about social support. (Social support is regarded as naturally existing resources that act to prevent disorder by either buffering the effects of stress or by meeting the individual's fundamental needs for meaningful human attachment; see Greenblatt et al., 1982).

Even behaviorists are now realizing that the production and maintenance of improvements in child behavior problems are not always guaranteed by dealing with the immediate environmental contingencies of those behaviors. Environmental events temporally distant from the child's behaviors, and their stimulus contingencies, exert control over these stimulus–response interactions. Clinicians are attempting to bolster these environmental events [called "setting events" (Wahler and Graves, 1983)] and the support networks that are available to clients, a tactic that will be discussed in a later section of this chapter. The residential treatment center by definition is a social support system for a child, and, like any system, it needs regular monitoring and bolstering. There is no reason why the necessary tools cannot be developed to assess "atmospheres" and social support systems in children's centers.

Meaningful Quality Assurance Studies

The Joint Commission on Accreditation of Hospitals, a body now accrediting many residential treatment centers, requires that ongoing quality assurance studies be performed by those agencies it accredits (see Chapter 12). It requires the ongoing collection and evaluation of information about important aspects of patient care, both to identify opportunities for improving care and to identify problems that impact on such care. Each department or service is required to participate in evaluating its own performance against objective criteria developed by the service itself.

If, for example, it is agreed that the child with no controls should have pleasurable activities with minimal frustration, that frustration should be made into objective issues, and that the relationship aspects of recreational activities should predominate, then the following guidelines should be observed. First, recreational activities should never be contingent upon acceptable behavior. Second, initial activities should be those that require the development of a new skill, such as record playing, tumbling, simple card games, well-known table games, crayoning, and storytelling. The activities should be those in which the child needs no extra help or support, waiting and taking turns is minimized, there is no element of danger, and impulse control is minimal. The games also should include those with high-powered "it" roles, such as "red light–green light," "Simon says," or "statues," where the child can experience mastery. Third, food and rhythm should be involved whenever possible.

If analysis of the recreational programming for children with no controls reveals that they are involved in treasure or scavenger hunts, relay races requiring concentration, dodge ball, or even "hide and seek," then the recreational program is not achieving its objectives for such children. Games involving impulse control, such as relay races requiring concentration, or those requiring frustration tolerance, such as treasure hunts, may be accepted for some children with variable controls, but are inappropriate for those with no controls. If it is also found that children are being deprived of recreational activities because of disruptive or aggressive behavior (denial of activity or excessive time-out from the activity), then recreational staff have "forgotten" the stated objectives of their service for children arrested at that particular level of development.

As stated earlier, the clinician's main task in residential centers is to help design and monitor the milieu plan for each youngster and to develop overall milieu approaches for children subgrouped into meaningful treatment categories. Evaluation, then, is the continued ongoing formal assessment of whether the milieu plans are being implemented—it is quality assurance! Returning to the developmental chart presented earlier, observational and coding techniques can be developed to assess whether a child diagnosed as emotionally arrested at between two and three years of age is truly getting the optimal learning conditions, teaching techniques, and milieu techniques designed for his developmental level. (See for example, Braun et al., 1969, who analyzed teaching styles of persons working with disturbed children.) Are the staff tolerating food fads and encouraging gross motor physical activity? Is punishment kept to a minimum on the living unit?

If the goal for ego-impaired children is to support the development of defenses and to develop coping skills, do staff know concretely what this means for their behavior? If they say to the child who storms away from an activity, "You always run away when things get tough," rather than "I'm glad you didn't destroy anything; color for a while since this usually calms you down, and I will check with you shortly," then they're not supporting defenses but actually tearing them down! (See Van Ornum and Mordock, 1983.) I have observed that the majority of workers (including highly trained clinicians) need a manual of clinical procedures that includes concrete ways to respond to children in various situations. Staff behaviors, including verbal ones, can be classified as therapeutic, neutral, and antitherapeutic, with the manual giving examples of staff behavior falling into each of the three classes for various selected situations that occur regularly in treatment settings. In the example cited, the first statement would be considered antitherapeutic because it confronts the child with his defense and implies disapproval of its use; the second is therapeutic because it actually supports leaving the scene (as opposed to use of the more primitive defense of destruction) and concentrates on helping the child to get less upset (helps develop a coping skill). Saying nothing or asking the child what got him upset could be considered neutral responses, although the latter often gets the child more upset because he usually does not know why he got upset, or does not want to admit his weaknesses (loss of face—an undesired experience). If all the members of a treatment team reviewed the extent to which they were able to use therapeutic responses to a child over the course of a three-month period, they each would be more aware of the reasons why individual children have or have not advanced developmentally.

Earlier we commented that residential treatment centers vary in their clinical effectiveness. It is easy for a center to slip into the practice of simply providing education (after all, the children are far behind in school) and child care (after all, the children have few concrete skills), "forgetting" that the children are disturbed. Education and care predominate over treatment, and the center functions like a normal child-care institution rather than a treatment setting. It can be enlightening for staff to visit residential centers that serve scholastically and athletically capable children or adolescents, where educational and recreational needs are minimal, if not nonexistent.

Problems other than failure to provide actual treatment also arise from time to time in residential centers, seriously diluting the effectiveness of planned milieus. These problems include communication difficulties (Caplan, 1966; Montalvo and Pavlin, 1966), misunderstanding of family reactions (Christ and Wagner, 1966), and staff burnout (see Chapter 14). Such problems do not have to become crises; ongoing assessment of their presence can result in their timely resolution.

SUPPORT NETWORKS

Although we have concentrated on the child and the milieu, equally intensive evaluative efforts need to be directed toward assessing a family's response to treatment and the family's need for supportive services. In many cases, family members do not actively participate in treatment efforts. Children from more disturbed families make less progress in residential treatment than children from less troubled families; typically it is most often these disturbed families that fail to respond to our efforts. Although it is beyond the scope of this chapter to discuss treatment approaches with multi-problem families, the data suggest that actually we temper our enthusiasm when it comes to *treating* families, and instead we advocate for other support services for children and families. Family systems theory was initially expected to make a significant impact on children's treatment (see Auerswald, 1969), but like all panaceas, it has not lived up to its promise.

A study of 356 admissions to a residential center (Mordock, 1978) revealed that 65% of the children had experienced separation from their families prior to admission, and a similar percentage experienced changes in their primary caretaker. Those separated had been so for 45% of their lives. They averaged 46 months away from home prior to admission and had 3.3 changes in prime caretaking agent. Only 40% of children were living at home at the time of their admission. In addition, about half the children's sibling were also placed outside the home (Mordock, 1978). All these families had received considerable service from other community and child care agencies, and yet the child still experienced one or more placements.

While 67% of 93 families studied in 1970 (Mordock, 1978) were viewed as cooperative by agency staff, outside supports were needed to sustain 80% of the families, with 65% needing mental health services. Mistrust, poor self-esteem, and denial of problems were present in 68%. In approximately 40% of the cases, parent problems, rather than parental child-rearing problems per se, were responsible for the child's placement away from home. Similarly, Quinton and Rutter (1984) report that contrary to the current belief that parent training programs can help multi-problem families, parenting is not an attribute of an individual independent of his or her current life situation, and breakdown in parental functioning seldom occurs in response to current disadvantages alone. Parenting problems were strongly associated with marked psychiatric impairment in one or both parents, and with marital difficulties. In addition, parenting was affected by the presence of other life stressors, such as the availability of social supports, qualities of the spouse, the extent to which child rearing was shared, time available, and housing conditions. It was noted that:

> The stresses caused by poverty and poor circumstances are amenable to amelioration through appropriate social policies, but the stresses caused by marital problems may be more intractable. (Quinton and Rutter, 1984, p. 246)

During the children's stay in placement, many families dissolve so that the child returns to either a single parent or a parent with a new paramour, while none returns to a former foster home (Mordock, 1978). As a result, only 44% of children in the Mordock study returned to their families following treatment, and, of these, 32% needed additional group care at a later date. Twenty-eight percent of the children were discharged to foster care, and of these, only 24% spent time with their families during their youth. Forty-five percent of those originally placed in foster care were later transferred to group care, and all were still in group care at follow-up or discharged to independent living. Twenty-one percent were initially discharged to group homes with 50% returning to parents or relatives after an extended period in the group home. In summary, close to 60 percent of the children discharged from residential treatment needed group care (group home, child care institution, or psychiatric center) at some time following their discharge (Mordock, 1978).

Studies of hospitalized adults reveal the dissolution of the patient's network of support following placement. This network collapse is attributed to both antagonistic attitudes of collaterals and the patient's impaired social competence (Lipton et al., 1981). It is clear that this phenomenon also occurs for children, as both families and communities are quick to reclassify a child admitted to a residential center as "theirs" rather than "ours" and can resent the child's return to the community. Parental attitudes expressing a sense of relief are associated with poor outcomes whereas separation difficulties are associated with positive outcomes (LaBarbera et al., 1982). Mordock (1978) concludes:

The supports, but not necessarily the services, received by the child are more significantly related to his eventual outcome than the degree or kind of emotional disturbance he displayed at either admission or discharge. Unless the child showed extremely disturbed or bizarre behavior, his outcome could not be predicted from his behavior. (pp. 227–228)

This result has been reported by others for adult populations (Goering et al., 1983; Billings and Moos, 1985).

Although it now is popular to laud network intervention as the solution to children's problems, social workers in residential care have been involved in such work for many years (Specht and Glasser, 1963). In addition, Cohen and Adler (1986) state:

Indeed, successful network interventions must be viewed as an unhurried, long-term effort. The fact that the project staff identified distrust of professionals and a lack of sensitivity to one's personal network as major impediments indicated that considerable rapport and education may be required before a network procedure can be implemented. (p. 287)

Monitoring Treatment Planning

Evaluative efforts should also include monitoring of treatment team planning. The monitoring of discharge planning falls into the category of network assessment. What makes a particular supportive environment work? What type of children do well in foster homes, group homes, etc.? Because of pressures to discharge children from residential centers as quickly as possible, inappropriate discharge plans often are made. I propose that agencies should develop concrete criteria against which to validate a discharge plan. One such set of criteria, which I developed from research findings and experience, appears in Table 2.

Table 2. Criteria for monitoring treatment plans for discharge.

I. Discharge Plan (evaluated after one year in treatment for long-term cases)

To Own Home—The following should have occurred:
1. Child has had parental contacts at residence in last six months.
2. Child has visited home in last six months.
3. Child has had extended period of stay at home in last six months (four or more days).
4. Child has received frequent telephone calls, letters, photographs from psychological parents.
5. Record reflects efforts of staff to encourage parent contacts of all types.

WARNING FLAGS
1. Child has been away from home for over 50% of his life.
2. Child has other siblings placed outside the home.
3. Mother has moved during the last year.
4. Sibling has been placed within past year.

To Foster Home—The following should have occurred:
1. Child has visited in last six months with adults who are potential foster home parents.
2. Child has had contact (mail, telephone) with an adult who is a potential foster home parent.
3. Record reflects discussion with parents of possibility of foster home placement for their child.

WARNING FLAGS
1. Child's predominant family identification is with his natural family.
2. Child had a series of unsuccessful foster home placements prior to admission and has not discussed his history while in placement.

To Group Home—The following should have occurred:
1. Child has spent over 50% of his life in group care but has a natural family.
2. Child has had a series of unsuccessful foster home placements and has never verbalized his feelings about these placements.
3. Parents have rejected past efforts at foster home placements and have interfered with placements that have taken place.

Adoption—The following should have occurred:
1. Child's history is sufficiently free of severe psychopathology and, therefore, will not require frequent mental health intervention in future years.
2. Child is freed for adoption.
3. Child has had no contact with his natural parents for several years.
4. Child has no psychological parents.

WARNING FLAGS
1. Child can be freed for adoption but has been in foster home for a number of years, and foster parents reject idea of adoption.
2. Child had previous long-term placement in a foster home in which death of a parent or encroaching old age contributed to the breakdown of placements.
3. Child has verbalized his past history and his feelings related to historical events.

II. Discharge Plan (evaluated when discharge is pending)
    To Own Home—The following should have occurred:
    1. Child has had extended period of stay at home (four or more days).

2. Record reflects parent's report of ability to manage and care for child during extended stay.

WARNING FLAGS
1. Visits home were characterized by short stays followed by transfer to relatives.
2. Child has never verbalized reasons for his placement.

To Foster Home—The following should have occurred:
1. Child has had volunteer placements in family setting during period of stay, and record reflects that these stays are relatively trouble-free.
2. Record reflects efforts to elicit child's feelings about foster home placements.
3. Child has some notion of agency's responsibility for him and how this responsibility is carried out.
4. Record reflects that agency has kept image of natural parent alive in child's mind.
5. Record reflects efforts to clarify visiting arrangements between natural and foster parents.
6. Record reflects that both natural and foster parents have discussed stages a child goes through in reacting to foster home placement.

WARNING FLAGS
1. Child has had different volunteer placements during his stay.
2. Child relates no feelings about foster home placement.
3. Child has unmarried mother and has been placed early in life.
4. Child cannot verbalize a conception of foster parent's motivation for caring for him.
5. Natural parent is reluctant to meet with foster parents.
6. Child's recent behavior is free of signs of splitting the mother figure with good and bad images, concrete expressions of which are:
   a. Physical attacks on maternal figures.
   b. Hate and love notes written or verbalized to parent figure.

To Group Home—The following should have occurred:
1. Child needs diluted emotional relationships.
2. Child's behavior is very unpredictable and subject to wide mood swings.
3. Child's behavior problems suggest considerable need for agency support of community facilities in which the child will be enrolled.
4. Natural or psychological parents reject idea of foster home placement after efforts to win their acceptance of idea.
5. Child has experienced loyalty conflicts between agency parent figures and natural or psychological parents.
6. Child has visited group home within past three months.
7. Natural or psychological parents have visited group home within past three months and received orientation to group home program.
8. Child has verbalized his feelings about group home placement.

Adoption—The following should have occurred:
1. Child has had successful volunteer placements with parent figures.
2. Child is sufficiently freed from ties to psychological parents.
3. Child has verbalized desire for adoption and has realistic expectations of parent figures.
4. Child has verbalized and discussed past history with staff.
5. Child has formed attachments to agency staff.

Inspection of Table 2 indicates that a child is a good risk for foster care when discharge is pending if he has discussed foster home placement, has had trouble-free volunteer placements, can describe his mother and his relationship with her, and so on. The clinical record should reflect that these critical events have occurred, and quality assurance staff could assure their presence by regular sampling of records.

Although evaluative efforts should continue, there exists a host of data (See Mordock, 1978, pp. 225–237) indicating that extended group care and foster care are a necessary part of the treatment of seriously ego-impaired children. Effective treatment of some children takes considerable time when one is working with tenacious resistances and early fixations. As Masterson (1976) states, "When we find briefer means of development then we will have briefer forms of therapy" (p. 95). Other children need group care not because they present behavior management problems, but because they cannot tolerate the close interpersonal relationships characteristic of foster or adoptive homes. Evaluative efforts should focus on identifying the types of children who will most need continued group care, clarifying to others why this is so, and not apologizing for this fact simply because it appears costly. The cost of caring for a child in a group home or even in a small children's home throughout his youth is less than the annual salary of some professional athletes and corporation presidents!

Skuse (1984) concluded, after an in-depth study of three young children raised in an extremely deprived family and then transferred to a group living situation:

Secondly, it is shown that placement in a nuclear family is not necessary for substantial gains to be made in intellectual, emotional or social functioning. Louis has spent the last decade in a small children's home, albeit with a consistent caretaker. (p. 40)

The children Mordock (1978) studied did quite well as adults, indicating the cost-effectiveness of extended group care. Moreover, the majority of those children had been separated from their families prior to intake. Prentice-Dunn et al. (1981) also reported that following discharge, children living in group homes, in the care of an agency, in foster placement, or with relatives showed more positive changes than those living with one or both of their biological parents.

One reason why children do better in these less traditional living arrangements than in their own families is that the alternative caretakers not only provide more stability but also function as effective advocates for the child in the community. Agency staff or relatives help the child and the community through the periodic crises that characterize these children's lives. They attend meetings, both planned and emergency, at schools, intercede on the child's behalf with police, arrange for participation in after-school recreational or vocational programs or operate such programs themselves, and make other interagency contacts on the child's behalf—all tasks that the multi-problem family usually is unable to do for its child.

To conclude, evaluative efforts in residential centers should now focus less on outcome and more on monitoring treatment environments. We have already established that children generally improve in residential treatment—close to 60% are judged to have done so in the Mordock (1978) study. What is needed is refined assessment of the children's adaptive functioning from a developmental viewpoint and evaluation of factors contributing to improvement, as well as monitoring for the continued presence of these factors along the lines suggested in this chapter.

SUGGESTED READINGS

To assist those desiring more knowledge about developmental assessment of children, to generate thinking about the types of treatment environments or milieus necessary for children, and to familiarize the reader with evaluative efforts in residential treatment, a suggested list of supplemental readings, organized under three headings, follows the references cited at the end of this chapter. This bibliography is by no means complete, but is merely a list of those works I have found helpful, in addition to the classic works in the field, in stimulating my interest, providing food for thought, and answering my specific questions over the years. Most of the articles and books listed are not recent ones. Whether this phenomenon is due to waning enthusiasm among professionals for residential services (such services have taken a back seat to developments in community mental health) or to difficulties in implementing what has already been proposed is anyone's guess.

REFERENCES

Adessa, S. and Laatsch, A. (1965). Extended residential treatment: eight year anxiety. *Social Work, 10,* 16–24.

Albert, A. (1959). Reversibility of pathological fixations associated with maternal deprivation in infancy. *Psychoanalytic Study of the Child, 14,* 169–185.

Auerswald, E. H. (1969). Changing concepts and changing models of residential treatment. In G. Caplan and S. Leboviei, eds., *Adolescence, Psychosocial Perspectives,* New York: Basic Books.

Baenen, R. S., Stephens, M. A. R., and Glenwick, D. S. (1986). Outcome in psychoeducational day school programs: a review. *American Journal of Orthopsychiatry, 56,* 263–270.

Beardslee, W. R., Jacobson, A. M., and Power, S. (1985). An approach to evaluating adolescent adaptive processes: scale development and reliability. *Journal of the American Academy of Child Psychiatry, 24,* 637–642.

Beres, D. (1952). Clinical notes on aggression in children. *Psychoanalytic Study of the Child, 7,* 241–263.

Beres, D. (1956). Ego deviation and the concept of schizophrenia. *Psychoanalytic Study of the Child, 11,* 164–235.

Beres, D. (1965). Ego disturbances associated with early deprivation. *Journal of the American Academy of Child Psychiatry, 4,* 188–205.

Billings, A. E. and Moos, R. H. (1985). Life stressors and social resources affect post-treatment outcomes among depressed patients. *Journal of Abnormal Psychology, 94,* 140–153.

Bloom, B. S. (1964). *Stability and Change in Human Characteristics.* New York: Wiley.

Bowlby, J. (1977). The making and breaking of affectional bonds. I. Aetiology and psychopathology in light of attachment theory. *British Journal of Psychiatry, 130,* 201–210.

Braun, S. J., Holzman, M. S., and Lasher, M. G. (1969). Teachers of disturbed preschool children: an analysis of teaching styles. *American Journal of Orthopsychiatry, 39,* 609–618.

Caplan, L. M. (1966). Identification, a complicating factor in the inpatient treatment of adolescent girls. *American Journal of Orthopsychiatry, 36,* 720–724.

Christ, A. E. and Wagner, N. E. (1966). Introgenic factors in residential treatment: a problem of staff training. *American Journal of Orthopsychiatry, 36,* 725–729.

Cohen, C. I. and Adler, A. (1986). Assessing the role of social network interventions with an inner-city population. *American Journal of Orthopsychiatry, 56,* 278–288.

Crenshaw, D. A., Bowsell, J., Guare, R., and Yingling, C. I. (1986). Intensive psychotherapy of repeatedly and severely traumatized children. *Residential Group Care and Treatment, 3,* 17–36.

David, H. P., ed., (1972). *Child Mental Health in International Perspective: Report of the Joint Commission on Mental Health of Children.* New York: Harper and Row.

Ekstein, R. (1962). Special training problems in psychotherapeutic work with psychotic and borderline children. *American Journal of Orthopsychiatry, 32,* 569–583.

Ekstein, R. (1967). *Children of Time and Space, Action and Impulse.* New York: Appleton-Century-Crofts.

Fineberg, B., Sowards, S., and Kettlewell, P. (1980). Adolescent inpatient treatment: a literature review. *Adolescence, 15,* 913–925.

Freud, A. (1965). *Normality and Pathology of Childhood.* New York: International Universities Press.

Geleerd, E. R. (1946). A contribution to the problem of psychosis in children. *Psychoanalytic Study of the Child, 2,* 273–291.

Goering, P., Wasylenki, L. W., and Freeman, S. J. (1983). Social support and post-hospital outcome for depressed women. *Canadian Journal of Psychiatry, 28,* 612-618.

Goldfarb, W. (1970). *A Follow-up Investigation of Schizophrenic Children.* New York: Jewish Board of Guardians.

Gould, R. (1972). *Child Studies through Fantasy.* New York: Quadrangle Books.

Greenblatt, M., Becerra, R., and Serafetinides, E. A. (1982). Social networks and mental health: an overview. *American Journal of Psychiatry, 139,* 977-984.

Grieger, R., Mordock, J. B., and Breyer, N. (1970). General guidelines for conducting behavior modification programs in public school settings. *Journal of School Psychology, 8,* 259-266.

King, C. H. (1976). Counter-transference and counter-experience in the treatment of violence prone youth. *American Journal of Orthopsychiatry, 46,* 43-52.

Klein, B. and Mordock, J. B. (1975). A guide to differentiated developmental diagnoses with a case demonstrating its use. *Child Psychiatry and Human Development, 5,* 242-253.

Kohlberg, L., LaCrosse, J., and Ricks, D. (1972). The predictability of adult mental health from childhood behavior. In B. B. Wolman, ed., *Manual of Child Psychopathology,* New York: McGraw-Hill.

Konstantareas, M. M. and Humatidis, S. (1984). Aggressive and prosocial behaviors before and after treatment in conduct-disordered children and their matched controls. *Journal of Child Psychiatry and Psychology, 25,* 607-620.

LaBarbera, J. D., Martin, J. E., and Dozier, J. E. (1982). Residential treatment of males: the influential role of parental attitudes. *Journal of the American Academy of Child Psychiatry, 21,* 286-290.

Lipton, F. R., Cohen, C. I., Fischer, E., and Katz, S. E. (1981). Schizophrenia: a network crisis. *Schizophrenia Bulletin, 7,* 144-151.

Martion, L. H., Pozdnjakoff, I., and Wilding, J. (1976). The use of residential care. *Child Welfare, 55,* 269-277.

Masterson, J. F. (1972). *Treatment of the Borderline Adolescent: A Developmental Approach.* New York: Wiley.

Masterson, J. F. (1976). *Psychotherapy of the Borderline Adult: A Developmental Approach.* New York: Brunner/Mazel.

Matsushima, J. (1979). Outcomes of residential treatment: designing accountability protocols. *Child Welfare, 58,* 303-318.

Menninger, R. W. (1977). Psychiatric treatment: what is quality and how do we measure it? *Bulletin of the Menninger Clinic, 41,* 181-190.

Montalvo, B. and Pavlin, S. (1966). Faculty staff communication in a residential treatment center. *American Journal of Orthopsychiatry, 36,* 706, 711.

Moos, H. R. and Fuhr, R. (1982). The clinical use of sociological concepts. *American Journal of Orthopsychiatry, 52,* 111-122.

Mordock, J. B. (1970). Developmentalist or behaviorist: a reaction to Allen Ross. *The Clinical Psychologist, 24,* 11-12.

Mordock, J. B. (1978). *Ego Impaired Children Grow Up: Post-discharge Adjustment of Children in Residential Treatment.* Special monograph in commemoration of the Silver Anniversary of The Astor Home for Children, Rhinebeck, N.Y.

Mordock, J. B. (1979a). Evaluation in residential treatment: the conceptual dilemmas. *Child Welfare, 58,* 293–302.

Mordock, J. B. (1979b). The separation–individuation process and developmental disabilities. *Exceptional Children, 46,* 176–184.

Mordock, J. B. (1986). The inadequacy of formal measures of child adjustment during residential treatment. *Residential Treatment for Children and Youth 42,* 55–73.

Mordock, J. B. (1987). Evaluating the dually-diagnosed. In F. Menolascino and R. Fletcher, eds., *The Care and Treatment of the Dually-Diagnosed.* Baltimore: The John Hopkins University Press.

Mordock, J. B. and Phillips, D. (1971). The behavior therapist in the schools. *Psychotherapy: Theory Research and Practice, 8,* 231–235.

Nagera, H. (1963). The developmental profile: notes on some practical considerations regarding its use. *Psychoanalytic Study of the Child, 18,* 511–540.

Prentice-Dunn, S., Wilson, D., and Lyman, R. (1981). Client factors related to outcome in a residential and day treatment program for children. *Journal of Clinical Child Psychology, 19,* 188–191.

Quinton, D. and Rutter, M. (1984). Parents with children in care. I. Intergenerational continuities. *Journal of Child Psychiatry and Psychology, 25,* 231–250.

Rabkin, L., Weinberger, G., and Klein, A. (1966). What made Allen run? The process of communication in residential treatment. *Journal of the American Academy of Child Psychiatry, 5,* 272–283.

Rank, B. and MacNaughton, D. (1956). A clinical contribution to early ego development. *Psychoanalytic Study of the Child, 5,* 53–65.

Rausch, H. L. (1959). Observational research with emotionally disturbed children: session I. 3. On the locus of behavior-observations in multiple settings within residential treatment. *American Journal of Orthopsychiatry, 29,* 235–241.

Rinsley, D. B. (1974). Residential treatment of adolescents. In S. Arieta, ed., *American Handbook of Psychiatry,* Vol. II, 2nd revised edition. New York: Basic Books.

Risley, T., Sajwaj, T., Doke, L., and Agras, S. (1975). Specialized day care as a psychiatric outpatient service. In E. Ramp and G. Semb, eds., *Behavior Analysis: Areas of Research and Application.* Englewood Cliffs, N.J.: Prentice-Hall.

Schopler, E., Brehm, S. S., Kinsbourne, M., and Reichler, R. J. (1971). Effect on treatment structure on development in autistic children. *Archives of General Psychiatry, 24,* 415–421.

Silver, L. B. (1976). *Professional Standards Review Organizations: A Handbook for Child Psychiatrists.* Washington, D.C.: American Academy of Child Psychiatry.

Skuse, D. (1984). Extreme deprivation in early childhood. I. Diverse outcomes for three siblings from an extraordinary family. *Journal of Child Psychiatry and Psychology, 25,* 523–541.

Specht, R. and Glasser, B. (1963). A review of the literature in social work with hospitalized adolescents and their families. *Social Service Review, 37,* 295–306.

Stiffman, A. R., Jung, K. G., and Feldman, R. A. (1986). A multivariate risk model for childhood behavior problems. *American Journal of Orthopsychiatry, 56,* 204–211.

Tanguay, P. E. (1984). Towards a new classification of serious psychopathology in children. *Journal of the American Academy of Child Psychiatry, 23*, 373-384.

Van Ornum, W. and Mordock, J. B. (1983). *Crisis Counseling of Children and Adolescents.* New York: Continuum.

Wahler, R. G. and Graves, M. G. (1983). Setting events in social networks: ally or enemy in child behavior therapy. *Behavior Therapy, 14*, 19-36.

Weil, A. P. (1956). Some evidences of deviational development in infancy and early childhood. *Psychoanalytic Study of the Child, 11*, 292-299.

Weinstein, L. (1974). Evaluation of a program for reeducating disturbed children: a follow-up comparison with untreated children. Final report. Bureau for the Education of the Handicapped, UNDHEW Project Nos. 6-2974 and 552023.

Weitzman, J. (1985). Engaging the severely dysfunctional family in treatment: basic considerations. *Family Process, 24*, 473-485.

Wood, M. E., ed., (1975). *Rutland Center Model for Treating Emotionally Disturbed Children.* Athens, Ga.: Rutland Center.

SUGGESTED READINGS

Developmental Assessment

Specific Readings

Bemporad, J. R. (1972). Cognitive growth and childhood psychopathology: the concept of finality. *Child Psychiatry and Human Development, 3*, 63-67.

Fraiberg, S. (1960). On the sleep disturbances of early childhood. *Psychoanalytic Study of the Child, 5*, 285-309.

Freud, A. (1963). The concept of developmental lines. *Psychoanalytic Study of the Child, 18*, 245-265.

Korner, A. F. and Opsvig, P. (1966). Developmental considerations in diagnosis and treatment—a case illustration. *Journal of Child Psychiatry, 5*, 594-616.

Meers, D. R. (1966). A diagnostic profile of psychopathology in a latency child. *Psychoanalytic Study of the Child, 21*, 483-526.

Nagera, H. (1966). Sleep and its disturbances approached developmentally. *Psychoanalytic Study of the Child, 21*, 391-447.

Neff, B. and Hayward, R. (1971). Reciprocal contributions between psychoanalysis and education. *Journal of Child Psychiatry, 10*, 204-241.

Ruebush, F. K. and Waite, R. R. (1962). Oral dependency in anxious and defensive children. *Merrill-Palmer Quarterly, 7*, 181-190.

Sandler, J. and Rosenblatt, B. (1962). The concept of the representational world. *Psychoanalyic Study of the Child, 17*, 128-145.

Santostefano, S. (1971). Beyond nosology: diagnosis from the viewpoint of development. In H. H. Rie, ed., *Perspectives in Child Psychopathology.* Chicago: Adline, Atherton.

Shane, M. (1967). Encopresis in a latency boy: an arrest along a developmental line. *Psychoanalytic Study of the Child, 22*, 296-314.

General Readings

Beres, D. and Obers, S. J. (1950). The effects of extreme deprivation in infancy on psychic structure in adolescence: a study in ego development. *The Psychoanalytic Study of the Child, 5,* 212–235.

Daunton, E. (1969). *The Therapeutic Nursery School.* New York: International Universities Press.

Edgcumbe, R. and Burgner, M. (1972). Some problems in the conceptualization of early object relationships: Part I. The concepts of need satisfaction and need-satisfying relationships. *The Psychoanalytic Study of the Child, 27,* 283–314. Part II. The concept of object constancy. *The Psychoanalytic Study of the Child, 27,* 315–338.

Erikson, E. H. (1969). *Identity and the Life Cycle.* New York: International Universities Press.

Fraiberg, S. (1959). *The Magic Years.* New York: Charles Scribner's Sons.

Freud, S. (1953). Three essays on the theory of sexuality. *Standard Edition, 7,* 125–245. London: Hogarth Press.

Furth, H. G. (1970). *Piaget for Teachers.* Englewood Cliffs, N.J.: Prentice-Hall.

Hartmann, H. (1958). *Ego Psychology and the Problem of Adaptation.* New York: International Universities Press.

Jacobson, E. (1964). *The Self and the Object World.* New York: International Universities Press.

Kestenberg, J., Marcus, H., Robbins, E., Berlow, J., and Buette, A. (1971). Development of the young child as expressed through bodily movement I. *Journal of the American Psychoanalytic Association, 19,* 746–764.

Khan, M. M. R. (1963). The concept of cumulative trauma. *Psychoanalytic Study of the Child, 18,* 296–306.

Lichtenberg, P. and Norton, D. (1970). *Cognitive and Mental Development in the First Five Years of Life: A Review of Recent Research.* Rockville, Md.: National Institute of Mental Health.

Mahler, M. (1963). Thoughts about development and individuation. *Psychoanalytic Study of the Child, 18,* 307–324.

Mahler, M. (1972). On the first three sub-phases of the separation individuation process. *International Journal of Psycho-Analysis, 53,* 333–338.

Rosenthal, M. J. (1962). The syndrome of the inconsistent mother. *American Journal of Orthopsychiatry, 32,* 637–644.

Sandler, J. and Jaffe, W. G. (1967). The tendency to persistance in psychological function and development. *Bulletin of the Menninger Clinic, 31,* 257–271.

Stein, M. (1974). Educational psychotherapy of preschoolers. *Journal of American Academy of Child Psychiatry, 13,* 618–634.

Wolfenstein, M. (1969). Loss, rage and repetition. *Psychoanalytic Study of the Child, 24,* 432–460.

Methodological Issues and Descriptive Studies

Bauer, N. and Krivohlavy, J. (1974). Co-operative conflict resolution in institution-alized boy dyads. *Journal of Child Psychology and Psychiatry, 15,* 13–21.

Breitmeyer, R. G., Bottum, G., and Wayner, B. R. (1974). Issues in evaluative follow-up for a residential treatment program. *Hospital and Community Psychiatry,* *25,* 804–806.

Chandler, M. J., Greenspan, S., and Barenboim, C. (1974). Assessment and training of role-taking and referential communication skills in institutionalized emotionally disturbed children. *Developmental Psychology, 10,* 546–553.

Dinwiddie, F. W. (1974). Reciprocity of emotional transactions: a crucial issue in residential care and treatment. *Child Care Quarterly, 3,* 119–124.

Durkin, R. P. and Durkin, A. B. (1975). Evaluating residential treatment programs for disturbed children. In M. Guttentag and E. L. Struening, eds., *Handbook of Evaluation Research* Vol. II. Beverly Hills, Calif.: Sage.

Hagamen, M. B. (1977). Family support systems: their effect on long-term psychiatric hospitalizations in children. *Journal of the American Academy of Child Psychiatry, 16,* 53–66.

Heinicke, C. M. and Westheimer, I. J. (1965). *Brief Separations.* New York: International Universities Press.

Johnson, H. L., Nutter, C., Callan, L., and Ramsey, R. (1976). Program evaluation in residential treatment: some practical issues. *Child Welfare, 55,* 279–287.

Masten, A. S. (1979). Family therapy as a treatment for children: a critical review of outcome research. *Family Process, 18,* 323–335.

Minuchin, S., Auerswald, E., King, C. H., and Rabinowitz, C. (1964). The study and treatment of families who produce multiple acting-out boys. *American Journal of Orthopsychiatry, 34,* 125–133.

Owen, G. (1974). Residential treatment of young offenders: the boys' perspectives. *British Journal of Criminology, 14,* 318–335.

Shyne, A. W. (1976). Evaluation in child welfare. *Child Welfare, 55,* 5–18.

Talmach, J. (1985). "There ain't nobody on my side": a new day treatment program for black urban youth. *Journal of Clinical Child Psychology, 14,* 214–219.

Tizard, J. and Tizard, B. (1974). The institution as an environment for development. In M. P. Richards, ed., *The Integration of a Child into a Social World.* London: Cambridge University Press.

VanScoy, H. C. and Bordelon, K. J. (1974). Patients' perceptions of the residential treatment staff: revisited. *Adolescent, 9,* 237–244.

Whittaker, J. K. (1974). Evaluating residential treatment. *Child Care Quarterly, 3,* 195–196.

Wolkind, S. N. and Rutter, M. (1973). Children who have been "in care"—an epidemiological study. *Journal of Child Psychology and Psychiatry, 14,* 97–105.

Wolkind, S. N. (1974). The components of "affectionless psychopathy" in institutionalized children. *Journal of Child Psychology and Psychiatry, 15,* 215–220.

Follow-Up Studies

Alderton, H. (1969). A comparison of the follow-up studies of Children's Aid Society wards and non-wards treated in a children's psychiatric hospital. *Canadian Medical Association Journal, 100,* 1035–1042.

Allerhand, M. E., Weber, R. E., and Haug, M. (1966). *Adaptation and Adaptability: The Bellefaire Follow-up Study.* New York: Child Welfare League of America.

Davids, A. and Salvatore, P. (1976). Residential treatment of disturbed children and adequacy of their subsequent adjustment: a follow-up study. *American Journal of Orthopsychiatry, 46,* 62–73.

Doron, R. (1972). Clinical observations of juvenile psychopathology. *Psychologie Francaise, 1,* 3–9.

Groeschel, B. J. (1974). Social adjustment after residential treatment. In D. F. Ricks, A. Thomas, and M. Roff, *Life History Research in Psychopathology,* Vol. 3. Minneapolis, Minn.: University of Minnesota Press.

Jones, F. H. (1974). A 4-year follow-up of vulnerable adolescents: the prediction of outcomes in early adulthood from measures of social competence, coping style, and overall level of psychopathology. *Journal of Nervous and Mental Disease, 159,* 20–39.

Levy, E. (1969). Long-term follow-up of former inpatients at the children's hospital of the Menninger Clinic. *American Journal of Psychiatry, 125,* 1633–1638.

Roberts, A. H., Erickson, R. V., Riddle, M., and Bacor, J. G. (1974). Demographic variables, base rates, and personality characteristics associated with recidivism in male delinquents. *Journal of Consulting and Clinical Psychology, 42,* 833–841.

Taylor, D. and Alpert, S. (1973). *Continuity and Support Following Residential Treatment.* New York: Child Welfare League of America.

14

Understanding and Coping with Burnout

Kevin J. Corcoran

Few topics in the behavioral and social sciences have been welcomed as enthusiastically as burnout. The subject was introduced in the professional literature just over a decade ago (Freudenberger, 1974), and has already been the focus of national conferences, several books, and numerous scholarly reports. In spite of this interest, there is generally no accepted theory of burnout, except that stress is considered to be one antecedent. Even the definition of burnout has been elusive (Corcoran, 1986a; Shinn, 1982).

The purpose of this chapter is to define burnout and review three major theoretical models: the organizational environment model, Maslach's interactional-phase model, and Harrison's social competency model. These concepts contrast in terms of the source of stress leading to burnout. Considered together, they provide valuable information for prevention and intervention.

DEFINING BURNOUT

One of the problems in understanding burnout is the term's frequent vernacular use. Burnout seems to apply to any situation where someone loses interest in an activity or topic. For example, we might lose a tennis partner because he or she has become "burnt out" on the game, or colleagues at work because they got "burnt out" by the emotional demands of helping people with problems. Although the terms are the same, these two examples of burnout are quite different.

Our understanding of burnout has also been hampered because the topic is similar to job satisfaction. Some writers simply dismiss burnout as a "reinvention" of the "job satisfaction wheel." Although job satisfaction and burnout are interrelated, they are not identical. The similarity of burnout and job satisfaction, as well as their difference, is seen when we realize that a dissatisfied practitioner may be burnt out, but a burnt-out practitioner is not necessarily dissatisfied with his or her job. In other words, for several reasons the burnt-out practitioner can no longer cope with the demands of work that may or may not be satisfying.

One might very well ask, "What, then, is unique about burnout?"

First and foremost, burnout is unique in terms of the actual experience. This is seen from anecdotal accounts by burnt-out workers and from more rigorous empirical research. Burnout is most frequently described as an emotional syndrome. Moreover, although there are at least six different instruments to measure burnout, the most common characteristic is a form of emotional fatigue or exhaustion (Corcoran, 1986a). The essential dimensions of these accounts of burnout is the *depletion* of the practitioner's emotional availability. For example, after a demanding group session a child care counselor may feel "drained" or "used up."

Burnout is also unique in terms of who is susceptible to becoming burnt out. Burnout is a syndrome specific to professions where one has face-to-face contact with people who have problems. A few of the more apparent examples are social workers, counselors, psychologists, nurses, teachers, physicians, and possibly psychiatrists. Less obvious professions subject to burnout are police, lawyers, the clergy, and people in funeral services.

The reason burnout is restricted to people-oriented professions is based on the defining characteristic, the depletion of emotional energies needed to perform one's job. This energy is used up as a consequence of emotional exposure to people with problems. Professions that do not demand emotional availability to others' problems and suffering may lose people because of dissatisfaction or disinterest, but *not* because the emotional energy required to do one's job has been exhausted.

Admittedly, some writers do not agree with this restricted application of burnout. Pines and her colleagues (Pines et al., 1981), in fact, leave burnout open to any professional, regardless of whether the job involves constant contact with other people. This view considers burnout as a more general occupational tedium.

The third characteristic unique to burnout is that it is considered a consequence of stress. This is an area of consensus in the literature. The theoretical postulation is that stress depletes a practitioner's emotional energy. The resulting lack of energy, in turn, has a detrimental effect on the practitioner and the delivery of services, as well as other areas such as one's family. The three models of burnout discussed below explain most of the sources of the stress that lead to burnout.

MODELS OF BURNOUT

The Organizational Environment Model

This model focuses on how burnout is due to stress from within the work environment. The stressors may be a result of formal administrative policies and procedures, or established social norms for employees, such as the formality with when one is expected to interact with a physician. The structure of the administration can also be stressful. For example, in residential treatment the chain of command between the child care counselor and administration may be so vast that the counselor senses a lack of availability, appreciation, or opportunity for advancement. As Pines and her colleagues (Pines, 1982) have shown, this type of rigidity is stressful to several types of workers, and is associated with burnout. Additional examples of stress from the organization include seemingly endless "forms and paperwork," "red tape," and extensive caseloads. These factors have also been shown to predict burnout (Pines et al., 1981).

Probably the two most prominent organizational stressors that facilitate burnout are role conflict and role ambiguity. At least, these two stressors have had the most consistent empirical attention. These stressors are a result of a poorly defined job description that fails to delineate the parameters of one's position, responsibility, and expected performance.

Role conflict refers to the fact that a person's job, or role in an agency, consists of two or more competing demands. Moreover, these two demands are perceived to be incompatible. For example, role conflict in residential treatment may occur when a child care counselor is expected to be empathic, caring, and supportive toward an individual, and then may have to forceably escort that same person to a time-out or isolation room.

Role ambiguity, on the other hand, occurs when a worker has insufficient information about his or her job. The worker may have received a poor orientation to the position and thus is uninformed about a program's policies and procedures. This lack of clarity is stressful because the person is not certain of how to act in various situations.

Role conflict and role ambiguity are stressful because the practitioner is torn between incompatible roles and is at a loss as to what to do. The stress may deplete the practitioner's enthusiasm and emotional investment in helping people with problems. Consequently, the person is burnt out.

Other stressors also are considered in the organizational environment model. Examples include opportunities for promotion and physical variables such as the noise level. In general, this model focuses on the stressors found in one's work environment. These stressors thwart one's efforts to effectively help clients change, and deplete the emotional energy required for professional altruism.

The Interactional-Phase Model

This model has been the focus of Christina Maslach and her colleagues (Maslach, 1982; Maslach and Jackson, 1981). The label is used here because the model emphasizes the interaction between the practitioner and the client. The model also conceptualizes burnout as occurring in three phases.

This model restricts burnout to people-oriented professions. The major premise of the model is that burnout results from prolonged exposure to the stress of working with people's troubles. This exposure creates an emotional overload, which is first experienced as emotionally exhausting. For example, an intake worker in a residential facility for battered women may experience stress from the emotional overload of seeing others in pain, which in turn is emotionally draining.

This aspect of the burnout experience is called emotional exhaustion. It is the first phase in the burnout syndrome. Emotional exhaustion may be experienced in numerous ways, from feeling emotionally drained or mentally listless or to feeling "used up."

Once emotional exhaustion occurs, one is less able to give of him/herself. That is, a practitioner is less emotionally available. This sets up the second phase of burnout, depersonalization. Depersonalization is an effort to cope with emotional exhaustion by distancing oneself from the source of stress, namely, the client. These efforts to cope provide psychological detachment from the affective demands of working with people, which is seen as indifference and disregard.

Depersonalization may occur in numerous forms. Some common ones are to be rude or to derogate one's clients or coworkers. Other manifestations are seen when a worker is overly critical or makes humorous and sarcastic remarks about clients, or holds the client responsible for the causes of a problem (as with "blaming the victim").

Clearly, the practitioner who is depersonalizing clients is unlikely to provide effective service. This results in the third phase of burnout, a perceived decrease in one's personal accomplishments as a professional. This realization may lead to low self-esteem, depression, or other problems frequently found to be associated with burnout.

The Social Competency Model

This perspective, articulated by Harrison (1983), is similar to the organizational environment model, as it emphasizes the stressors of burnout instead of focusing on the syndrome itself. As a point of departure, Harrison notes the inverse relationship between a practitioner's perceived effectiveness and burnout; in other words, as people become more burnt out, they tend to report a decrease in their perceived competency.

The competency model asserts that people enter the helping professions highly motivated to help others. The desire to help clients change is based on the practitioner's belief that he or she has the ability to influence them. This is the person's perceived social competency, which refers to a belief about one's own ability to interact with clients and effectively deal with their problems.

At the beginning of the practitioner's career, this motivation and sense of competency are often overidealized, and the young helper may be overzealous. When confronted with the stressful facts that some clients may not want help, and that change is frequently slow or nonexistent, the practitioner begins to feel frustrated, disappointed, and eventually emotionally exhausted.

This type of stress can also result from other barriers the practitioner encounters in trying to help clients solve their problems. Examples of limiting factors include the severity of the problem, lack of local social programs or resources to address the problem, or one's professional skill or ability.

As a consequence of stressful barriers, the practitioner begins to question his or her social competency, the same competency that motivated the individual to enter the field in the first place. The loss of social competency causes the practitioner to feel less motivated to work, so that he or she emotionally withdraws and depersonalizes clients.

Research Findings

These three models of burnout differ in terms of the sources of the stress that produces burnout. The models have led to extensive research on the causes, consequences, and correlates of burnout.

The research tends to support many notions suggested by the different models. For example, Jayaratne et al. (1983) found that role ambiguity and role conflict significantly predicted emotional exhaustion and depersonalization. This finding was also reported by Pines and her colleagues. Pines and associates also observed that work overload correlated with occupational tedium (Pines et al., 1981).

Researchers have investigated other emotional and physical problems that seem to be a consequence of burnout. For example, burnout is correlated with depression, anxiety, feelings of irritability, and somatic complaints (Jayaratne and Chess, 1983, 1984a, b). Additionally, burnout has been shown to be associated with lowered self-esteem, sleep disturbance, a lack of physical health, feelings of hopelessness and loneliness, absenteeism, and a desire to find a new job (Caron et al., 1983).

These findings illustrate that burnout has a serious and immediate effect on practitioners. Research further suggests that burnout generalizes beyond the burnt-out worker, and impacts upon his or her entire family. For example, Jackson and Maslach (1981) found from a sample of policemen that burnt-out officers were more likely than other officers to display anger, spent more time away from the family, were less involved in the family, and reported more unsatisfactory marriages.

Finally, researchers have begun to examine the effect of burnout on the client–clinician relationship. For example, less skilled workers reported more burnout than workers who considered themselves skilled (Streepy, 1981). Additionally, burnout is associated with practitioners' negative impressions of clients' social and intellectual abilities (Corcoran, 1986b).

METHODS FOR PREVENTION AND INTERVENTION

One common theme in the anecdotal accounts and empirical reports on burnout is lack of a sense of control over stressors. In fact, burnout has been shown to relate to a general lack of perceived control (Caron et al., 1983). This lack of control may be general, in terms of feeling one is not able to cope with the stressors of burnout, or it may be specific, as in the case of feeling one is not able to effectively help a particular client. Two guidelines emerge from the theme of controlling stress: first, practitioners should develop appropriate methods for coping with stress; and second, they should become as knowledgeable and skilled in their practice as possible to decrease the stress of working with clients.

Stress, in its various manifestations, is an everyday phenomenon, and simply cannot be avoided. This is certainly true for the specific stress of the helping professions, which emotionally depletes workers. However, stress control is achievable by focusing on the three components of stress: the environment, one's cognitive reaction to the environment, and one's physical reaction. The techniques discussed below for coping with stress have been shown to impact on all three of these factors.

Coping with Stressors

In recent years a massive amount of attention has been given to developing methods for coping with stress. The techniques have focused primarily on reducing one's physical reaction to stress and altering the cognitive processes that interpret and label stressful events. When applied to the helping professions, relaxation techniques and cognitive restructuring are useful ways to minimize the effect of stress. The techniques are valuable because they can be applied to the emotionally depleting stressors found in helping clients change.

Relaxation techniques will help the practitioner cope with the physiological impact of stress. There are numerous forms of relaxation techniques, such as progressive relaxation, meditation, and hypnosis (Davis et al., 1982). Self-control relaxation seems best suited for dealing with the stressors of burnout because it can be used to cope with the immediate acute arousal that can occur on the job, such as feeling angry at a particular resident or one's supervisor. It can also reduce chronic stress reactions, such as feeling exhausted or drained each night after work.

The essential component of self-control relaxation is to learn to relax. This may be done by tensing specific muscle groups in the body, such as the arm or leg muscles, then relaxing them. Attention is then focused on the contrasting feelings and sensations between the tensed and relaxed states. One should progressively repeat this procedure with all muscles groups throughout the entire body. The outcome of this procedure is that one feels relaxed. Once this technique has been mastered, it is advisable to pair the relaxation state with a particular cognitive cue, such as the word "relax." This cognitive cue should be repeated during each of the relaxation states of the progressive relaxation procedure. The cognitive cue can then be used alone when one is exposed to a stressful situation, such as a hostile and demanding family session. This will reduce the stressful impact of the situation.

For relaxation training to be most effective in reducing the effects of stress, one must practice it periodically. Practitioners should consider practicing the relaxation procedures before and after work a few times a week.

The relaxation technique can also be used in conjunction with a behavioral hierarchy. Adopted from systematic desensitization of anxiety disorders, a behavioral hierarchy is a list of ten or twenty stressful events or activities that cause one to feel emotionally depleted. This list could include a particular client, a type of clinical problem, or any other circumstance where the practitioner experiences the stressors of burnout. The items are then to be arranged from least stressful and emotionally exhausting to most stressful and exhausting. Finally, the relaxation technique can be applied as one imagines each of the stressful events on the hierarchy. One should work the way up the hierarchy slowly, applying the technique to the least stressful events first, and repeating only a few events at a time. One should try to keep the items fairly consistent so that the hierarchy has an even gradation.

A second coping skill for dealing with the stressors of burnout is cognitive restructuring, which is an attempt to change the cognitive arousal that influences the intensity of one's reaction to stress (Emery et al., 1981). For example, a counselor might dislike a residential unit of juvenile delinquents and think that "these kids are just a bunch of punks and no-good hoods." This type of thought is self-defeating because it interprets an event as stressful and intensifies the reaction to stress.

Cognitive restructuring, in general, uses techniques that strive to correct self-defeating thoughts. Some common restructuring approaches include Albert Ellis's rational emotive therapy and various methods of cognitive-behavior therapy (Ellis, 1970; Rimm and Masters, 1979).

In terms of burnout, the essential components of cognitive restructuring are first to identify the cognitive distortion, or the self-defeating thought; then, once individuals recognize that they are having such thoughts, they make positive, self-enhancing statements. In other words, the technique is to replace the self-defeating thought with a self-enhancing or positive one. In order to be more effective, this procedure should be practiced first outside the stressful environment. Like relaxation training, cognitive restructuring can be used when one encounters stressors on the job. Cognitive restructuring should also be used when the practitioner has depersonalizing thoughts about a client. Here one should immediately replace the depersonalizing thought with one that evaluates the client positively. For example, an argumentative adolescent could be reframed as simply trying to establish self-determination or perhaps as one who knows no more effective communication style.

A third way of coping with job-related stress, which actually combines restructuring and relaxation, is to develop a proper cognitive perspective about work, in terms of what one does at work and away from it. For example, young practitioners, either paraprofessionals or professionals, are often overenthusiastic about trying to help clients, so that they become overly involved with the clients. A more appropriate perspective, one that is less stressful, is to realize that it is the client who is responsible for change. Moreover, the practitioner can facilitate change only if the client is receptive to it.

Similarly, the burning-out practitioner may need to develop a proper perspective about non-work-related events. The overenthusiastic counselor may let the career become his or her entire life. Because of the disproportionate commitment it requires, young workers fail to realize that work is only one aspect of life. Time away from work, hobbies, and other activities one enjoys provide ways to rejuvenate oneself in order to be emotionally available for clients. The burning-out practitioner needs to realize that recreation is essentially re-creation.

Although a good support system will help alleviate the stress of work, colleagues who socialize with each other after work may not experience stress reduction. All too often the focus of attention turns to clients, crises, and careers in such gatherings. The desire to "get away" from work and enjoy the company of peers to rejuvenate oneself may be a natural extension of a staff meeting or an informal case conference. But the activity is still work-related, even if the environment is unpressured and the format informal.

When one does choose to socialize with colleagues, efforts must be made to steer conversation to non-work-related topics. This may be more difficult than it seems because work is the obvious common interest in a group of colleagues. Consequently, it may take some ingenuity to keep the group from focusing on work. One technique I used with a group of colleagues in residential care was to limit the amount of time the group could discuss work-related issues. Anyone who brought up a work topic after the allotted time had to answer one personal question asked by the other group members. Not only did this help control the discussion of work, but the staff quickly became cohesive, learned about each other's interests, and were able to form a support group outside the workplace.

Enhancing Treatment Effectiveness

The second major guideline for coping with the stressor of helping people is to make the job of helping less stressful. One way to accomplish this is to transfer to another job within the agency in order to work with less difficult clients, or perhaps to transfer to an agency with a different type of client or one that uses a different treatment model. This is an avoidance method of coping, which is a perfectly reasonable intervention.

Another way to make work less stressful is to be as effective in one's practice as possible. If we are very effective or socially competent, the task of helping clients change is easier. Although this task is clearly a continuous process of professional growth and development, certain suggestions can be applied to practitioners working in residential treatment.

First of all, because role conflict and role ambiguity tend to predict burnout, supervisors, administrators, and practitioners need to develop clear and concrete job descriptions and program policies and procedures. By doing so, practitioners will learn the objectives of a program and their own responsibilities, and thus will be able to work more effectively with clients.

Supervisors can also help prevent burnout by providing opportunities for practitioners to become more knowledgeable and skillful at helping people change. The role of clinical skills in intervening in burnout has been investigated by Corcoran and Bryce (1983). In a quasi-experimental study of social work practitioners and a matched control group, workers' training in interpersonal interviewing skills helped to reduce burnout, while subjects not receiving the training became more burnt out between pre-test and post-test assessment periods. It may be appropriate to assume that their other practice skills may also reduce burnout by making practitioners more effective. Supervisors may also consider helping workers become more skilled by providing funds for them to attend professional seminars, offering *relevant* in-service training, or even providing release time for them to take graduate classes.

Supervisors may also help the at-risk practitioner by observing the early stages of burnout and providing task-oriented treatment (Tubesing and Tubesing, 1982; Freudenberger, 1982). More specifically, the supervisor may need to help the practitioners to master and utilize such coping skills as relaxation.

Another general method for decreasing stress in practice is to establish realistic goals with the client and then develop an effective treatment plan. The goals most likely will need to be both short-term and long-term. The treatment plan should be directly related to the goals, specific, and concrete. All three of these dimensions have been shown to enhance treatment effectiveness (Smith et al., 1980; Yideka-Sherman, 1985). This will not only reduce the stress involved in helping people, but will provide the practitioner with positive reinforcement as he or she sees that goals are reached throughout the course of treatment.

One final suggestion for enhancing effectiveness is to systematically evaluate the quality of the clinical services. As John Mordock discussed in Chapter 13, one viable method of evaluating effectiveness is with single-case research designs. As a consequence of numerous rapid assessment instruments designed to measure clients' problems, it is relatively easy for any practitioner to evaluate each and every client (Corcoran and Fischer, 1987).

By monitoring clients' progress and evaluating their own effectiveness, practitioners may become more skilled as they learn what techniques work with which clients. This feedback provides positive reinforcement for the use of effective techniques, while also allowing one to change an unsuccessful treatment plan. Both of these outcomes make helping people change more effective, so that, the practitioner finds his or her job less stressful which ultimately helps prevent burnout.

REFERENCES

Caron, C., Corcoran, K. J., and Simcoe, F. (1983). Intrapersonal correlates of burnout: the role of locus of control in burnout and self-esteem. *The Clinical Supervisor, 1*, 53–62.

Corcoran, K. J. (1986a). Measuring burnout: a reliability and convergent validity study. *Journal of Social Behavior and Personality, 1,* 107-112.

Corcoran, K. J. (1986b). The association of burnout and social work practitioner's impressions of their clients: empirical evidence. *Journal of Social Science Research* (in press).

Corcoran, K. J. and Bryce, A. K. (1983). Intervention in the experience of burnout: effects of skill development. *Journal of Social Science Research, 7,* 71-79.

Corcoran, K. J. and Fischer, Joel (1987). *Measurers for Clinical Practice: A Sourcebook.* New York: The Free Press.

Davis, Martha, Eshelman, Elizabeth R., and McKay, Matthew (1982). *The Relaxation and Stress Reduction Workbook,* 2nd edition. Oakland, Calif.: New Harbinger Publications.

Ellis, Albert (1970). *The Essence of Rational Psychotherapy: A Comprehensive Approach to Treatment.* New York: Institute for Rational Living.

Emery, Gary, Hollon, Steven D., and Bedrosian, Richard C. (1981). *New Directions in Cognitive Therapy.* New York: Guilford Press.

Freudenberger, Herbert J. (1974). Staff burnout. *Journal of Social Issues, 30,* 159-165.

Freudenberger, Herbert J. (1982). Counseling and dynamics: treating the end-stage person. In W. S. Paine, ed., *Job Stress and Burnout: Research, Theory, and Intervention Perspectives.* Beverly Hills, Calif.: Sage, pp. 173-185.

Harrison, W. David (1983). A social competence model of burnout. In B. A. Farber ed., *Stress and Burnout in the Human Services Profession.* Elmsford, N.Y.: Pergamon Press.

Jackson, S. E. and Maslach, C. (1981). After-effects of job related stress: families as victims. *Journal of Occupational Behavior, 3,* 66-77.

Jayaratne, S. and Chess, W. A. (1983). Job satisfaction and burnout in social work. In B. A. Farber, ed., *Stress and Burnout in the Human Services Professions.* Elmsford, N.Y.: Pergamon Press.

Jayaratne, S. and Chess W. A. (1984a). Job satisfaction, burnout, and turnover: a national survey. *Social Work, 29,* 448-453.

Jayaratne, S. and Chess, W. A. (1984b). The effects of emotional support on perceived job stress and strain. *Journal of Applied Behavioral Science, 20,* 141-153.

Jayaratne, S., Tripodi, T., and Chess, W. A. (1983). Perceptions of emotional support, stress, and strain by male and female social workers. *Social Work Research and Abstracts, 19,* 19-27.

Maslach, Christina (1982). *Burnout: The Cost of Caring.* Englewood Cliffs, N.J.: Prentice-Hall.

Maslach, Christina and Jackson, Susan E. (1981). The measurement of experienced burnout. *Journal of Occupational Behavior, 2,* 99-113.

Pines, Ayala (1982). Changing organizations: is a work environment without burnout an impossible goal? In W. S. Paine, ed., *Job Stress and Burnout Research, Theory and Intervention Perspectives.* Beverly Hills, Calif.: Sage, pp. 189-211.

Pines, Ayala M., Aronson, Elliot, and Kafry, Ditsa (1981). *Burnout: From Tedium to Personal Growth.* New York: Free Press.

Rimm, David C. and Masters, John R. (1979). *Behavior Therapy: Techniques and Empirical Findings,* 2nd edition. New York: Academic Press.

Shinn, M. (1982). Methodological issues: evaluating and using information. In W. S. Paine, ed., *Job Stress and Burnout: Research, Theory, and Intervention Perspectives.* Beverly Hills, Calif.: Sage, pp. 61–79.

Smith, Mary L., Glass, Gene V., and Miller, T. I. (1980). *The Benefits of Psychotherapy.* Baltimore: The Johns Hopkins University Press.

Streepy, J. (1981). Direct-service providers and burnout. *Social Casework, 62,* 352–361.

Tubesing, N. L. and Tubesing, D. A. (1982). The treatment of choice: selecting stress skills to suit the individual and the situation. In W. S. Paine, ed., *Job Stress and Burnout: Research, Theory, and Intervention Perspectives.* Beverly Hills, Calif.: Sage.

Videka-Sherman, Lynn (1986). *Harriett M. Bartlett Practice Effectiveness Project: Report to the NASW Board of Directors.* Silver Spring, Md.: National Association of Social Workers.

15

Combating Institutional Abuse

Nolan Rindfleisch

EMERGENCE OF THE ISSUE

Harmful acts of commission and omission affecting children and youths in residential facilities do not constitute a new phenomenon. However, the characterization of such events and omissions as abuse and neglect is relatively recent. It is a by-product of the pervasive disenchantment and hostility toward institutions for children that emerged in the 1960s, in part as a consequence of the deinstitutionalization movement. During the 1970s, institutions came under the further scrutiny of those who were deeply concerned about the treatment accorded incarcerated youths in secure settings (Wooden, 1976; Miller, 1981). By the late 1970s the Children's Defense Fund could report it found too many children in institutions. It also found that no state, among the seven its staff visited in a study of the status of children in out-of-home care, had set up guidelines to monitor and eliminate institutional abuse of children. The class action suit brought in behalf of Louisiana children sent to Texas. *Gary W. v. State of Louisiana,* highlighted a serious example of the abuse and neglect of some of the children who were placed out of state, primarily in private residential facilities in Texas (Knitzer and Allen, 1978).

This combination of events led to what private providers of children's residential care and treatment came to regard as an anti-institution bias. This bias was reflected in the 1980 child welfare reforms whose provisions limited the size of public institutions in which federal funds could be expended to twenty-five beds. The standard of least restrictive environment placed increased pressure on child placement agencies to use residential placements as a last resort.

By the late 1970s a continuum of attitudes toward the issue of institutional abuse and neglect had emerged, and constituted the environment in which policy would be formulated, resident protection programs developed, and protective services implemented. The perception of institutional abuse and neglect issues held by providers, child protection professionals, and advocates of deinstitutionalization seemed to fall along a continuum, defined by the following views:

- Type I—In defense of residential facilities: abuse and neglect are impossible. Those who hold this view argue the extreme position that professional standards of care and small facility size make child maltreatment impossible.
- Type II—Provider prerogatives are paramount: a narrow definition. Those who hold this view prefer not to refer to situations of child maltreatment as abuse and neglect. They prefer to call maltreatment a training or personnel selection problem that should be handled internally.
- Type III—Children's rights are paramount: a broad definition. In this view, violations of a child's rights are seen as abuse and neglect. It is highly unlikely that a residential facility could operate without violating the rights of children through individual acts of commission/omission or through administrative policies.
- Type IV—Institutions are the most restrictive environment: close them all. This view holds that placement of a child in a residential facility itself constitutes abuse and/or neglect. The act of placement is seen as harmful to the child because it removes a child from a less restrictive environment and allows placements to occur in organizations that cannot be reformed (Rindfleisch and Rabb, 1984a).

PROTECTION AFTER PLACEMENT

Between 1930 and 1965 the number of children placed in institutions, especially child welfare institutions, declined, but the number appears to have bottomed out and increased somewhat since the midsixties. Partly as a result of deinstitutionalization, this later period has seen phenomenal increases in the use of community-based care, especially for status offenders and the mentally retarded. The number of children placed in foster family care increased substantially between 1961 and 1978, from 260,000 to 350,000 (Thomas, 1982).

Shyne and Schroeder's (1980) study of social services being delivered to children and their families indicates that the percentage of children in residential care as a percentage of the total number of children receiving social services dropped between the years 1961 and 1977 from 12% to 4%. The actual number of children in residential care increased, however, from about 52,000 in 1961 to about 70,000 in 1980. The rate of utilization of residential group care increased also, from 10/10,000 children in the population to 12/10,000 children in the population (Shyne and Schroeder, 1980; Rindfleisch and Rabb, 1984b).

Once in placement, children and youths are presumed to be in an environment superior to that from which they were removed; and so they are not thought to need protection beyond that provided by state licensing activities. Providers of residential group care reinforce this perception by claiming that they intend to benefit the children and youths placed with them for care and treatment. Justification by intent, rather than by outcomes achieved, is rooted in several commonly espoused standards, which in their general effect reduce the number and types of incidents definable as abuse and neglect to the vanishing point. Thomas (1980) identifies four justifications for service activities undertaken in residential institutions:

1. The doctrine of "in loco parentis" is often used to justify the exercise of vaguely defined but wide-ranging powers to act as parents for children in care.
2. The concept of "in a child's best interest" is applied broadly by juvenile courts to decide matters on behalf of children within their jurisdiction.
3. The presumption of "best professional judgment" asserts that therapeutic or corrective interventions have been conducted in line with the state of the art.
4. The argument of "lack of resources" claims that service providers are doing the very best they can with what they have.

Thomas's definition of institutional abuse and neglect is framed in relation to these tendencies to justify doing harm on grounds of good intentions and lack of resources. Institutional abuse is "unjustifiable intrusion upon a child's person, privacy or liberty and institutional neglect is any failure to make advance provision for the protections and sustenance necessary to support normal growth and development as established by written codes, state of the art knowledge and/or local community standards." Institutional abuse is perceived as a consequence of the unwarranted exercise of administrative authority, and institutional neglect is perceived as a consequence of administrative failure to act in accord with knowable standards, notwithstanding proclamations of intent, disclaimers of administrative ignorance, or lack of resources. This view is held even though most adverse events may be traced initially to acts or omissions of particular direct care staff or other employees occurring on the grounds of the institution (Thomas, 1980).

A search of appellate cases was conducted by Toomey and Rivera to assess court responses to institutional abuse and neglect. They found twenty-seven cases, but only four were directly related to this issue. Based on their analysis, they urged that state institutional abuse and neglect statutes be drawn clearly so that the courts can react swiftly and justly. Murray conducted a review of federal court decisions concerning the constitutional rights of children to freedom from harm, to treatment, and to placement in the least restrictive environment. She concluded that institutional practices involving failure to provide, use of corporal punishment, isolation, and misuse of psychotropic drugs, from a constitutional perspective may be clearly labeled abusive in public facilities; and on the basis of the *Gary W.* decision, it is suggested that these practices are constitutionally offensive when employed in private facilities admitting children in state protective custody (Toomey et al., 1984).

Recent years have seen a substantial increase in the number of lawsuits seeking money damages from child welfare institutions. Liability is based on violations of duties of care that are assumed when the child becomes a resident of a facility. Liability of an employer is based on vicarious liability. This means that an employer can be liable for the acts of his/her employees if the employees are acting within the scope of their employment (Toomey et al., 1984).

What provisions have been in place in residential facilities to assure the protection of children and youths after placement? Rindfleisch conducted a national survey of children's residential institutions in 1981 to answer this question. The data were obtained from the providers of residential group care themselves and was supplemented by data obtained in 1982 from local child protection agencies in counties where 1700 enumerated children's residential institutions were located.

Preferred resident protective practices consisted of an "open door" policy by the administrator, program monitoring techniques such as professional rapport with residents, critical incident reporting, and daily logging of unusual events. Many had developed residents' rights statements and had advanced the cause of children's rights by enforcing these rights in their programs. The respondents were not supportive of introducing third parties, such as resident advocates, into the setting or of using certain resident-dependent casefinding techniques such as hotlines or complaint boxes to bring residents' concerns about their safety and security to the attention of the administrator or other designated person.

The results of this survey of residential institutions provide an initial estimate of the size of this problem on a national basis. There were 2692 complaints of abuse and/or neglect of residents in 1979 reported by the residential respondents, with 40% of the respondents indicating they had not received any complaints. The average complaint rate for the ten federal Health and Human Services (HHS) regions was 39 complaints per 1000 children in care. These rates varied from 55 per 1000 children in care in the Southwest Region and 54 per 1000 children in care in New York and

New Jersey to the low side of 25 per 1000 and 30 per 1000 children in care in the Middle Atlantic and South Central regions, respectively. For every 1000 residents, an average of 39 presumably serious adverse events could be expected to occur annually. These data seemed to confirm the possibility that harm to residents could occur in a field in which most facilities were doing a good job.

It seems clear, however, that the profile of the residential facilities surveyed was not congruent with the stereotype of the most notoriously deficient institutions that fueled the deinstitutionalization movement of the late 1960s. The average number of residents per facility in this survey was forty-one. Their average length of stay was one year. Public residential facilities were not very numerous. On the other hand, large-size (over seventy-five beds) facilities had 35% of the residents in care. Seclusion/isolation rooms were used in about 18% of the facilities. Such rooms were used more frequently in large facilities than in smaller facilities. Also, the staff–resident ratio grew less favorable as the size of facilities increased (Rindfleisch, 1984).

REPORTING MALTREATMENT OF RESIDENTS

There appear to be three types of barriers to discovering what harmful events occur in residential institutions that require a protective response. The first type stems from a general absence of consensus regarding just what acts and omissions require protective intervention. A second type grows out of the differing perspectives held by resident advocates on the one hand and the professionals who are responsible for the care and treatment of residents on the other. The third type of barrier to willingness to take protective action is organizational in nature; for although children's facilities espouse certain resident protective practices, actual reporting of resident maltreatment has been negligible (Russell and Trainor, 1984).

A useful approach in beginning to sort out what should be a resident protective issue was proposed by Harrell and Orem (1980), who suggest that adverse events be classified in terms of the following four questions: Is the event optimal? Is the event appropriate? Is the event legal? Is the event harmful? If an adverse event violates a court order or consent decree or is judged to be harmful, in all likelihood it is a resident protective issue.

The question of what constitutes abuse and neglect was addressed empirically by Rabb and Rindfleisch (1985) through a study of how serious twenty-four adverse events were judged to be by 540 respondents, including direct care staff, supervisors and clinical personnel, administrators, board members, child placement staff, and foster family care providers.

Besides learning about the relative seriousness of these adverse events, the researchers wanted to learn what factors seemed to influence the evaluation of their seriousness. What effect on the evaluation of seriousness did certain contingent factors have, such as (1) where the event occurred, (2) whether there was a consequence for the resident, (3) whether there was a consequence for the resident, (3) whether the adult had a limitation and (4) whether the resident was difficult to manage.

Of the twenty-four events evaluated, the following events were found to be the most serious: (1) adult gives double dose of medication to control behavior; (2) adult has sex with a youth; (3) adult smokes pot with a youth; (4) adult administers humiliating punishment for bedwetting; (5) adult strokes youth's thigh in a suggestive manner. In nine of the twenty-four events, significant differences in seriousness occurred when the adult was depicted as a parent, compared to when the adult was depicted as a residential facility employee. Stricter standards were held for employees in eight events. However, a less strict standard of behavior was held for employees, compared to parents, in cases of ignoring a youth and locking a youth in a room for an hour. The presence of a negative consequence for the youth led to events being judged to be more serious in only six events.

However, the seriousness of five of the events was influenced to a moderate extent by the four contingencies enumerated above. These events were: (1) youth is locked in the quiet room for one hour; (2) youth's earache is ignored; (3) youths are left to fight it out; (4) meals are denied as punishment; (5) adult pushes youth who falls down stairs. These results suggest that there is less agreement among the respondents about how to evaluate events involving neglect and seclusion.

However, judgments of the seriousness of the other nineteen events were affected only to a minimal degree by the contingent factors that were presented, suggesting that a substantial consensus exists with respect to about 80% of the events presented. The strong influence of contingent factors on evaluation of use of the seclusion room highlights the salience that out-of-control residents holds for employees in residential facilities (Rabb and Rindfleisch, 1985).

Use of seclusion or exclusionary time-out is perhaps least well understood in terms of its impact on residents and its potential for being harmful. Miller examined residents' perceptions of the seclusion room by obtaining drawings and comments about seclusion from forty residents. He shared these results with residential staff. Only one third of the drawings contained people. In general, the drawings revealed an emphasis on locks and security, aggressive themes, and punitiveness. He reported that children's perceptions of seclusion disturbed administrators of the program, as did complacency among staff for accepting its use as effective when the same children would be secluded repeatedly (Miller, 1985).

Evaluation of the seriousness of adverse events is not a straightforward process, though substantial consensus regarding which adult actions or omissions are more serious can be discovered through research. If a sufficiently serious adverse event has been recognized, what else needs to be present to increase the likelihood that protective action will occur?

Rindfleisch (1987) conducted a study of the factors that might contribute to the willingness of residents, residential employees, and child protective personnel to take protective action in behalf of residents. The willingness to report was influenced by the type of maltreatment that occurred. Physical and sexual events led to an increase in willingness to report. Other types of maltreatment such as harmful restraint/control, moral and emotional maltreatment and failure to provide led to lowered willingness to report. When a child care worker and social worker were depicted in an event, in contrast to a supervisor, more willingness to report was evident. Higher levels of assessed seriousness of the events led to increased willingness to report. However, the effects of these factors were modest when compared with the effects of three items that tested the respondents' commitment to report adverse events: willingness to report even if reporting (1) threatened the agency's funding, (2) resulted in anger from one's peers, or (3) led to the loss of one's job. Being a resident increased the willingness to report, but being a direct care worker, an administrator, or public child welfare worker reduced the willingness to report.

Subsequent to this study, a statewide demonstration of the effectiveness of alternative approaches to detecting and reporting possible maltreatment was undertaken in Ohio. Four casefinding methods were defined for introduction into residential facilities. These casefinding models were: child advocate within the line of authority; complaint box accessible to staff and residents; child advocate outside the line of authority; and a hot line accessible to residents and staff. These mechanisms were accepted as feasible by the cooperating residential facilities.

The two approaches that generated the most investigations were the child advocate outside the line of authority and the hot line. These findings tended to confirm initial assumptions that residents would be more likely to report, and that an internal child advocacy mechanism would lead to higher willingness to report. The hot line was not well received by child protective agencies, in part because of the volume of work that was generated. The internal child advocate outside the line of authority was accepted by both residential facilities and child protective agencies (Shafer, 1985).

ETIOLOGY OF THE PROBLEM

Despite the controversy of the past twenty years about the future use of residential environments for children, initial progress has been made in conceptualizing the problem and assessing the factors that contribute to the frequency and severity of abuse and neglect in residential facilities.

An early formulation by Gil (1979) influenced the thinking of researchers interested in this issue. Gil identified three forms of institutional abuse: system abuse, program abuse, and individual nonfamilial abuse. Included in the broad definition of system abuse are the kinds of abuses perpetrated on children by a system that allows them to drift through many placements. Program abuse is abuse and neglect due to specific institutional policies or conditions. Individual nonfamilial abuse is maltreatment committed by an employee of an institution against a child in the institution.

In addressing the problem of individual nonfamilial maltreatment, Gil proposed to apply the intrafamilial model of child abuse proposed by Helfer and Kempe. This model for understanding child abuse and neglect establishes three interacting factors in the occurrence of most child abuse and neglect cases: (1) an individual's potential, (2) the "identified" child, and (3) the crisis (Gil, 1979).

Harrell and Orem (1980) integrate the system and program levels with the individual level of analysis in their proposed model of institutional abuse. Their view of the factors contributing to institutional abuse and neglect incorporates six levels: the children, including group size; the adults; the atmosphere; the allowable sanctions; the available supports; and the institutional milieu. This formulation of the problem was based on institutional child protection experience, in part derived from the implementation of several demonstration programs sponsored by the National Center on Child Abuse and Neglect.

Rindfleisch conducted a study of the factors contributing to the seriousness of adverse events identified by designated staff in cooperating child welfare institutions. The study was conducted over a seven-month period and involved forty facilities in six states, 935 employees, and 196 adverse events. The study assessed the relative ability of about eighty factors suggested by the above-described views of the problem to explain the seriousness of adverse events in these residential facilities (Rindfleisch and Foulk, 1984).

It was found that more serious adverse events occurred when there was a bidirectional interaction involving residents who were less recently visited and meetings that were held too frequently (e.g., daily) between direct care staff and administrative/treatment staff. Events were also judged as more serious when staff were older, had fewer children of their own, had higher levels of personal life stress, had less say in treatment decisions, were in facilities that had higher direct care staff turnover rates, and had less opportunity for promotion. The finding regarding too frequent meetings runs counter to the assumed relationship between this factor and the seriousness of adverse events. Further research will be needed to clarify whether these results are an artifact of the sample or validly reflect general relationships between the frequency of meetings and the seriousness of adverse events.

In order to gain a better understanding of the etiology of institutional child maltreatment, 232 allegations of child abuse and neglect that occurred in facilities operated by the New York State Office of Mental Health were investigated. The study focused on administrative policy decisions, patient census and admissions, seasonal influences, staffing levels, and identifiable one-time disruptions in daily routines as potential contributors to institutional abuse. A four-variable model for predicting the number of reports of abuse and neglect made per month resulted. There was a curvilinear increase in the number of reports over the thirty-four-month period of the study; staff–resident ratio and months in which changes in schedule occurred such as June and September also contributed to the number of reports made monthly (Blatt and Brown, 1986). Although these studies confirm some assumptions about the factors contributing to the frequency of maltreatment reports and to the seriousness of such reports, much remains to be demonstrated regarding the determinants of this problem.

SOCIAL RESPONSE TO THE PROBLEM

Widely publicized discoveries of sexual abuse in day care in 1984 were only the latest development in a lengthening series of horrendous events and conditions that date back twenty-five years to the period when child rights advocates and proponents of deinstitutionalization began to highlight dramatically the problem of abuse and neglect in institutions. Protection and advocacy agencies emerged during the seventies to counter the dehumanization and disrespect for the abilities and wishes of persons with disabling conditions endemic in institutions for the mentally ill and developmentally disabled. Litigation has been the heart of the protection and advocacy movement's strength, although its activities are broader than litigation alone (Sundram, 1984; Ohio Legal Rights Service, 1984–1985).

In 1976–1977, two national conferences on institutional care were held.

Both were influential in setting directions for the coming decade. One was sponsored by the National Center on Child Abuse and Neglect (NCCAN), the other by the Child Welfare League of America (CWLA).

The National Conference on the Institutional Maltreatment of Children was held on the assumption that residential institutions would continue to care for children and youths, that protective strategies needed to take into account limited resources, and that no single "cure" was likely to be effective. Participants agreed that many institutions were too large, inadequately staffed and funded, and too isolated from the community and from the families of the residents (National Center on Child Abuse and Neglect, 1978; Garrett, 1979).

The CWLA Group Care Conference focused mainly on issues affecting residential facilities in the child welfare field. Two of these issues concerned residents' rights and organizational design. The conferees recommended that each group care facility develop a code of rights for the children in its care. They also proposed that no institution exceed fifty children, that living groups not be smaller than eight or larger than fourteen, and that child care staff receive adequate remuneration, recognition, and training (Mayer et al., 1978).

Before the passage of the Child Abuse Treatment and Prevention Act in 1974, state-administered licensing programs constituted the main protection available against the risks to the safety and security of children and youths served in out-of-home care by the child welfare system. An early formal recognition of the need to address the issue of abuse and neglect was reflected in licensing standards developed by the Interstate Consortium on Residential Child Care. The Consortium's work provided guidelines for residential facilities in casefinding and managing instances of abuse and neglect of residents. Standards quite similar to those of the Consortium were incorporated into model licensing rules for residential child care institutions by the Child Welfare League of America (Interstate Consortium on Residential Child Care, 1980; Child Welfare League of America, 1983).

The National Center on Child Abuse and Neglect (NCCAN) moved away from the previously influential idea that institutional care was by definition abusive. Beginning in 1977, NCCAN, through its rule-making authority, required states that were eligible for its basic grant program to investigate complaints of abuse and neglect of residents, extended its definition of "persons responsible for the welfare of a child" to include institutional employees, and provided that an independent investigation be conducted in those cases in which a child protective agency might have a conflict of interest. In the period 1979–1984, NCCAN sponsored fifteen research, demonstration, and training projects on abuse and neglect in residential facilities. The purpose of these projects was to increase experience in protecting residents and to develop resources for prevention and correction of this problem.

In response to reported allegations of child sexual abuse in day care centers, Congress enacted Public Law 98-473 in October 1984. Also in October 1984, Congress extended and amended the Child Abuse Treatment and Prevention Act as Public Law 98-457, the Child Abuse Amendments of 1984. One of the amendments involved a change in the definition of "person who is responsible for the child's welfare" to include persons who are employees of a residential facility or a staff person providing out-of-home care. Eligibility for basic grants now requires by law that states provide for the reporting of allegations of abuse and neglect emanating from institutions and day care centers. To be eligible for basic grant funds, states had until late in 1987 to bring their statutes or regulations into conformity with the federal statute. These changes will effectively shape programs for the protection of institutional residents into the 1990s.

Until 1985 the states had provided uneven and minimal programs to protect residents in child welfare institutions. State officials as late as 1983 expressed little dissatisfaction with what they were doing. They were painfully aware that any efforts to promote reporting of resident maltreatment would lead to a volume of work they would be unable to manage with the resources they anticipated. Many public urban agencies had already developed programs to deal with maltreatment in out-of-home care, and to this extent had moved on this problem in advance of their own state agencies. Generally, the states had to "stretch" intrafamilial statutes to cover the institutional situation. In the face of underreporting and denial of the problem, serious events, when they occurred, were often dealt with at the community level in an atmosphere of fear, crisis, and uncertainty because an organized approach to handling the problem usually did not exist. The actions of the parties involved took on an ad hoc quality. If the event was reported in the media, the whole episode took on a political dimension as well (Rindfleisch and Rabb, 1984a).

The absence of well-organized and disinterested residential child protection services has resulted in substantial insecurity on the part of administrators of facilities; they are justifiably concerned that they do not know what to expect if they communicate to the designated protective agency the occurrence of an adverse event that they think warrants protective intervention.

Notice of Proposed Rule Making, Child Abuse and Neglect Prevention and Treatment Program, P.L. 98-457, 45 CFR Part 1340, Office of Human Development Services, H.H.S. April 24, 1985.

As states develop and strengthen their resident protection programs, the following framework, at a minimum, should be considered:

1. State statutory language should specifically reflect the residential environment and setting.
2. Nonlocal staff should be involved in all investigations of maltreatment allegations, especially in states in which child protection is locally administered.
3. Reporting of institutional maltreatment should be monitored by a state-level office or agency other than the department responsible for resident protection operations.
4. Licensing and protective roles should be formally defined to include a clear division of work and compatible policies regarding confidentiality of maltreatment reports.
5. Operational definitions of reportable events should be developed between child protective agencies and residential facilities at state and/or community levels.
6. Personnel who constitute child protective units should be specialized, trained, permanent staff members who can establish and maintain long-term, open, and constructive relationships with residential facilities.
7. Residential facilities should organize a resident protective casefinding process that promotes a flow of information to administration and the child protective agency regarding adverse events, especially those that require protective intervention.
8. The state agency should organize its central register so that the name of resident, name of employee, and residential facility are included in reports of maltreatment, and so that data regarding resident maltreatment can be accessed readily for administrative and research purposes.
9. The state should have a continuing program of training in identification, reporting, and investigation of alleged resident maltreatment. This training should follow the formulation of policy, not precede it or serve as a substitute for policy making.

Legislative Initiative in New York

In June 1985 the New York legislature acted to extend the provisions of existing child protective statutes to out-of-home and residential sites in line with the federal changes of October 1984. Careful preparation of these changes had been under way for five years through demonstration and research work sponsored by the federal child abuse and neglect

agency (New York State Senate, 1983). The legislation provides for definitions of abuse and neglect specific to residential sites and applicable to all
residential facilities in the state. It defines employees as persons responsible for the welfare of the resident, and calls for investigations to be made
by the State Department of Social Services, and, in the case of institutions
for the mentally retarded and mentally ill, by the State Commission on
Quality of Care for the Mentally Disabled. A determination that some
credible evidence of maltreatment exists, and that a report is "indicated,"
must be made within ninety days of the date of the report. Existing due
process provisions regarding notification to subjects of a report, expungement
of records, and fair hearing rights were also extended to the situation of
residential employees. The issue in the fair hearing process is whether or
not a report submitted to the central register should be expunged.

When a report is "indicated," the act provides for administrators of
residential facilities to propose a plan of correction and to do this in
cooperation with state licensing and child protective units in cases where
there has been noncompliance with licensing standards or state abuse
and neglect statutes. The act also provides for a single statewide telephone number or hot line, an annual report, and specialized training for
staff who will conduct investigations (Child Abuse Prevention Act, 1985).

Implementation of State Programs

The spirit or philosophy guiding the implementation of state institutional
child protection programs may make the difference in whether any statute,
however comprehensively and specifically drawn, can be made to work.
Thomas (1985) is persuasive when he argues that state child protective
services are entering an environment within which they possess no immediate credibility, no claim to expertise, and no reputation or track record
to fall back on. In the short run, states may be tempted to adopt the
quasi-adversarial approach they have developed for dealing with child
maltreatment in the family/community context. This would be a serious
mistake because residential facilities are capable of undermining the
work of state departments in ways not available to the average family
perpetrator. Also, workers in state child protective services will find their
knowledge about how to deal with child maltreatment to be of minimal use
in the residential context. It would be far better if the quasi-adversarial
approach were replaced with a more collaborative approach. At the same
time, the public child protection service workers must understand that
because residential care is a sponsored, planned professional enterprise,
the defensive assertion that an adverse event is traceable to a lack of
resources must be discounted, as the probable consequences of a lack of

resources for residents were foreseeable. Also, administrative culpability should be assessed in all alleged incidents of abuse or neglect because staff with the greatest responsibility for day-to-day care are typically given the least authority in child-rearing and treatment decisions (Thomas, 1985).

The protective and advocacy agencies do not participate in placement of individuals in the residential institutions and group homes they monitor. However, child protective agencies in departments of social services typically place children in foster family homes and residential institutions as the legal custodian, fund these placements, and protect these same children after placement. These arrangements may constitute a conflict of interest situation. Plans for dealing with possible conflicts of interest on the part of protective agencies vary from state to state. In the long term, residential facilities will be better served by development of the most independent investigative arrangements possible.

Child Caring Agencies Handbook. The Ohio Association of Child Caring Agencies, with support from the Ohio Department of Human Services Basic Grant funds, developed a handbook containing guidance for residential facilities on protecting the child in residential group care. This guidance takes the form of about eight standards that encompass definitions of several types of maltreatment and procedures for reporting, investigating, and correcting incidents of resident abuse and neglect. The assumption upon which this guidance is based is that residential facilities should have an active and participatory role in the full range of activities that aim at identifying, managing, and preventing abuse and neglect in residential facilities. It is assumed that resident protection services will be conducted as social services and not exclusively as law enforcement.

This annual describes elements of the physical setup and staffing that are believed to contribute to neglect in residential care. It also describes how methods of control such as those involving physical pain and aggression, seclusion, and medication should be used, in the interest of minimizing the risk of the occurrence of resident maltreatment. It calls for a formal definition of residents' rights, a formal grievance procedure, and a system of child advocacy.

Resident protective activities are outlined in the second half of the manual. Development of a reporting system is proposed as crucial to maintaining a growth milieu and as a means of assuring the safety and security of residents. A reporting system allows staff to bring to the attention of the administration any incident that appears abusive and requires an investigation to substantiate its validity. Such reports are to be directed to the administrator or to a person designated by the administrator. In addition, daily logging of positive and negative resident behavior is proposed as a way to flag potential problems. Behaviors that should be noted in critical incident reports are specified, and all physical interventions or restraints are to be reported as critical incidents.

Formal procedures for conducting an internal investigation are proposed. They call for immediate investigation of alleged abuse and/or neglect by the designated staff person, and at the same time require giving notice to the child protective agency. Procedures for ensuring that the staff member involved does not work directly with the child involved until the investigation is completed, for assuring the protection of the child as a first priority during an investigation, and for including the resident's advocate in all phases of the investigation are also proposed.

The focus of corrective action is mainly on the employee. Such action, when undertaken in cooperation with the child protective agency, must respect the due process rights of both child and staff member. Confidentiality during the investigation and corrective action phase should be strictly adhered to, for the protection of the resident and the staff member. Finally, the manual calls on all facilities to adopt and disseminate to their staff a written policy regarding personnel who have been named in an allegation of abuse or neglect. This policy should include indication of when staff will be notified of the allegation, staff rights to legal representation, and the possible temporary reassignment of staff within the facility pending disposition of the report (Colson, 1982).

Implementation Issues for Residential Institutions

There are dilemmas at several levels within residential facilities with regard to carrying out resident protective activities. Administrators who operate closest to the facilities' constituencies have difficulty seeing adverse events as abuse and neglect. Direct care staff fear that the administration is coming down on them, tying their hands when resident protection services are presented. Staff are reluctant to be regarded as tattle tales, and fear getting bad reputations from false allegations.

Clinical directors want a safe environment in which residents can report, and in which staff are not driven underground by such reports. Union representatives typically regard allegations of abuse or neglect as clear grounds for advocating for their members. Whereas statutes provide for the confidentiality of the identity of the reporter, due process argues for the right to confront accusers. When internal policies and procedures such as those outlined earlier are initially introduced, staff see them as a new intrusion on their autonomy and security.

Clinical directors and trainers have problems keeping seasoned staff sensitized to how residents probably feel about potentially abusive methods. For example, seclusion is too often used as a control technique, and it comes to be seen as a normal part of the program. The potential for inconsistent application of the policies and procedures for remediating resident maltreatment is always present, as are the fear and the possibility that a punitive corrective response will follow the determination that abuse or neglect has occurred.

Suggested Responses. In order to cope with the relative unpredictability of what might befall a residential facility in the event of a reportable maltreatment incident, administrators should maintain an active, if not aggressive, environmental strategy. It should be aimed not at warding off the threat of outside intervention by denying that a serious adverse event could occur within one's establishment, but at seeking out compacts and protocols with the independent investigative agency in an effort to regularize and make predictable what takes place when a report has to be made. It is important for the administrator to become comfortable with and supportive of this issue, so that staff can become comfortable with and supportive of it also.

Once policy has been formulated, trainers have the opportunity to help all staff understand state statutes, the way they are applied locally, and the policies and procedures operating within the facility. It is important that staff be involved when the resident protection program is presented to residents so that staff hear what residents hear. In this way, residents can approach staff with their questions about the protective program. Once these policies and procedures are established, they are presented to new staff as existing program and are not seen as a new intrusion into their work lives.

One approach to minimizing threats to staff morale from residents making reports is to adopt a team model of operating, in which all feel responsible for what happens on all shifts. This requires that the organizational structure be relatively flat, and that administrative and other staff have their offices physically near the living units so they can be easily and quickly involved with each other regarding everyday interaction with residents. This has the effect of opening up staff–resident interactions to observation by others with a minimum of threat.

In the area of taking corrective action, it is important that agency policies be consistently administered, and that a continuum of corrective responses be used beyond termination of employees. A residents' rights committee or special procedures committee should be developed to plan corrective actions. The way this committee may be best constituted is not clear at this time, but representatives of direct care staff should be regular participants. Professionals in progressive residential facilities urge that meetings of the rights/procedures committee focus on fact-finding—on learning about the adverse event, its consequences, and its precipitants.

The meeting should be conducted in such a way as to minimize finger pointing and assessing of blame.

Prevention and management of resident maltreatment should start with an administrative stance or guiding philosophy about how residents will be treated, and how staff members will work with each other. From the beginning, administrators should be supportive of all staff and, with them, try to learn from work mistakes in which residents are harmed. This is especially important in the present context, in which many facilities find themselves providing care and treatment to the more challenging and difficult children and youths. Nor should administrators expect that their agency will be perfect and without work mistakes. However, if an employee is involved in repeated adverse events with residents, and these events appear to reflect punitive attitudes toward residents, then administrators should terminate the employment of that staff member.

Constructive use of physical intervention, skill in crisis management and control, and staff turnover constitute three areas of continuing challenge for a personnel strategy that aims at minimizing the occurrence of serious adverse acts and omissions, as well as enhancing program effectiveness. Training materials on crisis prevention and control have been developed by the Family Life Development Center at Cornell University (Nunno, undated; N.Y. State Child Protective Services, 1981). It remains crucial, however, that staff be aware that if they put their hands on a resident, the chance of injury is great, and that physical intervention should be used in a preventive way and not merely as a control maneuver.

Efforts to improve the tools available to residential facilities for child care staff selection have been undertaken by Ross and Hoeltke (1985). They have developed a selection interview protocol based on the assumption that outstanding individuals in every endeavor have configurations of strengths and talents that, once known, can be used to provide a valid basis for predicting the success of others choosing to enter that endeavor. These strengths and talents are conceptualized as life themes. They report that their interview guide predicts job performance in the settings used in their study.

The challenge of prevention is especially compelling in the residential care field because the effects of service activities are largely foreseeable, because these effects lie within the control of those who design and lead residential facilities, and because the ethic of "first do no harm" is basic to all human service practice.

Several strategies in combination will be required to reduce the severity of adverse events in residential facilities. These include: an environmental approach that brings about frequent contact with residents by outside persons; a design of staff-resident and direct care staff-administration relationships that reduces the likelihood of adversarial struggles, which result when relationships are oriented to power and authority; systematic monitoring of staff-resident interaction to obtain early warning signs of trouble; and a personnel strategy that emphasizes successful selection, support, and ongoing training of employees. In a broader sense, prevention of resident maltreatment should be undertaken not as an end in itself, but as a means of increasing the effectiveness of residential programs (Ross, 1983; Thomas, 1984).

CONCLUSION

The most negative impacts of the deinstitutionalization movement are probably a thing of the past for the residential group care field. During the past decade, systematic efforts have been undertaken to develop research findings and practical experience that would support the development of workable preventive and remedial programs to address the problem of institutional maltreatment. In 1985–1987, the states were developing improved programs of resident protection, in part through modifying their abuse and neglect statutes. Everywhere—and especially in those states in which the residential group care leadership has been involved in research and program development efforts—there is a substantial commitment to create residential institutions as environments in which children can benefit from care and treatment in complete safety. Federal agencies and private national organizations must continue to provide leadership so that the goal of harm-free care for residents can become an enforceable standard everywhere.

REFERENCES

Blatt, E. R. and Brown, S. W. (1986). Environmental influences on incidents of alleged child abuse and neglect in New York State psychiatric facilities: toward an etiology of institutional child maltreatment. *Child Abuse and Neglect, 10,* 171–180.

The Child Abuse Prevention Act of 1985, an Act of the People of the State of New York, 1985–86 Regular Sessions; amends several statutes in relation to investigation, prevention, and treatment of child abuse and child maltreatment in residential care (June 27, 1985).

Child Welfare League of America Inc. (1983). Suggested state licensing models for placement and care of children. Document prepared by the Child Welfare League of America under contract with the Children's Bureau, Administration for Children, Youth and Families, Office of Human Development Services, U.S. Department of Health and Human Services.

Colson, Virginia (1982). Guidelines for protecting the child in residential group care. Final report of Demonstration Grant number 5022-C from the Ohio Department of Human Services, Child Protection Bureau.

Garrett, J. (1979). Institutional maltreatment of children. *Journal of Residential and Community Child Care Administration, 1,* 57-68.

Gil, Eliana (1979). *Handbook for Understanding and Preventing Abuse and Neglect of Children in Out-of-Home Care.* Prepared by the San Francisco Child Abuse Council and the San Francisco Department of Social Services Pilot Project titled Prevention of Abuse and Neglect of Children in Out-of-Home-Care.

Harrell, Sharon and Orem, Reginald, C. (1980). *Preventing Child Abuse and Neglect: A Guide for Staff in Residential Institutions.* DHHS Publication No. (OHDS) 80-30255, U.S.D.H.H.S., Washington, D.C. 20201.

Interstate Consortium on Residential Child Care (1980). *Residential Child Care Guidebook.* New Jersey Department of Human Services, Trenton, N.J. 08625.

Knitzer, Jane and Allen, Mary Lee (1978). *Children without Homes.* Washington, D.C.: Children's Defense Fund.

Mayer, Morris. F., Richman, Leon H., and Balcerzak, Edwin A. (1978). *Group Care of Children Crossroads and Transitions.* New York: Child Welfare League of America.

Miller, D. (1985). A child's view of the seclusion room. *Journal of Child and Youth Care Work, 1,* 44-49.

Miller, Jerome (Spring, 1981). Thoughts on institutional abuse. In *Legal Response: Child Advocacy and Protection,* a newsletter of the American Bar Association, Young Lawyer's Division.

National Center on Child Abuse and Neglect (1987). *Child Abuse and Neglect in Residential Institutions: Selected Readings on Prevention, Investigation and Correction.* DHEW Publication No. (OHDS) 78-30160, Washington, D.C.

The New York State Child Protective Services Training Institute (1981). Therapeutic techniques in crisis control for the child care worker. Unpublished manual prepared by the Family Life Development Center, Cornell University, Ithaca, N.Y. 14853.

New York State Senate, Subcommittee on Child Abuse (Sept. 1983). Protection of children in residential care. A study of abuse and neglect in child care institutions in New York State. Final report of Grant #90-CA-802A to the National Center on Child Abuse and Neglect, Jules Kerness, project direct.

Nunno, Michael. Child care worker's handbook (draft). Family Life Development Center, Cornell, University, Ithaca, N.Y. 14853.

Ohio Legal Rights Service, Annual Report. (1984-1985). Unpublished report for the year 1984-1985 of the designated Protection and Advocacy Agency, Columbus, Ohio 43215.

Rabb, J. and Rindfleisch, N. (1985). A study to define and assess severity of institutional abuse/neglect. *Child Abuse and Neglect, 9,* 285-294.

Rindfleisch, N. (1984). Residential facilities in child welfare: some dimensions of safety and risk for children and youths. Unpublished paper based on a report of the Institutional Child Protection Project sponsored under Grant No.

90-CA-803-01-02 by the National Center on Child Abuse and Neglect. Available from the College of Social Work, The Ohio State University, Columbus, Ohio 43210.

Rindfleisch, Nolan (1986). Some factors influencing reporting behavior in residential child care settings. Chapter 3 in *Protecting Children from Abuse: Professional Ethics and Responsibilities* edited by Susan J. Wells and Ann Maney (in press). Philadelphia: Preager Publishers, 1987.

Rindfleisch, N. and Foulk, R. (1984). Factors that influence the severity of adverse events in residential facilities. Unpublished paper based on Vol. VI of the final report of the Institutional Child Protection Project conducted at the College of Social Work, The Ohio State University under Grant No. CA-803-01-02-03 and sponsored by the National Center on Child Abuse and Neglect.

Rindfleisch, N. and Rabb, J. (1984a). Dilemmas in planning for the protection of children and youths in residential facilities. *Child Welfare, LXIII,* 205–215.

Rindfleisch, N. and Rabb, J. (1984b). How much of a problem is resident mistreatment in child welfare institutions? *Child Abuse and Neglect, 8,* 33–40.

Ross, A. L. (1983). Mitigating turnover of child care staff in group care facilities. *Child Welfare, LXII,* 63–67.

Ross, A. and Hoelthke, G. (1985). A tool for selecting residential child care workers: an initial report. *Child Welfare, LXIV,* 46–54.

Russell, Alene and Trainor, Cynthia (1984). *Trends in Child Abuse and Neglect: A National Perspective.* Denver: American Humane Association, Children's Division.

Shafer, Jean (1985). Protection of children in institutional care project. Final report of Demonstration Project of the Ohio Department of Human Services submitted to the National Center on Child Abuse and Neglect, Administration for Children, Youth and Families, Office of Human Development Services, Department of Health and Human Services, Washington, D.C.

Shyne, A. and Schroeder, A. (1980). *National Study of Social Services to Children and their Families, Overview.* Publication No. (OHDS) 80-30149, U.S.D.H.H.S., Washington, D.C.

Sundram, J. D. (1984). Obstacles to reducing patient abuse in public institutions. *Hospital and Community Psychiatry, 35,* 238–243.

Thomas, George (1980). A contemporary definition of institutional abuse and neglect. Unpublished paper presented at the Region VII Conference on Institutional Abuse and Neglect, Kansas City, Mo. and sponsored by the Region VII Child Abuse and Neglect Resource Center, University of Iowa, Oakdale, Iowa 52319.

Thomas, George (1982). Residential child maltreatment: an unrecognized problem in the United States. Unpublished paper presented at the Fourth International Congress on Child Abuse and Neglect, Paris, France. Available from George Thomas and Associates Ltd., Box 152, Athens, GA 30603.

Thomas, George (1984). The problem of residential child maltreatment and its prevention. Unpublished paper presented to the State Conference on Residential Child Maltreatment, Baton Rouge, La.

Thomas, George (Apr. 1985). Shaping a role for state child protective services in institutional child maltreatment prevention. Unpublished paper presented as a subplenary address at the New York State Conference on Child Abuse and Neglect, sponsored by the Family Life Development Center, Cornell University in Albany, N.Y.

Toomey, B., Rivera, R., Murray, J., and Rindfleisch, N. (1984). Child abuse and neglect in residential facilities: the law and the courts — Part I and Part II. Vol. 2 of the final report of the Institutional Child Protection Project sponsored under Grant No. 90-CA-803-01 by the National Center on Child Abuse and Neglect. Available from the College of Social Work, The Ohio State University, Columbus, Ohio 43210.

Wooden, Kenneth (1976). *Weeping in the Playtime of Others*. New York: McGraw-Hill.

Index

About the Editors

Charles E. Schaefer, Ph.D., is a Professor of Psychology and Director, Psychological Services Center, Fairleigh Dickinson University, Hackensack, New Jersey. Dr. Schaefer is the founder and Chairman of the Board of the Association for Play Therapy, a national organization that includes international membership. He is a Fellow of both the American Psychological Association and the American Orthopsychiatric Association. Among Dr. Schaefer's publications are the outstanding books *Handbook of Play Therapy, The Therapeutic Use of Child's Play,* and *The Therapeutic Powers of Play.* He co-edited the book *Play Therapy Techniques.* Dr. Schaefer maintains a private practice with children and their families in Hackensack, New Jersey.

Arthur J. Swanson, Ph.D., is Clinical Psychologist on the Children's Inpatient Unit of the Psychiatric Institute, Westchester County Medical Center and is Director of Psychology Externship Training. He is also Assistant Professor of Psychiatry at New York Medical College and Director of Research for the Child and Adolescent Division. He is the author of articles on treatment outcome, group therapy, self control, and firesetting in children. Dr. Swanson maintains a private practice in Ardsley, New York.